2011

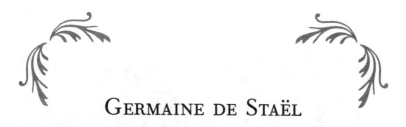

GERMAINE DE STAËL

&

BENJAMIN CONSTANT

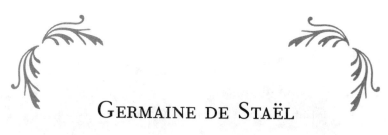

Germaine de Staël

&

Benjamin Constant

A Dual Biography

RENEE WINEGARTEN

Yale University Press
New Haven and London

Published with assistance from the Annie Burr Lewis Fund.

Designed by Mary Valencia.
Set in Fournier type by Keystone Typesetting, Inc.
Printed in the United States of America by
R. R. Donnelley, Harrisonburg, Virginia.

Library of Congress Control Number: 2007940634
ISBN-13: 978-0-300-11925-1
ISBN-10: 0-300-11925-9

A catalogue record for this book is available from the British Library.

The paper in this book meets the guidelines for permanence and durability of the
Committee on Production Guidelines for Book Longevity of the Council on
Library Resources.

10 9 8 7 6 5 4 3 2 1

Frontispiece: Benjamin Constant, pencil drawing by Firmin Massot (Coll. château
de Coppet [Suisse]); Madame de Staël, from a pastel by Jean-Baptiste Isabey
(Musée du Louvre, Paris / Réunion des Musées Nationaux / Art Resource, NY)

To the memory of my husband, Asher Winegarten,
and my parents, Sydney and Debbe Aarons

Thus piteously Love closed what he begat
The union of this ever-diverse pair!
These two were rapid falcons in a snare,
Condemned to do the flitting of the bat.

George Meredith, *Modern Love*

CONTENTS

⁓ *Prologue* ⁓

ON DECEMBER 13, 1830, the day after Benjamin Constant's funeral, a
friend recalled the deceased's extraordinary association with Germaine de Staël: "You have not known Mme de Staël at all," declared
the historian Sismondi, "if you have not seen her with Benjamin Constant. By means of a mind equal to hers, he alone had the power to put
all her intelligence into play, to make her grow more great through
their combat, to awaken an eloquence, a depth of spirit and thought
that were never manifest in all their brilliance except opposite him, just
as he was never truly himself except at Coppet."[1] The singular, dazzling conversational jousts that took place between them, at Germaine
de Staël's home close to Lake Geneva, left an indelible impression on
all those who were privileged to witness them. This was indeed the
most famous and significant liaison and literary and political partnership before the union of Simone de Beauvoir and Jean-Paul Sartre
in the twentieth century, but it was more fraught, fiery, and tempestuous than theirs, and more closely and directly involved in positive
action in the political arena.

The relationship between Germaine de Staël, the most outstanding, innovative, and notorious woman writer of the age, and Benjamin

Constant, who would become known as a highly important political thinker and liberal politician, endured on and off for almost seventeen years, from 1794 until 1811, with lingering repercussions up to her death in 1817 and, indeed, after her demise. It embraced a stormy love affair, a close union of minds and ideas, and a formidable partnership of equals—an association of no little relevance to our era as well as their own through their devotion to the cause of liberty.

In an age when sensibility was prized, Germaine was seen as a whirlwind of boundless nervous energy, activity, sympathy, warmth of heart, and enthusiasm; or perhaps as a lake whose waters were constantly ruffled. By contrast, Benjamin was regarded as sharp-tongued, calculating, even cold and withdrawn, yet beneath the surface he was often in turmoil, assailed by a mass of contradictory impulses. He would lay claim to sensibility when charged with a lack of it. Both were ambitious for fame, eager to live life to the fullest; both heard "Time's wingéd chariot" hurrying at their heels. She adored Paris and its diversions, its theaters and concerts, while he was fond of the countryside and its pursuits, and liked to keep a dog by his side; she enjoyed society and the variety of social intercourse, while he preferred solitude and thought there was a barrier between people that prevented them from ever really knowing each other.

Added to the mixture of their interests, ambitions, and aspirations were the dreams, obsessional needs, demands, and instabilities of "this ever-diverse pair." She, although disillusioned in her hopes for private and public happiness, was ever in quest of *le bonheur,* incompatible as she found it to be with *la gloire;* he, worldly yet indecisive, was torn between her exciting and demanding brilliance and his desire for a quiet life of ordinary domesticity. It was the dilemma that Germaine would evoke in her novel *Corinne:* whichever style of life Benjamin was leading, he felt he wanted the opposite.

What attracts one person to another is often complicated, mysterious to outsiders, and dependent on the moment: it cannot be attributed to a single element of passion or self-interest but is rather a subtle mélange. The strange and convoluted drama of Germaine and Benjamin's relationship was played out during a period of momentous upheavals and sudden changes. They aspired to be and often were committed actors who had a role in what was taking place on the public stage. Born into the challenging world and new ideas of the eighteenth-century Enlightenment and the last decades of the ancien regime, they were both in their early twenties when the French Revolution erupted in 1789. The Revolution would dominate their thoughts and their lives. By the time they met in 1794, not long after the end of the Terror, they had each accumulated a wealth of experience. How uncertain and unsafe their world was! The rise of the First Republic and the precarious Directoire; the ascent of "the savior of the Republic," General Bonaparte; his transformation into the Emperor Napoleon; his European wars; his increasingly authoritarian regime and his Corsican vendetta against Germaine; the long and bitter struggle to overthrow him, in which Germaine participated as eventually did Benjamin before his volte-face; the double defeat of Napoleon and the double restoration of the Bourbon monarchy with the ever-encroaching forces of reaction—all this occurred within a mere twenty years and inevitably affected the course of the relationship.

Unfortunately, it is impossible to recover the tenor of the conversational encounters between Germaine, whose manner of talking was regarded as exceptionally brilliant, and Benjamin, whom some considered the greatest wit since Voltaire. Germaine's father, the controversial statesman Jacques Necker, was scarcely impartial, but his description of her as "a sort of phenomenon" nonetheless conveys some idea of her gift of improvisation as she passed rapidly from subtle ideas and acute political reasoning to a tone of courtesy and gaiety.[2] All who knew her, including Benjamin, were agreed on this point, and many remarked on the kindly way she contrived to bring out those who were present: she was always eager to recognize and encourage potential. Her fascinating talk was one of the many qualities that so captivated Benjamin when he first met her.

The numerous letters Germaine and Benjamin are known to have written to each other, which would have filled many volumes, are mainly lost or destroyed. Of the very small number that survive, some do not show either of them in the best light. There remain, however, the many letters addressed to family and friends in which they confided their thoughts and feelings. Thus, it is largely through their own words—not always to be taken at face value—that their intriguing story is told here. With the additional insights, comments, and judgments of members of their intimate circle, the contours of their relationship begin to emerge. Particularly invaluable is Benjamin's private diary, which caused a great stir among leading writers when it was first published toward the end of the nineteenth century, for this is one of the most penetrating documents ever penned by a man who was fascinated by himself and his innermost being, and who noted down every passing thought and feeling, no matter how fleeting or contradictory it might be. Some hints about the liaison may also be deduced from their autobiographical writings and their fictional works, provided one prudently keeps in mind Proust's dictum that the writing self is not the same as the everyday self.

My debt to many distinguished scholars who have devoted themselves to the study of Germaine de Staël and Benjamin Constant, respectively, is of course considerable. Among them is Béatrice W. Jasinski, whose monumental edition of Germaine's letters was unfortunately cut short at the year 1809 with volume 6. The correspondence of Benjamin edited by C. P. Courtney, Dennis Wood, and others remains, at the time of this writing, incomplete. Otherwise the letters of both writers are dispersed in various separate collections. Authorities I have consulted in the fields of literature, biography, history, politics, and the history of ideas are gratefully acknowledged in the Notes and the Bibliography.

To venture to probe two major writers in tandem presents a particular challenge because the literary genus is, of its nature, slippery. Many have discussed the liaison from the side of one party or the other, but hitherto, as far as I know, it has not been extensively treated in depth as an entity for its own sake. It is not at all unusual for some who write about Germaine de Staël, and who favor her, to find it difficult to utter a good word about Benjamin Constant—the influential nineteenth-century critic Sainte-Beuve started this trend. Vice versa, some who are impressed by Benjamin and his work take his side and cannot refrain from blaming Germaine for his ills and misfortunes. Neither of them, whatever their genius, was a paragon of virtue, and their vagaries were all the more human for that. Here is an attempt, then, to keep an even hand and to treat them both with equal dispassion.

Through their own words it should be possible to discover to some degree who was indebted to whom and in what way, even if their intellectual debt to each other remains difficult to unravel. Over the years, many myths and prejudices have become attached to the depiction of their union and disunion. To try to remove some of the varnish and over-painting from the double portrait of this extraordinary pair is the aim pursued in the following pages.

CHAPTER ONE

⟐ *A Chance Encounter* ⟐

IT WAS "BY CHANCE," Benjamin Constant was later to affirm, that he met for the first time a great celebrity. Filtering his own experience through that of the narrator of his unfinished autobiographical novel *Cécile*, he described his encounter with "the most famous person of our age through her writings and her conversation. I had never seen anything comparable."[1] That encounter between Benjamin Constant and Germaine de Staël, daughter of Jacques Necker, the egregious former finance minister to Louis XVI, was to have an enduring influence on his life—as it did on hers—and on the course of European literary culture and political thought. It was Benjamin who would make the first moves in a strange, mutually enriching, and ultimately stormy relationship. The tie between these two brilliant innovators and advocates of "the new ideas" lasted nearly seventeen years, marking him even after her death and leaving their names permanently entwined in the eyes of posterity.

When they met for the first time, on September 18, 1794, neither of them was in the first flush of youth. She was born in Paris of Swiss parentage on April 22, 1766; he was born in Lausanne of Swiss parentage on October 25, 1767. They were both in their late twenties, she being slightly the elder. They were neither inexperienced nor un-attached. Both were married.

The excesses of the French Revolution could not be far from anyone's mind, for their first meeting took place about two months after the fall of Robespierre and the end of the Terror in France. The occasion was a social gathering at Montchoisi in Switzerland, the pleasant country retreat of Benjamin's cousin, Constance Cazenove d'Arlens, and her husband. Montchoisi was situated on a hillside just outside Lausanne, overlooking gardens, meadows, and Lake Geneva. The autumn air in that region of the Canton of Vaud was balmy and pure. Germaine had just come from taking a sad farewell of her secret lover, the handsome Swedish republican conspirator Count Adolph Ribbing, who had been involved in the plot to assassinate Gustavus III and had departed to settle in Denmark. At that moment her thoughts were full of Ribbing.

Germaine had been friendly with Constance Cazenove d'Arlens for many years and knew her cousin Rosalie de Constant, yet she had never met their first cousin, Benjamin. Indeed, there was no reason why the celebrated Germaine de Staël, with her glittering connections among noted thinkers and writers of the Enlightenment as well as among crowned heads in France and Sweden and the highest ranks of the French aristocracy, should have been aware of Benjamin. He moved, as it were, on the fringes of her acquaintance and had been living abroad for several years at the court of the Duke of Brunswick.

Benjamin, however, was certainly aware of Mme de Staël even before he met her, and he was not at all favorably inclined toward her after hearing all the malicious tittle-tattle about "*la trop célèbre*" that was current in his family circle in Lausanne. When he was in Paris in the 1780s, living ostensibly under the guardianship of the eminent writer and publisher Jean-Baptiste Suard, who was a long-standing friend of the Neckers and their daughter, he could easily have been presented to her. Benjamin's adventurous cousin, Charles de Constant, known as "Chinese Constant" because of his travels to the Far East, was in Paris at the same time, and he took the opportunity to visit her in her new salon on several occasions. But Charles had been bored there, feeling that nobody took much notice of him among the crowd, and he made adverse comments about Mme de Staël, although he admitted that she had spoken kindly to him. Perhaps Charles's disgruntled view of her as a pedantic parvenue dissuaded Benjamin from attempting to meet her. In 1793, a year before the fateful encounter with Germaine, Benjamin roundly declared that he was not interested in the lady: "I shall not be running after Mme de Staehl [*sic*]. I do not know what to say to someone who does not interest me." In a separate statement, he reaffirmed his total indifference: "I have not seen Mme de Staël, nor am I curious about her."[2]

While in Paris, early in 1787, Benjamin had met and had fallen under the influence of the embittered Dutch-born novelist Isabelle de Zuylen, Mme de Charrière, familiarly known as Belle. Theirs was a warm platonic relationship between an ambitious young man and a distinguished female author twice his age. Belle, the author of *Caliste*, a novel that Germaine deeply admired, did not care for Germaine or her writings. When, in August 1793, Germaine called in person at Belle's home, a manor house at Colombier, and lavished praise on her work, Belle let Benjamin know that she had little esteem for Mme de Staël, her story "Zulma," or her essay on the trial of Marie Antoinette, which she found ill written and inappropriate. Benjamin shared Belle's poor opinion of Germaine's apology for the unfortunate queen, considering it affected when it should have been moving, and he said nothing at the time to counter Belle's snide remarks about Germaine. The aristocratic Mme de Charrière was impressed by Germaine's powers of speech, seduced and charmed by her amiable manner, but, she said, the charm did not last. According to Belle, later remembering Germaine's visit, there her caller was, "priding herself on her wit as if she had none, on titled friends as if M. de Staël had picked her up yesterday at a dressmaker's, and on Paris society like some provincial female who had spent only six weeks there. . . . She is a woman who is pleasant to listen to, but it would be madness to want to have any closer connection with her than with Molé [Jean-François Molé, a well-known actor at the Comédie Française] when he is playing brilliantly the most attractive role possible. No reality is to be found there. We shall often amuse ourselves recalling her together."[3] All the same, Belle felt that it was high time Benjamin met her. Indeed, she urged him to see Mme de Staël as "a curiosity." She had no idea of the tremendous impression that the living and breathing Germaine would make on him.

A rude awakening was in store for Belle, however, as she was about to see herself supplanted by another. On September 26, a week after his first meeting with Germaine, Benjamin decided to call on his new acquaintance at her family mansion at Coppet, just outside Geneva. "My trip to Coppet was pretty successful," he informed Belle excitedly. Not having found Germaine at home, he galloped after her, caught up with her carriage, and was invited to join her. "I settled myself in her carriage, and traveled here with her from Nyon, supped, breakfasted, dined, supped, breakfasted again with her, so that I saw her very closely and, above all, heard her. It seems to me that you judge her very severely," he told Belle. "I believe her to be very energetic, very imprudent, very talkative, but also kind, trusting and confiding in others in good faith. One proof that she is not solely a talking machine is the lively interest she takes in those of her acquaintance who are suffering."[4] He cited as an example of Germaine's humanitarian instincts how, after three vain and costly attempts, she had succeeded in rescuing a woman who detested her from the prisons of the Revolution in France. This was in all likelihood vicomtesse de Laval, erstwhile mistress of Germaine's former lover, comte Louis de

Narbonne. Benjamin did not yet realize the extent of Germaine's secret maneuvers to rescue her friends and acquaintances and support them now that they were refugees.

He went on, trying to convince Belle that Germaine's positive qualities had been overlooked, that she used her energy "to do good. And so I believe her to be more than a Molé, and I am not convinced that she lacks reality." As a concession to Belle, however, he echoed part of her criticism: "What you say of her absurdities is true. She quotes great aristocrats like a newly arrived parvenue, and, as you say, she talks of Parisian society like a woman from the provinces. But I do not think that she prides herself on her wit. She feels that she has a good deal of it, she has a great need to talk, to confide in others, recognizing neither limit nor prudence. That is perhaps the source of what you hold against her, if your reproach is founded. She praises people too much because she wants to please them in order to confide in them unreservedly. When they are no longer there she naturally retraces her steps. It cannot really be called a betrayal." He added, significantly, "I am far from thinking about a relationship because she is surrounded by too much company, she is too active, too pre-occupied; but this is the most interesting acquaintance I have made in a long time."[5] The idea of a relationship, then, had already crossed his mind only a few days after meeting her.

What Germaine and Benjamin discussed during their succession of breakfasts, dinners, and suppers is not known, apart from one telling item: the freedom of the press. In Benjamin's account to Belle, Germaine expressed surprise that a certain paper, *Le Tableau de la dernière quinzaine*, had not been closed down. She and her beloved father, Jacques Necker, had been badly treated in its pages. Worse still in her eyes, this journal favored her bête noire, Robespierre, and the Jacobin Terror, which she excoriated. Nonetheless, Benjamin spoke up for the unrestricted freedom of the press—it was indeed one of his first principles and would remain so to the end. Germaine did not hold his opinion against him, said Benjamin; on the contrary, she tolerated the way that he opposed her vigorously in public, in the middle of a grand dinner at Rolle, on a subject that touched her amour propre and her peace of mind. (She was probably more concerned, in fact, about the attack on her father than that on herself.) In Benjamin's view, she had shown merely "an intolerant intention," and in any case, unbeknownst to them at the time, the paper had indeed been silenced.[6] Here he was, already hastening to her defense, as he would often have occasion to do in the future.

By October 21, Benjamin was finding it impossible to agree at all with his old friend's opinions of his new friend. In particular, he defended Germaine's taste for lavishing praise on all and sundry: "On the contrary, since I know her better, I have great difficulty in not ceaselessly singing *her* praises, and displaying my interest and my admiration to everyone I address. I have rarely seen a similar combination of astonishing and attractive qualities, so much brilliance, rightness, so wide and active a benevolence, so much generosity, a form of courtesy so gentle and constant in society, so much charm, simplicity, lack of constraint in her intimate circle." Carried away by his enthusiasm at being received privately along with her close friends, Benjamin added tactlessly, "She is the second woman I have encountered who could have replaced the whole world for me. You know who was the first." This unfortunate remark was hardly likely to placate Belle. A proud woman does not like to hear that she is not unique and that she has a successor—especially after having been told that she is herself one of a kind. "How much I love you! How I feel that you alone suit me completely," he had told Belle only a few months earlier. Now he informed her that "Mme de Staël has infinitely more wit in intimate conversation than in society: she knows how to listen—something neither you nor I imagined—and she responds to the wit of others with as much pleasure as to her own. She brings out those of whom she is fond with her clever, acute attentiveness, something that proves as much kindness as intelligence. Finally, she is a Being apart, a superior Being, one of a kind perhaps to be found in a hundred years, so that those who associate with her, know her, and count themselves her friends, should not ask for any other form of happiness."[7] In short, in the course of a few weeks, Benjamin had fallen passionately under her spell. But it would be a very long time before his feelings were returned.

Notably, in the course of his dithyramb Benjamin made no mention of Germaine's physical attributes or attractiveness. He would not share his views on that aspect until many years later, and after many vicissitudes, by way of *Cécile*. Instead, he concentrates on her extraordinary gifts of intelligence, charm, charisma, and infinite goodheartedness. It was generally agreed that Germaine was not beautiful by the standards of the day. Her father had candidly told her so and advised her to concentrate on her intelligence. Since intellect was commonly regarded as a masculine preserve, she was seen as lacking in feminine qualities, meaning softness and pliability. She was dark when the beauties of the day were fair, her build was stocky rather than svelte, her movements forceful rather than elegant. All were agreed, however, on her marvelously expressive eyes: they were "exceptionally magnificent," according to her cousin, Albertine Necker de Saussure.[8] Then there was the fascinating way she talked, which made her listeners forget everything else. The fine "speaking" portrait by Jean-Baptiste Isabey, thought to date from 1790–1792, just a few years before Benjamin met her, shows her with fashionable shoulder-length, free-flowing hair, wearing a high-waisted muslin dress fastened under the breast with a cameo set on a wide velvet ribbon. The portrait may well be flattering, for Isabey was a friend, but it is nonetheless wonderfully animated, perhaps the only portrait to capture that particular quality of hers.

And what did Mme de Staël think of Benjamin Constant, who had so rapidly fitted into her brilliant intimate circle? For her, looks were important. She saw a tall, willowy, slightly stooping man who had damaged his eyesight through too much reading by candlelight and whose appearance struck her as distinctly unprepossessing. Some even thought him downright ugly, as did Belle after they had grown distant. All the same, from the start, Germaine considered his intellect so remarkable that she fully expected him to be a great liberal philosopher, a second Montesquieu, a talent capable of producing a work akin to *The Spirit of the Laws.*

"I found here this evening," she wrote to her distant beloved Count Adolph Ribbing from Montchoisi on September 18, the day of her fateful meeting with Benjamin, "a man of great wit called Benjamin Constant . . . not very good looking, but exceptionally intelligent."[9] In short, in modern parlance, Benjamin was not her type, as she wanted to make clear. Besides, Germaine was not unattached; Benjamin had joined a sort of imbroglio that involved the recent arrival in Switzerland of her former idol, Louis de Narbonne, and the departure of her present idol, Adolph Ribbing. Germaine always favored good looks, preferably associated with high birth and physical courage, such as she had found in the comte de Narbonne, a dazzling figure in pre-Revolutionary society, or in the dashing Count Ribbing. By October 8, she was informing Ribbing that she had a new suitor: "I must tell you that M. Benjamin Constant, gentleman attached to the court of His Highness the Duke of Brunswick, twenty-six years old and outstandingly ugly, has fallen in love with your Minette [Germaine's pet name among her family and intimate friends]. We shall keep his letters for you and hide his face, which would add little merit to my sublime indifference."[10] So Germaine, unlike Benjamin, was not launching into raptures. She wanted Ribbing, an infrequent correspondent, to know that someone else valued her love, but that he had no rival and that she was utterly indifferent to Benjamin's attempts to pay court to her. Although the letters from Benjamin to which she refers are lost, some idea of their tenor can be gleaned from the wild and desperate tone of those he later addressed to Anna Lindsay and Juliette Récamier.

During the months that followed, Benjamin's frustrated passion grew in intensity. Germaine had only to be found straightening Ribbing's portrait for Benjamin to fall in a faint. From the mansion she was renting at Mézery, she wrote to Ribbing with a touch of coquetry:

> M. Constant, of whom I have already spoken, I think, has conceived a passion for me that is beyond description, he is at death's door and overwhelms me with so much misery that it deprives him of his one charm—a very superior mind—and inflicts on me a kind of compassion that both wearies me and reminds me that my Adolph perhaps never, never loved me so deeply. If you hear that M. Constant, gentleman attached to the court of His Highness the Duke of Brunswick, aged twenty-seven, as red haired as members of the royal house of Hanover, has killed himself at Bois de Céry, which he has just rented in order to spend his life in my garden or in my courtyard, do not believe that it is my fault. I have truly praised him for his work entitled *The Spirit of Religions* [an early draft of the immense study that was not to be published until many years later] which really reveals a talent comparable to that of Montesquieu; and forgetting entirely that his appearance is an invincible obstacle even for a heart not already yours, he has completely lost his senses.[11]

At that time many enjoyed and were thoroughly familiar with the famous scenes and characters in dramas that were performed not only in theaters but also in the great houses of the nobility or the private homes of the well-to-do literati. Germaine loved the theater: from the age of twelve she had written plays and acted in them. A famous actress, Mlle Clairon, had taught her diction and declamation. Indeed, although he could not know it, these desperate scenes of Benjamin's echoed the impassioned pleas of Germaine's letters to Narbonne, in which she threatened to take poison for death was preferable to life without her beloved. Benjamin was pursuing a dramatic strategy frequently employed in French classical tragedy where the hero tries to persuade the heroine to yield by arousing her pity with his readiness to die. He was imitating heroic Rodrigue in Corneille's *Le Cid,* whereas Germaine had imitated abandoned Hermione in Racine's *Andromaque.*

Benjamin's scenes, moreover, were being played out while numerous guests, refugees from the Terror, sheltered under Germaine's protection at Mézery, a large, isolated estate surrounded by trees that comprised two country houses or mansions, one with a fine terrace and views over the mountains of the Jura. Germaine had settled there with her friends, who included representatives of reform, moderate French aristocrats who had resigned their privileges at the beginning of the Revolution, and supporters of constitutional monarchy. Among them were now her former lover Narbonne, who was still her lover in the public eye; his past and future mistress, Mme de Laval; and her son, Germaine's faithful friend, Mathieu de Montmorency. In addition there were many distinguished visitors, notabilities, savants, and neighbors who came to dinner or to stay. "I am living with the surviving ruins of France," said one of these visitors, the liberal magistrate Charles-Victor de Bonstetten, as he hastened to enjoy their society before, so he presumed, it disappeared forever.[12]

It was not until late October that Germaine finally told her dear friend Mathieu de Montmorency about her secret preference for Ribbing, doubtless without confessing that she had been his mistress. Once again she related to the absent Ribbing how she had been shattered by the manifest despair of Benjamin, "who wanted to move me by some tragic scene or other, while reminding me of what is obvious, that M. de Narbonne's moodiness wearies and annoys me." She reported how she had told Benjamin roundly that she loved the best of men and hoped to devote her life to him. "I shall spare you the outbursts that this remark elicited. . . . Maybe I acted wrongly but I felt sick to hear him talk of love. . . . Today I do not even want to be loved by another."[13] She remained obsessed with Ribbing and fully intended to stay loyal to him.

And so it went on throughout the winter of 1794–1795 and into the spring of 1795. Ribbing, who replied rarely to her long, loving letters, was informed, "M. Constant, from whom I distance myself, writes five letters a day to me."[14] Kept at a distance or not, Benjamin was accepted as a trusted member of her entourage, for in November 1794 he accompanied her on a short visit to Coppet to see her father, who liked him. By December, she was reporting that Benjamin, who had indeed long suffered from periods of ill health and nervous debility, was "falling into a consumption. His passion for me moves me to pity. . . . He has a very ready wit but it is painful to look at him, especially since this unfortunate love is killing him."[15] Meanwhile, Benjamin sought to oblige her in any way he could; for example, he wrote to his protector in Brunswick to try to obtain a post there for one of her learned protégés. In January 1795 he was still "that unfortunate Benjamin Constant," always in attendance, staying in her house at Mézery, being admitted to her room, and being shown the door whenever his frenzy was deemed excessive. At the same time, Germaine herself was close to despair. For a very long while she went on harboring delusions: that Ribbing would soon return to Switzerland; that they would find a secluded country retreat there; that he would accompany her to France where, since divorce was now permitted under the revolutionary law of 1792, they could rid themselves of their respective spouses and finally marry. They would live happily ever after, and she would be Countess Ribbing instead of baronne de Staël. Ribbing remained deaf to her wild schemes and fantasies.

Benjamin's "scenes" continued to wear Germaine down with their appeal to her compassion, where—as he had discovered—she was most vulnerable. She recognized the element of manipulation in his conduct, but she was moved all the same. In one sense she felt sorry for him; in another she doubted his sincerity. In March she wrote to Ribbing that he "smashes his head against my chimney-piece when I beg him to leave my room."[16] This procedure of Benjamin's was not new: he had employed similar "acts of theatrical frenzy," as he would call them, when he was eighteen and courting the wife of an English diplomat, Mrs. Harriet Trevor, a coquette in her thirties. It was how he thought a lover ought to behave. Such was his display of violent despair with Mrs. Trevor that it reduced him to "a sort of fever that more or less resembled the passion I had only wished to pretend. . . . There I was rolling on the ground and striking my head against the wall." And all he gained was "a kiss on somewhat faded lips," he remembered with characteristic self-mockery.[17]

By the spring, what with her struggles with Benjamin, whom she deemed intelligent but "mad," and her quarrels with Narbonne, who ultimately settled for Mme de Laval, Germaine was yearning to escape. But Benjamin's banging his head on the fireplace was the least of the drama. One night at Mézery in March 1795 loud cries and groans could be heard coming from Benjamin's room: the servants who entered were sure that he was lying at death's door. He had consumed what the critic Sainte-Beuve would qualify as "the Coppet dose" of opium. His one wish was to take a fond farewell of his beloved before passing to a better world.

This was by no means Benjamin's first attempt at suicide as an unsuccessful lover. At the age of nineteen he had tried it when paying extravagant court to sixteen-year-old Jenny Pourrat, to whom he had

written to propose an elopement although she was contentedly betrothed to another. He was so shy that he had barely addressed a word
to her in person about the passion he thought he felt. "As it happened, I
had with me a little bottle of opium," he later recalled, expounding
with typical irony. "I endlessly repeated that I wanted to kill myself
and almost arrived at believing it, although deep down I had not the
least urge to do so. . . . I swallowed my opium. I do not think there was
enough of it to do me much harm." The girl's astonished mother,
deeply worried, plied him with antidotes, and he soon recovered. Then
sensible Mlle Pourrat appeared, dressed for the Opera: it was June 8,
1787, the first night of Beaumarchais's *Tarare*. Mme Pourrat invited him
to join them, he accepted, "and so that all should be tragicomic in this
affair, my poisoning concluded with an evening at the Opera."[18]

The scene enacted at Mézery in 1795 when he was twenty-seven
also belonged to the realm of tragicomedy. Unfortunately, Benjamin
himself omitted to leave an account of this particular attempted suicide
in his customary self-mocking style. An eyewitness who was an habitué
of the Coppet circle, the agronomist Frédéric Lullin de Châteauvieux,
conveyed with relish what he saw and heard to the diplomat Jacques de
Norvins, who consigned it with equal amusement to his *Mémorial*,
published many years later. Having awakened most of the household
with his groans, the moribund Benjamin managed to speak to Germaine's girlhood friend, Catherine Huber, now Mme Rilliet-Huber,
who arrived with Châteauvieux: "Oh! Madame, tell her I am dying for
her sake. . . . In the name of one who is dying, beg her to come and
hear my last farewell, if there is time, and let me die after having seen
her once more." Roused by Mme Rilliet-Huber, Germaine was moved
to exclaim, "It is a matter of life and death, I am coming with you." All
those who were staying at Mézery were by now in Benjamin's room
when she arrived there. "Wretched man! What have you done?" she
cried, and called for a doctor. Benjamin sensed that it was time to come

back to life. "Oh! It is you, it is you," he whispered. "You recall me to life for an instant." "Live, live, dear Monsieur Constant, I beg you," urged Germaine. "Since you command it, I shall try to live," murmured Benjamin, seizing her hand and implanting on it a long kiss. The following day Mme Rilliet-Huber told Châteauvieux how afterward Germaine washed her hand thoroughly in scented water, confessing to her friend, "I feel I have a physical antipathy to this man that nothing can overcome."[19] In the end the two women could not help laughing at Benjamin's rapid return to life.

The houseguests, gathered to witness Benjamin's demise, were amused or ironic. Her increasingly devout friend Mathieu de Montmorency could not conceal his aristocratic disgust: "This fellow who does nothing but disturb this household and who dishonors it with a suicide should be thrown out of the window."[20] Details of the bizarre scene, which conforms to the pattern of Benjamin's previous attempt to kill himself for unrequited love, spread outside the intimate circle. "When you play jokes of that sort, you should die of it, for the honor of the lady," an acquaintance of Germaine's, General de Montesquiou, remarked acidly to the novelist Mme de Montolieu.[21]

In spite of his efforts, Benjamin did not yet win the day. But his "services" to Germaine, his willingness to run her errands and do her bidding, earned him a place as a most cherished friend and escort. Thus, he simply continued in his patient pursuit. What ultimately allowed him to succeed—apart from his dogged persistence—was not so much his oft-displayed suffering and his melodramatic excesses but his utter devotion in obliging her in every possible way. He was also helped by some news that came in January or February 1796: that Ribbing, on arriving in Paris armed with Germaine's letters of introduction to all her associates in *le grand monde*, had attached himself to the famous beauty Pulchérie de Valence, who, Germaine claimed indignantly, was nothing but a woman of easy virtue. This was the final blow to Germaine's hopes for perfect bliss with her idealized but recalcitrant lover.

In the spring of the previous year, well aware that she was losing hold of Ribbing just as she had lost hold of Narbonne, she had told the elusive Swede, "It is a spell cast on my life: those I do not love cling to me, those I do love cast me aside. . . . I have had troubles enough with the dreadful scenes of death and illness that Benjamin Constant has performed for my benefit. It is cruel to make someone else also suffer, when one is oneself so unhappy."[22] The "oneself" in this instance is Germaine, and these words indicate her growing reluctance to remain the source of Benjamin's misery, even though she patently did not feel for him what she felt for Ribbing. For her, the main charm in life was to be loved, and without this warmth everything seemed hateful. After Ribbing's betrayal she was on the rebound. Her infatuation with the studious journalist François de Pange, a friend of the lyric poet André Chénier (who perished in the last days of the Terror), came to nothing when she learned that he was about to be married. But Benjamin was still there, still in attendance, to console her.

Finally, after a pursuit that lasted some eighteen months, Benjamin triumphed over Germaine's physical antipathy. Everyone who knew them well, from Germaine's perceptive cousin Albertine Necker de Saussure to their mutual friend, the ravishing beauty Juliette Récamier, agreed that it was a meeting of minds. But was it love? Who can say? Love takes many forms. Certainly, their sensibilities were attuned; they both shared the same morbid dread of death, the same delectation in suffering, the same inclination to melancholy. Benjamin was ecstatic at his triumph, which presumably occurred sometime in the spring of 1796 and which far exceeded any of his previous—or later—triumphs. The woman he was to call "the most famous person of our age through her conversation and her writings" was his at last. They made no secret of their affair. Benjamin's name was constantly on her lips. He touched her neck affectionately and called her his little kitten. It was enough to raise eyebrows in straightlaced Swiss society.

What of their spouses?

The union of Germaine Necker with Eric Magnus de Staël-Holstein, which took place when Germaine's father was in office, was for her in some respects a last resort and a marriage of convenience. It proved a great if anticipated disappointment. She was not in love with him, nor he with her. She did not want to leave France, and it has been said that she married Paris and he married her father's millions. The Neckers were faithful Protestants, and it was not easy to find a suitable match in Catholic France, where Protestant citizens had been expelled toward the end of the previous century. On January 14, 1786, nineteen-year-old Germaine was married to her Swedish suitor, who was her elder by seventeen years. Most girls of her day were married at sixteen to much older men, marriage being largely a matter of status, money, and property. In her case, however, there had been not only the long search for an acceptable Protestant spouse of some standing but also protracted negotiations between Jacques Necker and the Swedish crown concerning a title and the Paris embassy for M. de Staël. The ceremony took place in the chapel of the Swedish embassy in the rue du Bac. It was followed by Germaine's presentation at court, where Louis XVI and Marie Antoinette received her graciously.

By all accounts Staël was neither a brilliant intellect nor a man of exceptional talent. A young Hanoverian doctor, Erich Bollmann, had some cruel fun at his expense: he claimed that Germaine's husband was so dim that he "would not be capable of inventing a dish of potatoes."[23] The testimony of Staël's secretary at the Swedish embassy, Nils von Jacobsson, is all the more telling because it comes from a man who was utterly devoted to him. He painted an unvarnished picture of Germaine's husband. Staël, he wrote candidly in his private diary, was not of high birth, was not well educated, and had no money. He cut a fine figure, though, and he had a way with the ladies. True, many at the Swedish court felt that he lacked the essential qualities for a diplomatic career. For instance, he could not write with ease and elegance. But he spoke persuasively and inspired trust. In society at Versailles, said Jacobsson, he acquired "a certain tact" that concealed his ignorance and a pleasing manner that imitated the tone of the salons and passed for intelligence.

It was another matter entirely when he found himself in Germaine's circle of wits, intellectuals, and savants. There, observed his secretary, he was thoroughly out of place. "In my opinion," noted Jacobsson, "this marriage caused his misfortune, because of the utter disparity in intellect and feeling between husband and wife." He continued, "Here is a man who, at twenty, probably aspired to nothing more than the command of an infantry regiment. . . . Ambassador at thirty-five, he marries the wealthiest heiress in France, daughter of the man of the age, so to speak, who inspired such popular enthusiasm that he was placed above the greatest ministers of the past. . . . He marries her and from that moment it is downhill all the way."[24] It is a devastating picture of plausible mediocrity.

As for his finances, Staël was never able to keep them under control. According to Jacobsson, he had very large debts when he married, which his father-in-law Necker promised to settle. But his financial affairs were like a sack with a hole in it, and "if he had in his purse the whole of Necker's fortune it would not have prevented him from ending in ruin."[25] His wife became his only resource and support, but he did not like having to appeal to her generosity any more than she was pleased to have to deal with his constant indebtedness. By the time Benjamin Constant encountered Mme de Staël, she and her husband were living virtually separate lives. M. de Staël was attached to his mistress, the famous actress Mlle Clairon, considerably his senior, who had very expensive tastes. Mme de Staël pursued her fondness for a kind of flirtatious friendship that was often barely distinguishable from love (as the French call it so succinctly, *amitié amoureuse*) with a succession of attractive men. Being financially independent meant that she could live more or less as she wished. From the beginning of her engagement it had been obvious both to her father and to herself that Staël was cold, lacking in temperament, unlikely to inspire the enthusiasm and passionate love she sought—and found for a while, or thought she found, in Narbonne and Ribbing. Benjamin's insistence on playing the part of the poet or sensitive soul dying of love, which had long been a feature of the literature and music that delighted her, surely contributed in part to arouse her imaginative sympathy for him.

Whereas Germaine's marriage had been a matter of slow European diplomacy over several years, Benjamin's union in May 1789, at the age of twenty-one, was undertaken on impulse, without deep reflection. He saw marriage as a panacea, a solution to his problems, such as his intense boredom at the petty court. His bride was Wilhelmina von Cramm, lady-in-waiting to the Duchess of Brunswick and his elder by nine years. The duchess appears to have encouraged the match between her protégée and the duke's young chamberlain. The couple gave the impression of being quite happy at first. Benjamin often spoke of "my Minna," and he brought her to Lausanne to introduce her to his family. To his relief she met with their approval. But the marriage was soon on the rocks. Minna was thoroughly at home in court ceremonial and intrigue, whereas Benjamin, rebellious and full of contempt for such trivialities, was not. She had no interest whatsoever in his learned pursuits, and she was doubtless as shocked as other members of the conservative German court by his eccentric behavior, his boldness in speaking ill of a number of its dignitaries, and his unconcealed sympathy for the French Revolution.

By February 1794 Benjamin and Minna were separated. He

discovered that Minna had taken a lover, a Russian prince, and that she was expecting a child he knew was not his. He sued for divorce, behaving in a chivalrous manner by taking all the blame and, in consequence, further blackening his reputation with the duke and duchess and most of their courtiers. But Benjamin did not lack consolation. Apart from the prostitutes he knew from his youth, there was a young actress named Caroline and also the unhappily married Charlotte von Marenholz (née von Hardenberg).

When Benjamin Constant encountered Mme de Staël at Montchoisi, however, he forgot everyone else, including Charlotte, his mistress. His divorce would not become legal until a year later, on November 18, 1795; after that, Benjamin was in effect a free agent and able to remarry. Germaine, on the other hand, was still tied, and subject to endless gossip. She largely behaved in private as if she were free, while being seen in public as the notorious wife of the Swedish ambassador, a position that had afforded her some protection in difficult political circumstances during the Revolution. This status as *madame l'ambassadrice* was, perhaps, the main advantage of her union with Staël.

She had given Staël a daughter, Gustavine, who unfortunately died in infancy in April 1789. Her two sons, Auguste and Albert, bore her husband's name, but they were in fact the offspring of Narbonne, as she declared in her letters to him. With his customary lordly insouciance, he appears to have taken little interest in their welfare. Handsome, elegant, cultivated, quick-witted, seductive Narbonne was a *grand seigneur* with a distinguished military career, widely believed to be one of the numerous illegitimate descendants of Louis XV, and a godson of Louis XVI. Germaine's liaison with him was a formative element in her life and her outlook. It probably began in 1788. Its fire, which she fed with her impassioned letters to him, lasted for several years before its embers expired finally in 1794. There may have been previous amorous episodes in her life—with the gallant military tactician, comte Hippolyte de Guibert, for instance, or with Charles-Maurice de Talleyrand, the future power broker—but this was her first serious and deeply passionate love affair. It caused a rift with her disapproving parents, especially her mother, the daughter of a Swiss pastor, who uttered constant reproaches and never forgave her.

The affair with Narbonne was also partly the source and inspiration for Germaine's first major work, *De l'influence des passions,* a discourse on the influence of the passions upon the happiness of individuals and nations, written at a time when the very idea of the pursuit of happiness was new, following the revolutions in America and France. The book is obliquely autobiographical, and a number of her contemporaries perceived its personal character. Henri Beyle, for instance, who had not yet become Stendhal the novelist, thought *De l'influence des passions* was her best book and, despite his enduring reservations about her style, urged his sister Pauline to read it: "She is a passionate spirit describing what she has felt."[26] Germaine had embarked on writing it in 1792, though it was not published until 1796 and even then remained incomplete. She wrote it in response to a double disillusion, not only with Narbonne but also with the fearful course that the Revolution was taking into the Jacobin Terror.

Some of the book's confessional passages, while referring to men in general, clearly allude to the attitude and conduct of Narbonne. "At twenty-five," she declared in the foreword, elaborating on the woman's point of view, "your fate is decided in many ways, and men then consider if it suits them to bind theirs to it; if they see less advantage in this than they thought . . . at the exact moment when they have decided to distance themselves from you they want to justify themselves for the wrong they are doing you; they look for faults to absolve themselves of the greatest of them; those who are guilty of ingratitude deny your devotion, they pretend you are demanding."[27] She complained in the section "On Love," "Nature and society have disinherited half of

humankind: strength, courage, genius, independence, everything belongs to men. . . . According to the opinion of an unjust society the laws
of morality itself seem to be suspended in the relations between men
and women. . . . In fine, they [men] can have received from a woman the
benefits, the tokens of devotion which would bind together two masculine friends, two companions in arms, and which would dishonor one
of them if he were to prove capable of forgetting these; [yet] they can
have received such tokens from a woman, and extricate themselves
from everything."[28] These words would prove applicable not solely to
Narbonne.

Germaine had good reason for her bitterness at her lover's increasing reserve and ultimate desertion. It was she who had converted
the monarchist Narbonne to liberalism and propelled him to be appointed minister of war in 1792. She supported him, rescued him at
great risk to herself when she was pregnant, and saved his life when
the revolutionaries were after his blood, as he acknowledged many
years later. During the upheavals in Paris between August 10 and the
outbreak of the massacres on September 2, 1792, she hid Narbonne in
the Swedish embassy. One morning she learned that a notice denounc-
ing him had been affixed at the corners of the rue du Bac. A search
party duly arrived. "M. de Narbonne, as an outlaw, died that very day
if he was discovered," she recalled, "and, whatever precaution I took, I
knew perfectly well that if the search was carried out thoroughly he
could not avoid capture. At all costs I had to prevent this search; I
gathered my strength and I felt at that moment that one can always
govern one's emotion, however violent it may be, when one knows
that it places the life of another person at risk." She realized that she
had to convince the men of the search party that they were putting the
whole nation in danger by entering the Swedish embassy. "With death
in my heart I had the courage to make jokes about the injustice of their
suspicions. . . . I accompanied them to the door. And I gave thanks to

God for the extraordinary strength He had lent me at that moment; all the same, the situation could not have been prolonged, and the least chance sufficed to condemn an outlaw who was so well known for having recently been a minister."[29] Through the good offices of young Dr. Erich Bollmann, who risked his own life, Narbonne escaped to England, where Germaine eventually joined him. She provided him with funds throughout their liaison, found shelter for him and their friends in a colony she set up at Juniper Hall in Surrey, and, in short, gave him every token of a single-minded devotion so great that it even exceeded her feelings for her father at the time. She expected gratitude and did not find it. Her reproaches and attempts at moral blackmail in her letters did not produce the desired result. He was slipping away from her. Nonetheless, Narbonne was still living in exile under her protection at Mézery when she met Benjamin.

The affair with Narbonne's successor, Ribbing, was more brief, and it was not on the same level, although she was marked by his republican ideas. She met him in July 1793, and the liaison lasted from the spring of 1794 until September of that year when he departed for Denmark. It lingered on for two years during his absence, chiefly through her passionate letters, until early in 1796, when his betrayal contributed to Benjamin's victory.

What did Germaine de Staël see in Benjamin Constant? For a long while it was primarily the agile conversational give-and-take and the intellectual pursuits they shared, in addition to his exemplary devotion. Her distinguished aristocratic friends, such as Mathieu de Montmorency, who had fought in the American War of Independence with Lafayette, could not understand or appreciate what she saw in him. "He is a man of very superior intellect," she reminded Ribbing as late as January 23, 1796, assuring him yet again that love did not come into it, while adding, "There are few who, as regards social intercourse,

accord so well with my tastes in conversation and, above all, in literature. So much for his personal attractions. As for his virtues, he is
devoted to me as no man on earth would be, given the conditions I
impose on him. He is entirely lacking in strength of character and
physical charm, and I cannot conceive of love without one of these
attributes. . . . I think strength of character is the ideal quality. . . .
Intellect alone does not make a marriage, happiness in love, any more
than does great talent on the fortepiano."[30]

Even clearer is a letter to Ribbing written on March 10, 1796,
where she becomes more specific while using the euphemisms of the
day. Speaking again of Benjamin to claim that he was not her lover, she
declared, "He has a great taste for my best talent, wit. He shares
in those literary occupations with which I fill the empty hours of a
woman's life, and finally, I think I told you, under the seal of secrecy,
and despite my distaste for such a subject, how during the divorce
proceedings his wife gave as a reason the wretched state of his health.
It seems to me that he lies outside the course of love, at least love that
one inspires."[31] Generously, Benjamin had told his wife to charge him
with every shortcoming and misdemeanor, provided they did not stain
his reputation, and presumably impotence due to ill health was among
them. Germaine still seemed keen to diminish Benjamin's likelihood as
a lover in Ribbing's eyes, and perhaps she protested too much about his
possible limitations in that area. Yet she was perfectly and repeatedly
clear about being unable to conceive of love with a man who lacked a
strong, courageous, virile personality and a fine appearance.

What Germaine did perceive in Benjamin from the start was his
potential: here, she felt sure, was another important thinker, a second
Montesquieu. His father, Juste de Constant, and other members of his
family recognized his precocious talents—but for what? Was he destined for a literary career as a writer, scholar, historian, or philosopher,
or for a significant role in the administration of some German court?

They were still waiting for him to fulfill his promise. Germaine was always looking to share her life with some great man whose career she could promote, since that was the only role open to a woman with a keen interest in politics. To be the wife or companion of a gifted man who admired her father—for there could not exist another Jacques Necker—was her fondest dream.

Although he was a Swiss Protestant, her father had risen from banker and financier to the lofty and powerful position of virtual prime minister in Catholic France, where he was idolized as a savior for a time. Dismissed by Louis XVI and sent into exile on July 11, 1789, Necker was recalled a few days later after the fall of the Bastille. Germaine returned with him and her mother from Bâle, and she saw peasant women kneel in the fields as his carriage passed by. She would never forget the scene or the thrill she felt. On arriving in Paris it seemed to her as if the entire population of the city crowded into the streets: "Men and women shouted 'Long live M. Necker!' from windows and rooftops." When, from the balcony of the Hôtel de Ville, he spoke of peace for all French citizens whatever their party, he was greeted with wild popular acclamation. "I saw nothing more at that moment," Germaine recalled, "for I fainted from pure joy."[32] From then on, she sought to experience once again the *gloire* that had shed its golden light upon Necker, the *gloire* in whose rays she had basked. It was obvious from the beginning that her husband was never going to fulfill such a role. With Narbonne there were possibilities, and the place she procured for him as (short-lived) minister of war was the culmination of her efforts. Often she tried to convince the republican Ribbing that, if only he would put his mind to it, he could play a vital part in the new French Republic. Ribbing, however, was disillusioned with politics and disinclined to fall in with her ideas for him.

With Benjamin it was different: he was very ambitious, he loved books and reading, he ardently desired literary fame, and he spent many hours at his studies with a view to obtaining it. Germaine turned his head with her praises and her encouragement. Belle de Charrière, by contrast, had tried to moderate the heady flight of his ambition and, in his opinion, had tried to kill his desire for *la gloire littéraire:* "Even the shadowy trace of literary fame that you made every effort to kill within me," he told Belle on September 26, 1794, "has returned, and renders the future more attractive."[33] So it was after he met Germaine that he felt the habit of work was restored, and with it came the enthusiasm and the spirit of emulation that, in turn, inspired her. Where Belle showed little faith in humankind, Germaine was a firm believer in the worth of human striving and the possibilities for human progress. At first Benjamin was just one of the many friends Germaine loved to stimulate, encourage, and draw out to their best advantage.

When Benjamin met Germaine, she was already a great celebrity, whereas he was as yet unknown to the general public. Although he had previously scorned such notoriety, he was dazzled when he finally met her. She was, moreover, *"la fille de M. Necker,"* a famous statesman now living in retirement who might be regarded as either a charlatan or a demigod but was so wealthy that he had been able to lend millions to the royal exchequer. Germaine might be bourgeois in origin and hence regarded as a parvenue by some members of the Swiss upper class, but her present status as the wife of the Swedish ambassador to France, and as a woman who had witnessed or been concerned in great revolutionary events there, contrasted with Benjamin's more limited political experience as a member of the Vaudois gentry, excluded from positions of power by the ruling class in Berne.

She had been actively engaged in matters he had only read or heard about. She knew personally a number of the leading figures on the revolutionary scene, partly because they had at one time sought or enjoyed Necker's patronage and partly because she entertained a wide circle in her salon as *madame l'ambassadrice.* In addition, she had proved herself courageous, resourceful, and energetic in rescuing people from the Terror, while Benjamin had merely pondered the situation from Germany. Her status was indeed dazzling, and to cap it all, she was wealthy. The thorny question of finance would figure prominently in their future relationship. Since his youth Benjamin had been a gambler, and by the time he met Germaine he had already accumulated sizable debts. He was always to be much concerned about his inheritance, what he called "*ma fortune,*" in his letters to his father and other members of his family, as well as in his diary. Given all this—her charisma, fame, position, and standing—no wonder he thought that she was "a superior Being" and that he had never met anyone like her. There *was* no one like her. That was part of the attraction, and it would develop into part of the problem.

By September 1794, moreover, Germaine was already a well-known author. At twenty-two she had written a study of the writings and character of Jean-Jacques Rousseau that had caused a stir not only in France but also in England where, in *A Vindication of the Rights of Woman,* the revolutionary feminist Mary Wollstonecraft had criticized her reluctance to condemn the philosopher's condescension toward women and her failure to promote equality for her sex. Benjamin had read voraciously whatever came to hand, from the literature of antiquity to modern French, British, and German philosophy, but what he had written on moral or religious topics remained in manuscript, often unfinished and put aside. The new Montesquieu had not yet published anything of importance. In many ways, then, his position looked inferior to hers. If in the beginning he saw only the pleasures, advantages, and prospects in being closely associated with Mme de Staël, it was not until later, and under the pressure of dire public events, that he would begin to have second thoughts.

His eventual debt to her would be considerable. It was Germaine who focused and channeled his diverse and dispersed gifts. Before a political career was on his agenda, she encouraged him to write on political affairs for the public and guided and promoted him and his writings. She took him with her to Paris, where he would first become known for the pamphlets he published under her aegis during the Directoire. She introduced him not only to the intricacies of French political life but also to the immense network of her contacts, including important notabilities like abbé Emmanuel-Joseph Sieyès, who would prove so useful to him in his later career. With aid from her father she gave him considerable financial assistance, providing him with funds to help buy an estate outside Paris, ownership of property in France being an essential prerequisite for any political aspirant.

What man in the eighteenth century—or later—would be happy to admit to himself, let alone to others, that he owed his advancement to a woman? No doubt Benjamin would have made his way without her somehow, in some area of endeavor, but it would have been much more difficult for him to do so, and he would have advanced at a much slower pace. Without Germaine de Staël, what prospect would there have been for the Benjamin Constant of 1795, a modest Swiss-born chamberlain at the court of Brunswick, to gain a political foothold in France, where he was unknown, amid the often-corrupt intriguers and the bitter factional upheavals of the Directoire?

The seeds of future complexities and confrontations were already being sown even before those two great icons of French liberalism became intimate.

CHAPTER TWO

Prodigies

WHAT EMOTIONAL AND INTELLECTUAL BAGGAGE did Germaine de Staël and Benjamin Constant bring to the journey of their partnership? What family background and situation, what upbringing and education, molded their sensibility, individuality, and outlook on life?

Benjamin, like Germaine, was an only child. Anne-Louise-Germaine Necker was the sole issue of the marriage of Suzanne Curchod and Jacques Necker; Benjamin Constant was the sole issue of the marriage of Henriette de Chandieu and Juste Constant de Rebecque. The essential and dominating fact of Benjamin's early life was the death of his mother, a fortnight after his birth. Consequently, he was left to the tender mercies of his father, who, as a Swiss officer in the army of the Prince of Orange, was frequently absent on military service in the Low Countries. Benjamin's paternal grandmother, Rose-Suzanne de Constant, looked after him in the beginning, followed by his father's young mistress, Marianne Magnin. Constant, who wrote so much about himself, says remarkably little about his feelings for the mother he never knew, either because those feelings were too painful to be expressed or because her death and absence had become so remote. The consequences of her loss were nonetheless grave: although he was not neglected, as a small child he did not experience any truly close maternal tenderness and care. By contrast, Germaine was cherished. Mme Necker had only two major emotional concerns apart from the Deity: her husband and her daughter.

Benjamin's early life was ruled by a domineering father who wanted to do the best for his son but had little idea of how to go about it, relying on the odd advice of various colleagues and friends. Germaine, however, was in the hands of a loving but controlling mother. Her father was far too busy with financial and state affairs to concern himself with his daughter's upbringing when she was small.

Mme Necker had a plan: to turn her child into someone worthy of her husband and herself, someone extraordinary. She was a woman of considerable talent, keen to commit her thoughts to paper, but her literary ambitions were frustrated by her husband despite his own similar ambitions, which he fulfilled. As Suzanne Curchod—beautiful, cultivated—she was admired and courted in Lausanne, not least by the future historian of the decline and fall of the Roman Empire, Edward Gibbon, whose father resolutely refused to countenance "this strange alliance." "After a painful struggle I yielded to my fate: the remedies of absence and time were at length effectual," Gibbon wrote complacently in his memoirs.[1] The death of her father, a modest clergyman, left the jilted Mlle Curchod with very limited means: she was reduced to becoming companion to a lady and traveled with her to Paris.

There, she encountered among the friends of her benefactress a rising Genevan banker, Jacques Necker. Their marriage carried her from a subordinate position to one of prominence in Parisian society. Her love and admiration for her husband and his talents knew no bounds. Her salon, the chief purpose of which was to promote her husband's career, was frequented by many of the prominent men of letters, political thinkers, reformers, and *philosophes* of the Enlightenment. It was said that she herself never acquired the ease in repartee and the vivacity and polish in conversation that would distinguish her daughter. Some felt that there was always something rather stilted, reserved, and repressed about her. Prone to strict self-examination, she was also endowed with a morbid imagination. In particular, she was obsessed with the notion of premature burial after learning—on her charitable visits to hospitals—the fate of unfortunates who were buried before they were clinically dead.

This was the woman who was in sole charge of Germaine's education, for Mme Necker had decided to undertake the child's education herself, at home. In the second half of the eighteenth century it was not unusual for mothers to teach their own children, especially after Rousseau laid such stress on the importance of a caring mother in a child's early development. It was customary in France, however, to send a girl at about the age of six to a convent, where she would remain until leaving at sixteen to be married. A convent was out of the question for Mme Necker, a devout Calvinist. Besides, she felt herself to be well equipped for the role of teacher. Pastor Curchod had given her lessons in Latin and even taught her a little Greek, and her studies included geometry and physics. It was considered an exceptional education for a girl of her day.

Mme Necker's plan of education was to follow that of Rousseau's controversial *Emile ou l'éducation,* or so she said. Germaine, who was called Louise or Minette by her parents, was to follow the role of Emile himself, not that of Sophie, trained to be his helpmeet. In fact, Mme Necker subverted Rousseau: until he was twelve, when his studies were to begin, Emile was to enjoy a natural life with Sophie in the open air and to be kept away from religion and books. Mme Necker was not in favor of playmates and the open air but of "a sort of gymnastics of the intellectual faculties."[2] Reading books and commenting upon them from an early age provided flexibility in thinking, which was the key to a sound education. Benjamin, too, became an avid reader as a boy.

Books were a refuge, a solace, and studying a pleasure, even—in Germaine's later view—a source of self-esteem.

Germaine was only two years old when her mother introduced her to the Old and New Testaments and to works of piety. Mme Necker taught her daughter Latin and English, history, geography, mathematics, physics, and theology. As a girl she studied the great works of seventeenth-century French literature as well as more modern authors, and she was familiar with English poetry and fiction, from Milton and Gray to Fielding and Richardson. In 1776, when she was ten years old, her parents, accompanied by their friend Jean-Baptiste Suard, an authority on British literature and thought, took her on a journey to England. It served to confirm the passion for all things English that was then highly fashionable in French society and that she shared with her father and mother—and, indeed, with Benjamin also. There she met among other notabilities her mother's former suitor, Edward Gibbon, now a friend; saw with delight the great David Garrick in *Hamlet;* and was duly impressed on visiting the Houses of Parliament. Mme Necker was keen on the knowledge of languages, and Germaine was said to be fluent in English by the time she was twelve. She also had to answer questions like, "What is the best government?" Of the four types of European government—monarchical, aristocratic, democratic, and mixed—she chose the last because a government led by many is less risky than the rule of one man alone. A bad monarch could ruin his country, while in the past there had been independence under a mixed government. It is tempting to imagine that this answer foreshadows her future opposition to the rule of a dictator and her urge to independence.

The effect of this peculiar hothouse education was indeed to produce a prodigy, though one with whom Mme Necker was never quite satisfied. She was an extremely passionate woman who spent her life trying to suppress her passionate nature, aiming to keep it within the bounds of cool reason. She recognized the same impassioned emotionalism in Germaine and did her utmost to control it. Once, when her parents were briefly absent and she was left alone with the servants, the girl wrote a despairing letter to her mother in which she betrayed the perennial terror of an only child at the thought of being left permanently alone by the death of her parents: "My dear Mamma, I need to write to you. My heart feels tight, I am sad, and in this large house, which only a short while ago enclosed all I hold dear, and where my entire world and my future were confined, I realize that this expanse is too large for me, and I run into my little room so that my eyes can at least take in the surrounding emptiness. Your brief absence has made me tremble for my fate."[3] She was writing sometime between the ages of ten and twelve, but this dread of the void, of isolation and absence, would endure throughout her life. It would make her cling desperately to those she loved as she clung to her mother. And she would try to fill the black hole that her imagination conceived so vividly with endless discussions with her friends and ceaseless activity. Yet the sadness and melancholy, the ennui and anguish of existence, lurked beneath the effervescent gaiety she displayed in society, ready to pounce at any moment.

As the letter continued, she confessed to her mother all her faults and shortcomings: "Oh mamma, do correct me," she cried, as she begged her mother for permission to kiss her. "I shall take every care to subdue my whims and please you (if I possibly can) in every way."[4] That telling proviso in parenthesis points to her struggle to conform and her consciousness of failure, of never being able to fulfill her mother's demands and attain her high standards of conduct. She kissed her mother's letters and anticipated the boundless joy and ecstasy she would feel when they were reunited, then she hoped her mother would not be annoyed at this expression of feeling. Every moment of her life was consecrated to her mamma, she declared, and she vowed that her affection would increase and last to the end of her days. Mme Necker's response to her daughter's outpourings was deliberately cool: "Tell me that you love me and prove it by making your heart and your reason ever more perfect, by always sacrificing your character, and elevating your soul through religion."[5] Try as hard as she might, Mme Necker never succeeded as she hoped in forming a replica of herself, in curbing Germaine's natural warmth, impulsiveness, and vivacity.

In Mme Necker's strict regime Germaine took no exercise and had no companions of her own age until she was about eleven. Then, after much hesitation, Mme Necker found a suitable friend in the person of Catherine Huber, who was two years older than Germaine. When Mme Huber suggested an excursion to the Bois de Boulogne, Germaine trembled with fear lest her mother might say no. With reluctance Mme Necker acquiesced, but she fretted about the safety of the carriage and gave instructions about how to descend carefully from it. Germaine was so excited at the rare prospect of an outing without her mother that she kissed Mme Huber's hands and threw her arms about her neck. She did not see the woods, the other carriages, or the promenaders; "she saw only her own happiness and was concerned only with that," recorded Catherine Huber.[6] Here is the torrent of excessive emotion that Mme Necker called "the exaggeration of feeling" and strove in vain to subdue.

The hothouse regime finally affected Germaine's health. Her worried parents consulted the famous Dr. Tronchin. He prescribed country air and forbade books and reading. Germaine, accompanied by a governess and a maid, traveled to the château that her father had purchased in 1770 at Saint-Ouen outside Paris. According to Mme Necker's friend, the now-forgotten poet Antoine-Léonard Thomas, the house boasted a handsome terrace overlooking the Seine; he found the place very restful. Germaine thought it was the prettiest house in existence. She ran about in the great park and played games with

Catherine Huber who came to visit each week. It was not long before Germaine broke free of her mother's control, just at the time when her father began to take more interest in her, finding in his effervescent daughter a relief from the burden of matters of state. "Let's go and see Minette," he would say. Once, Mme Necker was shocked to find them chasing each other around the dining table with napkins wound around their heads like turbans. Gradually Germaine transferred her filial love to her father. "I love my father excessively," she was to write later in her portrait of him.[7]

The second part of Germaine's education took place in her mother's salon. This was Mme Necker's sphere: her husband put in a rare appearance but took no part in the conversation. Next to Mme Necker's armchair was a little stool where thirteen-year-old Germaine sat up straight, as she was instructed, just as she does in the famous drawing by Carmontelle. There, her hair is piled high, resembling a powdered wig, her tight bodice is heavily beribboned, and she looks as if about to speak. Catherine Huber recounted how four or five gentlemen once drew near to Germaine: one of them, wearing a little round wig, took her hands in his and kept them there, conversing with her as if she were twenty-five. This was abbé Guillaume Raynal, then about sixty years old, one of the most distinguished thinkers of the day and author of the important *Histoire philosophique et politique des établissements et du commerce des Européens dans les deux Indes,* which had appeared a few years earlier in 1774. It was a work that attacked tyranny and superstition: it would be placed on the Index, then later condemned to be burnt, and Raynal would have to flee into exile. An assembly of equally celebrated and farseeing writers and philosophers frequented Mme Necker's salon, including Jean-François Marmontel, the novelist and playwright; abbé André Morellet, the economist; Friedrich Melchior, Baron von Grimm, German by birth but French in taste and editor of the prestigious *Correspondance littéraire,* which circulated among the crowned heads of Europe, not least Catherine the Great; comte de Buffon, the distinguished naturalist; and Jean Le Rond d'Alembert, the eminent mathematician, and Denis Diderot, the multitalented and highly original essayist, storyteller, and art critic, who together founded the great *Encyclopédie,* an attempt to embrace all existing knowledge. Among the guests were many freethinkers and atheists, but the pious Mme Necker did not bar her door to anyone who could engage in "gymnastics of the intellectual faculties" or who might prove useful to her husband.

During dinner, Catherine Huber recalled, she and Germaine did not say anything, just listened.

> But you should have seen how Mlle Necker listened! Her gaze followed the movements of those who were speaking and she seemed to apprehend their ideas before they uttered them. She did not open her mouth and yet she appeared to speak, so expressive were her animated features. She was aware of everything, grasped and understood everything, even political subjects, which at that time provided one of the main topics of conversation. After dinner, many more people arrived. Each person, on approaching Mme Necker, said a word or two to her daughter, paid her a compliment or shared a joke. She replied with easy grace. Some took pleasure in provoking her, embarrassing her, or exciting her young imagination that already revealed its brilliance. Men who were most distinguished for their wit exerted themselves to encourage her to speak.[8]

The novelist Mme de Genlis, an authority on education, thought that Mme Necker brought up her daughter very badly by letting her spend so much time in her salon among the crowd of wits. To Mme de Genlis's disapproval they surrounded Mlle Necker and, while her mother's attention was elsewhere, discussed with her all sorts of subjects that were far beyond her years, including the passion of love.

Germaine's early contacts with some of the leading minds of the eighteenth century helped to shape and stimulate her own ideas. If Mme Necker encouraged the ability to seize, assimilate, and play with ideas at a young age, most vital to Germaine's intellectual development was her encounter with outstanding rebels and reformers. Here were those independent thinkers who were ready to question everything and accept nothing on authority, those fighters for justice, toleration, enlightenment, and "the new ideas" she herself would propagate so enthusiastically throughout her life. The influence of her father was also significant. Once she was in her teens, he treated her as a friend, some said like a lover, rather than as a daughter. And she confided to her diary how she wished she had been born at the same time he was, so that she could have been his wife. Certainly, she absorbed something of Necker's stance on reform, his desire for moderation, his dislike of theories and systems.

How different from Necker, ponderous, prudent, conscious of his own worth and that of his wife and daughter, was Benjamin's father! Juste Constant de Rebecque was imposing and severe but also erratic, unpredictable, rash, and distinctly odd. A military man from a military family (many of the Vaudois gentry, excluded from office by the rulers in Berne, offered their services to foreign armies), he dominated his son. Though fond of each other, they were sometimes tongue-tied when they were together, or else they argued, often about money. Of Juste's eccentricities perhaps the most notorious was his kidnapping of an intelligent little girl of nine named Marianne Magnin from her modest home, a crime that went unpunished and that he committed before his marriage to Benjamin's mother. He arranged for the girl's education in Holland, a country where she knew no one, and later made her his mistress and eventually his second wife. Benjamin did not discover until many years afterward that he had a half-brother and half-sister, a fact that led him worry even more about his inheritance. His feelings toward Marianne, who looked after him when he was a small child, veered between expressed gratitude for her kindness and private aggressiveness against "this harpy." Later Juste became embroiled in a lawsuit with his superiors which lasted many years and which, through his rash and imperious behavior, he finally lost. This lawsuit darkened Benjamin's life. Creditably, he made every effort to help his father, but his efforts were in vain. Much of the family property was confiscated, and Juste retired to France, to Brevans, near Dôle, claiming French citizenship as a descendent of Huguenots who had been expelled.

Benjamin's cousin Rosalie de Constant left a vivid portrait of her uncle. According to her, Juste cared less for his first wife than she for him: when she died in childbirth, they had been married for only two years, and she was soon forgotten. Benjamin was not brought up to cherish his mother's memory, declared Rosalie. "The third son of General Constant, named Juste, was imposing in appearance, very intelligent, and very eccentric. Mistrustful, secretive . . . he has the ability to inspire love . . . but also no one knows better how to wound and mortify people with his bitter irony."[9] Benjamin inherited his tone of irony, his caustic tongue. His father could not fail to note his son's precocious talents—Benjamin was as advanced at thirteen as most people are at thirty, thought Rosalie—and set about providing him with what he thought would be a most suitable education for a prodigy with prospects.

If Germaine's education was eccentric, Benjamin's was bizarre. Benjamin himself described it in *Le Cahier rouge* (so called from the red binding of his notebook), a memoir begun in 1811 and abruptly discontinued. This account of his early years, complemented by his letters to his grandmother, is as lively as a picaresque tale—ironic, amusing, and on occasion appalling in its implications. The voice of amused irony, adopted with hindsight, barely conceals an undertone of distress at a lonely and distorted childhood. A succession of unlikely or unpromising tutors, frequent coming and going between Switzerland and the Low Countries, a brief visit to London and Oxford, and many months spent at distinguished universities, first at Erlangen in Bavaria and then in Edinburgh, made up the scarcely credible story of Benjamin's education. Formal it was not, but somehow, from an early age, Benjamin acquired a deep love of learning and study, along with less reputable occupations that he acquired from the example of others, like gambling and a taste for prostitutes.

When he was not yet five his father engaged a German named Ströhlin as a tutor, who taught Benjamin Greek as a kind of game, and who beat him and then smothered him with affection to make up for it and prevent him from telling his father. This abuse was discovered, and Ströhlin thrown out. Next, after spending some time in Brussels, a lively place where officers like his father who were garrisoned at Bois-le-Duc came on leave, Benjamin, now seven, was taught by a Frenchman named La Grange, a regimental surgeon who proved to be thoroughly disreputable. A mediocre, ignorant, vain man, in Benjamin's opinion, he was also an atheist who took the boy to live with him in a brothel. He, too, was dismissed. Then Juste placed his son with his music master, who was a decent fellow but did nothing for the boy's education. Left to his own devices, Benjamin spent eight or ten hours a day in a *cabinet littéraire,* or lending library, reading whatever he found there, including erotic novels and irreligious works. His eyes suffered, and his eyesight was to trouble him throughout his life.

From 1776, the year Germaine visited England for the first time, his tutor was a former French lawyer who had left France under suspicious circumstances. M. Gobert lived in Brussels with a young woman he called his housekeeper. He taught Benjamin some Latin and history. Eventually, the scandal of his domestic arrangements and other matters aroused public gossip that reached the ears of Juste, who, at the end of 1778, took his son back to Switzerland, where he stayed at the family properties of La Chablière and Le Désert, near Lausanne, until the spring of 1779. Benjamin passed to another Frenchman, M. Duplessis, who turned out to be a defrocked monk trying to avoid the authorities and who later committed suicide. The boy spent over a year with him, partly in Switzerland and partly in the Low Countries, and made some progress. But the list is not complete: there would follow young Nathaniel May, who gave him lessons but was regarded more as a companion than a tutor; and then, finally, came a man of serious learning, M. Bridel, a member of the Protestant clergy. Altogether there were seven widely differing men in charge of Benjamin's education, usually chosen because someone had recommended them to Juste. And once Juste became disillusioned with an appointee he expressed his scorn and mockery in his son's presence.

From Brussels when he was twelve Benjamin wrote to his grandmother, Rose-Suzanne de Constant, for whom he felt genuine affection, describing how he rose at seven and after breakfast worked at translating Horace and had music lessons with M. Duplessis, followed by dancing lessons. After lunch, he read Quintus Curtius, wrote Latin verse, had a lesson on the harpsichord, played piquet, had his supper, and went to bed at nine. Sometimes he went to the theater. Twice a week he went out into *le grand monde:* "I have a fine coat, a sword, and I carry my hat under my arm. I act the grown-up as well as I can. I observe, I listen . . ."[10] He said he was not much taken with worldly pleasures but—ominously—he was fascinated by the gaming table. Gambling was one of the chief and ruinous diversions of the well-to-do society of the day, and Benjamin soon became addicted.

His health was never really sound: from an early age he suffered from feverish nervous attacks. "I wish my blood could be prevented from circulating so fast and could be given a more harmonious flow," he told his grandmother. "I have tried to see if music could produce this result, I play adagios and largos that would send thirty cardinals to sleep . . . but I do not know by what magic these slow airs always end by becoming prestissimo. . . . I believe, my dear grandmother, that this illness is incurable and will resist reason itself; I should have some spark of it because I am twelve and a few days, yet I am not aware of its empire; if its dawn is so faint, what will it be like at twenty-five?"[11] What an extraordinarily knowing letter for a twelve-year-old! It is self-regarding, self-aware, humorous, and aims to entertain as well as enlighten his grandmother about his activities.

What did Benjamin glean from this erratic and undisciplined education? He was reading Homer before he was nine, and between the ages of ten and twelve he added Cicero, Ovid, Horace, and other Latin authors as well as Roman history. He was acquainted with the principles of eighteenth-century philosophy and the work of materialists like Julien de La Mettrie, author of *L'Homme machine,* and especially Claude-Adrien Helvétius, a skeptical empiricist who criticized the church and its influence and preferred paganism to Christianity. As for Voltaire, the hammer of ecclesiastical obscurantism, superstition, and injustice, he was a friend of the Constant family, and Benjamin shared something of his brilliant use of irony as a weapon. Doubtless he was familiar with Voltaire's writings—for who was not? But he did not claim any particular connection with the author of the *Dictionnaire philosophique* as he did with Helvétius and his *De l'Esprit.* Nor, apparently, did he pay a visit to the sage of Ferney, unlike many members of cultivated European society, including Mme Necker, who took Germaine with her to see the great man.

In contrast to Germaine's sheltered existence, Benjamin's life was marked by early contact with the seamier side of human behavior through the conduct of his more disreputable tutors. Evidently missing from his upbringing was any stress on moral rectitude or any religious instruction of the sort that Mme Necker instilled into Germaine. Benjamin, however, was immensely interested in religion, though in his youth it was chiefly with a view toward combating what was called "prejudice" in imitation of his favorite *philosophes*. Both Germaine and Benjamin had early literary ambitions. He wrote a tragedy, *Dido*, and also a heroic novel, *Les Chevaliers*, about the battles of Charlemagne and his knights against the Saracens. His proud father saw to it that this novel was published in Brussels in 1779. Benjamin was twelve, more or less the same age as Germaine, who was then writing plays that were being performed at Saint-Ouen.

When he was thirteen, in 1780, his father took him to London, where they stayed only briefly, and then to Oxford. There is no record of him at the university, but he spent two months in the city, learning English. It was at this time that Juste engaged Nathaniel May, a young student at Lincoln College, who accompanied Benjamin for a year and a half in Switzerland and the Low Countries. Some while afterward Juste happened to meet again an elevated acquaintance, the Margrave of Anspach-Bayreuth (whose mistress at the time was the ubiquitous actress Mlle Clairon). He advised Juste to send his son to the University of Erlangen, founded some forty years before. There Benjamin acquired a good knowledge of German language, literature, and thought, dividing his time between serious study, attendance at court, dissipation, and the accumulation of gambling debts. By the time he was about sixteen he felt it necessary for his standing to keep a mistress, and he bizarrely chose a person of easy virtue whom he did not love and who did not grant him her favors. Benjamin's mockery of the ruler's wife, the Margravine, who had been gracious to him, reached her ears: she would later refer to him as having "the tongue of a viper."[12]

Juste decided to withdraw his son, who was no longer welcome at court, from Erlangen and took him to Edinburgh, where he had good friends. It was July 1783. After placing Benjamin in the home of a teacher of medicine, Juste departed. Benjamin enrolled at the University and so began what he called "the most pleasant year of my life."[13] Edinburgh was no longer seen as Auld Reekie, so called for its noisome alleys, but as the Athens of the North, a city endowed with noble buildings and renowned for its innovative writers and scholars like David Hume, Adam Smith, Adam Ferguson, and many others esteemed throughout the civilized world. Benjamin was far from being the only foreign student: the university attracted many who came from abroad to study medicine, law, or political economy.

Benjamin joined various university associations: notably, on November 18, 1783, he was elected to the Speculative Society, a well-known debating society with its own hall. He attended its sessions regularly. Among the many political and social issues that were debated, Benjamin voted yes on the question, "Was the execution of Charles I justifiable?" His opinions were already radical. He opened the debate on whether there should be universal toleration, and on November 23, 1784, he gave an address on the influence of pagan mythology on manners and character—a theme that would occupy him for many years, culminating in his book on paganism, *Du Polythéisme romain considéré dans ses rapports avec la philosophie grecque et la religion chrétienne*, published posthumously in 1833. Another question under debate was "Would it be to the advantage of society to permit women to have a learned education?" Even among these open-minded students, twelve voted no and only five voted yes, but Benjamin was the teller for the "yes" vote, indicating that his views on female education were liberal for the day.

He made a number of good friends in Edinburgh, and he would keep in touch with some of them. Interestingly, he does not mention any childhood friends in *Le Cahier rouge*. Like Germaine, he presumably had no friends of his own age in his early years. Among his new companions was the future polymath James Mackintosh, many years later a friend of Germaine's, who remembered the young man he called baron Constant de Rebecque in his memoirs as "a Swiss of singular manner and powerful talents."[14] Benjamin was also friendly with Malcolm Laing, who was to publish a notable *History of Scotland,* and he was particularly attached to John Wilde, a brilliant professor of civil law. Benjamin was later to be deeply saddened upon learning of Wilde's cruel fate as the inmate of a lunatic asylum. Wilde certainly had the measure of Benjamin's complex, changeable, and contradictory nature, describing him as "constant in versatility, in inconstancy constant."[15] It seemed to Wilde that his Swiss companion had drawn freedom with his first breath. Indeed, the months of personal liberty as a student in Scotland, without parental harassment, were crucial. These human relationships and contacts with the inquiring and liberal tradition of thought and discussion north of the border, this encounter with the Scottish Enlightenment, was to leave a profound mark on Benjamin's outlook. He said that his "Scottish politics" inclined him to the reforming party of the British Whigs, and he always kept a Scottish burr when speaking English.

Benjamin lived in Edinburgh for almost two years: all went well, except that when he departed, his gambling debts remained unpaid. After three weeks in London he traveled to Paris, where he arrived in May 1785, and rapidly fell in with bad company, leading a dissolute life and visiting prostitutes. He was eighteen. That same year, Germaine's marriage to M. de Staël was finally being settled. When Benjamin went to stay with the hospitable Jean-Baptiste Suard and his wife, Amélie, both well known in the publishing and literary life of Paris, he could meet at their gatherings many of the prominent writers who frequented Mme Necker's salon, including Morellet and Marmontel. The liberal proto-feminist philosophe, the marquis de Condorcet, was a great friend of the Suards; he and his young wife, Sophie, would often be found in their company. Benjamin's contact with the writers and philosophes who gathered in Mme Suard's salon—contact that would be repeated when he again stayed with the couple in 1786–1787—took place when he was much older than Germaine had been. Her memorable encounters with them had occurred at a more impressionable age.

Doubtless, the skeptical rationalism of these thinkers exerted an influence on Benjamin, but it was in a direction that he had already taken, through the books he had read in the *cabinet littéraire* and elsewhere, and through his encounter with the Scottish Enlightenment and its representatives. M. Suard, too, was familiar with Scottish thinkers: he had been friendly with David Hume (who died some years before) and corresponded with several others and translated their works. Benjamin followed suit by translating a chapter of the *History of Ancient Greece* by John Gillies, whose brother Adam he had met in Edinburgh: it was published as *Essai sur les moeurs des temps héroïques de la Grèce* in 1787. This serious effort appeared a year before Germaine's *Lettres sur les écrits et le caractère de Jean-Jacques Rousseau*, a more personal and wide-ranging work that had a far greater impact. Benjamin's head was full of projects that he began and then often discarded, unfinished, including a refutation of Jacques Necker's book on religion, *De l'importance des idées religieuses*. Nonetheless he accumulated a large amount of material in manuscript form that he would be able to draw on in later years.

Women now began to figure more prominently, according to Benjamin's account in *Le Cahier rouge*. At eighteen he had a very brief liaison in Brussels with gentle Mme Marie-Charlotte Johannot, a lady from Geneva who was so sweet and undemanding that twenty-five years afterward he still remembered her with particular regard. In contrast, his pursuit of flirtatious Mrs. Harriet Trevor in Lausanne and of indifferent Mlle Jenny Pourrat in Paris were, as he makes plain, perfect examples of what Stendhal would call *amour de tête,* or love in the mind, though none the less painful and despairing for that.

These "affairs" were on a different level—a nonintellectual level—than his friendship with Mme de Charrière. Benjamin and Belle were enchanted by the long conversations they held all day and well into the night. When he came to stay with her and her husband at their house at Colombier, the two friends sent each other notes from their respective bedrooms. They took tea together and indulged their pet dogs. When he caught some venereal disease Belle looked after him and helped him recover. Benjamin was deeply touched: not only was he fond of her, but also he admired her as a person of strong and unusual character and as the author of *Caliste.* In her fiction, she dealt with remarkable, venturesome women, misunderstood by a narrow society and let down by weak men subservient to convention and to dominant fathers. He was taken with Belle's originality and her spirit of independence that chimed with his deepest desires. They began to collaborate on a novel.

It was while under her libertarian influence that Benjamin undertook his most extraordinary adventure. On an impulse, just when he was expected to return to his reproachful father, twenty-year-old Benjamin set out from Paris for England on his own, without the servant who usually accompanied him, and with only thirty louis that he had borrowed from Belle. Hiring a post chaise and horses, he rode hard and reached Calais in twenty-two hours. In those days, as he pointed out in *Le Cahier rouge*—in sharp contrast with life under Napoleon in 1811—no passports were required for the crossing to Dover. On arrival in London with fifteen louis in his pocket, he spent two of them on a couple of dogs and a monkey, exchanged the monkey for a third dog, then sold two of the dogs for less than he paid for them. He visited London theaters and brothels; borrowed some funds from his father's banker; contemplated applying to John Adams—American diplomat and future president—for a permit to visit the United States; and set off via Newmarket across the country, partly on foot and partly on horseback, seeking assistance from some of Juste's associates and a few of his own, with varying success. By a circuitous route and after many vicissitudes he reached Edinburgh and was welcomed with much carousing by his old friends, including John Wilde. The return journey took him through Cumbria and Westmoreland, and he ended his travels convinced of the rose-colored view that England was "a garden," a land of wisdom and liberty, with clean inns and contented, reasonable inhabitants. During this escapade, which lasted over two months, he felt totally free, savoring "an unutterable feeling of well-being at my complete freedom." He valued being independent and on his own. As he was to write a few years later, "Literature and solitude, there is my true element."[16] It was one pole of his temperament.

With fear and trembling he returned to his father at Bois-le-Duc, dreading the reception that awaited him. He found Juste playing whist with his fellow officers. "Oh! There you are," said Juste, continuing with the game as if nothing had happened. In fact, Benjamin was hoping for a candid discussion about his future, but that never took place. There was, however, an unexpected and disagreeable surprise to come. His future had been decided: his father had found a post for him as chamberlain at the court of the Duke of Brunswick. Setting out on February 18, 1788, Benjamin arrived there on March 3. He would spend six long years of tedium in Brunswick, his duties often consisting of little more than having to seat people according to rank when the grand marshal was absent.

Belle and Benjamin corresponded throughout this period, and the two highly sensitive and susceptible beings read between the lines and scrutinized every phrase of their respective letters. No wonder, then, that "a few little clouds," as Benjamin called them, appeared on the horizon, in part because of the vagaries of the postal service.[17] In that era the post took a very long time: a letter despatched from Brunswick on March 7 reached Colombier on March 18, and Belle's reply of March 19 was in Benjamin's hands on March 30. Thus, the explanation of any ambiguous or ill-conceived phrase arrived too late to soothe some perceived wound or to restore lost harmony. Belle continued her motherly admonitions about Benjamin's conduct, which might have been tolerable to a man of twenty but were progressively irritating as he grew older. In her allusions to his shortcomings he could see yet another despotic yoke to be eluded.

Belle, too, might well have become wearied by his detailed analyses of his feelings and states of mind, by his concentration on himself and his doings. "I like speaking about myself," he owned. This pleasure in what he called "my chatter about myself" was one that he indulged immoderately.[18] And, to complicate matters, political differences arose. Brunswick was now one of the main centers in Germany where French royalist émigrés found refuge. Benjamin sympathized with their plight as refugees, but he could not bear the reactionaries among them. The Duke of Brunswick passed from having been regarded as an enlightened ruler to being one of the principal leaders of the counterrevolutionary invasion of France in 1792. In one notorious proclamation, he even threatened the French revolutionaries with extermination. While Belle, still privately a Dutch aristocrat, remained a moderate friend of émigrés she met in her region in Switzerland, Benjamin, out of a spirit of contradiction and a hatred of reaction, became an ardent and outspoken supporter of the Revolution, a position that proved too radical for Belle and one that certainly did not endear him to members of the ducal court.

Charles de Constant remarked in his diary in 1794 that he did not know what his cousin, a convinced republican, was doing in Brunswick as the chamberlain to a despotic duke. Yet the Brunswick years were not a total loss. For instance, Benjamin met there and became very friendly with a distinguished soldier and scholar of French descent, Jacob Mauvillon, whom he characterized as "the friend of liberty and enlightenment."[19] Mauvillon's sudden death in 1794 left him deeply distressed, and he determined to write a biography of his friend—an example of the quiet, scholarly existence that increasingly appealed to Benjamin. Great German libraries like the one at the university at Göttingen, whose professors he encountered, made a profound impression on him. Such was his own frenzy of book buying that when he left Brunswick he arranged for his treasured library of fifteen hundred books, culled from the three or four thousand that he had accumulated, to be forwarded to Lausanne. Building on the foundations he had laid earlier during his stay at Erlangen, he furthered his knowledge of German language, philosophy, history, and literature, an accomplishment rare among his educated French contemporaries. Indeed, he thought that German writings on philosophy and history were superior to anything written in French or English. He had developed, moreover, the aptitudes and habits of a scholar and a taste for quiet. The love of scholarship and a peaceful scholarly existence was one of the many conflicting elements that made up Benjamin's complex personality. When he met Germaine it was in the field of scholarship that his ambitions lay, his aim being to produce a great work on religion that would make his reputation "among a few scattered philosophes, lovers of toleration and liberty," or so he said.[20]

Even before he arrived in Brunswick, and especially under Belle's influence, Benjamin had adopted a superior, disillusioned air—the sort of ennui that was to become highly fashionable among young men and all the rage in literature. He made no secret of his scorn for the rest of humanity and indulged in double forms of irony, as Belle called them. He was not happy and said he never would be happy. The disappointment of his marriage to Minna, his sense of humiliation, and the long divorce proceedings increased his misery. He experienced dark periods of apathy during which the depression that overwhelmed him prevented him from stirring or doing anything at all. Why bother to move? What was the point when death awaited you at the end of everything, and after death, nothingness? These hours of "low spirits"—he used the English expression—were interspersed with occasional bursts of impulsive activity.

Benjamin was well aware of the strangeness of his upbringing and education. As he wrote to Belle on May 17, 1793, "I am fighting with all my strength against this indifference to vice and virtue which has been the result of my strange education and my even stranger life, and the cause of all my ills. As it goes against my character I shall easily overcome it. I am weary of being an egoist, of mocking my own feelings. . . . I wish to become trusting again, capable of belief and enthusiasm."[21] A year later, almost to the day, on May 24, 1794, only a few months before he met Germaine, he wrote to another confidante, his maternal aunt, the comtesse Anne-Marie de Nassau, using the same kind of language: "Believe me, my dear aunt, you wrong me by suspecting me of insensibility. Cast an eye again over my education, this wandering and disconnected life, these objects of vanity on which my childhood was weaned, this tone of irony that is my family's style, this affectation of making a mockery of feeling, of valuing only intellect and *gloire*, and ask yourself if it is surprising that my young brain was turned by all this. I have suffered from it too much not to reject it." He yearned to change.

He also now felt that indulgence in a sense of superiority was not worth sacrificing a moment of feeling. He continued: "I am tired of making fun of people. . . . Since this fine display of scorn has not made me happy, to the devil with the reputation of being superior to those who feel; if what makes one happy is folly, I prefer the folly of Enthusiasm to this fatal good sense, and even if it would be only out of egoism and calculation, I want to stop being calculating and egotistical. Return, then, passions I have deadened, simple and modest plea-sures I have rejected, common everyday virtues I have considered it meritorious to despise. Return, trust that I congratulated myself so foolishly on being without. Feelings of love, friendship, benevolence, happy candor that was torn from me by premature and pretentious lessons, return."[22] These strange and eloquent words—almost poetic in their final rhetorical invocation—are sandwiched oddly between a discussion on finance and an allusion to General Dumouriez, who abandoned his command and decamped to the Austrians, along with a statement of Benjamin's fondness for and high opinion of Mme de Charrière. Yet it seems plain that his words, whose intention is re-peated over the passage of a year, mark a departure, offering a tu-multuous welcome for "Enthusiasm," that counter to indifference and the quality most admired by Germaine, who would direct a famous paean to it at the end of her influential book on German culture, *De l'Allemagne*. With this letter to his aunt, Benjamin seems to be aiming in a new and more generous direction, as if preparing for his meeting with Germaine in September 1794.

To that encounter each one brought very distinct feelings and views concerning not only political matters but also love and marriage. That their spirits were attuned comes as no surprise, for both Germaine and Benjamin issued from the great forward flow of ideas and projects fostered by the eighteenth-century Enlightenment. Perhaps Germaine had greater faith than Benjamin in the virtues of its onward march. While he derived from the rational skepticism of Helvétius, she de-rived from the introspective emotionalism of Rousseau, who did not figure among Benjamin's favorite authors. Indeed, he would later op-pose Rousseau's notion of the General Will, a theory associated with what has been called "totalitarian democracy." In the matter of their education, if not in its manner, Germaine's had much in common with

Benjamin's, including the Anglomania of the day that in his case embraced all things Scottish. Benjamin, however, was more erudite; he had a stronger foundation in the literature of antiquity, in history, and certainly in German culture, which was unfamiliar to her at the time they met. No wonder she was impressed by his intellect.

Nonetheless, Germaine made up for any academic shortcomings with her greater political experience, acquired through daily contact with her father at a time when the world—and notably its writers, political figures, and philosophes—beat a path to his door. She was in Paris in the years immediately leading up to the French Revolution, and she witnessed a number of the decisive and tumultuous events that marked its early days and the whittling away of royal power. For instance, she was among the excited spectators on May 5, 1789, when the States General—the representatives of the nobility, clergy, and third estate—met for the first time since 1614, and she heard her father address the gathering. She was also present when the States General became the National Assembly, paying close attention to the speakers. She experienced, too, the high emotions aroused by Necker's dismissal and exile and his glorious recall.

Only a few months later, Germaine was present when the palace of Versailles was stormed. The morning of October 5, 1789, on hearing that armed members of the populace headed by a mass of hungry *poissardes*, or market women, were marching from the Hôtel de Ville to Versailles, she hurried by a side road to join her parents there. At the palace she heard gunshots and saw traces of blood on the floor—presumably that of the royal bodyguards who had been slain. The next day she witnessed the humiliation of Louis XVI and Marie Antoinette when, as virtual prisoners, they were forced to leave the splendors of Versailles for Paris and the rundown palace of the Tuileries, which had not been inhabited by a French king since young Louis XV had left it sixty-seven years before.

During this time, Germaine and her friends continued busily discussing everything that was going on, just as they had during the ancien regime: they still preserved high hopes from the revolutionary dawn, when it was bliss to be alive. She would look back on this time as the most brilliant age. Her salon in the Swedish embassy on the rue du Bac was widely admired; it played an important part in the general ferment as a place where the Constitution of 1791 was being formulated—and she could participate in the discussions. Among those who frequented her salon were Thomas Jefferson and other diplomats, Lafayette, Condorcet, Talleyrand (not yet a public figure), and Sieyès, the maker of constitutions whom she regarded as a great innovator. Soon, moreover, she was involved in obtaining Narbonne's appointment as minister of war.

On the eve of the fearful massacres that began on September 2, 1792, after having contrived to rescue Narbonne, Germaine set about trying to save other aristocratic liberal friends of hers, like the marquis de Jaucourt. Who was the right person to approach for help? She settled on Louis-Pierre Manuel, *procureur* of the Commune and one of the Jacobin leaders known to have literary ambitions. Fortunately, he proved to be amenable and found a way to save Jaucourt. Still, as the situation worsened, she had to accept that there was nothing to do but to leave Paris as soon as possible for Switzerland. Planning to collect a royalist acquaintance, abbé de Montesquiou, outside the city gates, she tried to leave. But, as she recalled in her reflections on the French Revolution, "some old women from hell," joined by a threatening crowd, suddenly blocked the path of her carriage, which was adorned with the Swedish coat of arms: they were convinced that she was absconding with the nation's gold.[23]

Germaine told how she was conveyed to the revolutionary committee of her area in the faubourg Saint-Germain and thence to the tribunal in the Hôtel de Ville. Progress was slow, and with one exception her guards remained unmoved by the fact that she was pregnant. At the place de Grève, where several victims had been massacred on August 10, "I stepped from my carriage into the midst of an armed multitude and moved forward under a vault of pikes. As I climbed the steps . . . a man aimed his pike at me. My guard protected me with his sabre; if I had fallen down at that moment my life would have been over."[24]

Brought before the apostle of virtue, Robespierre, the provincial lawyer with whom she had conversed at her father's two years before, she boldly spoke up for her right to leave Paris as the wife of the Swedish ambassador. Manuel vouched for her and then locked her and her maid in his office for safety: "We stayed there for six hours waiting for him, dying of hunger, thirst, and fear. The window looked out on the place de Grève, and we saw the murderers coming back from the prisons with bare, bloodstained arms and uttering dreadful shouts."[25] After nightfall Manuel returned, provided her with a passport, and led her home. The next day, Jean-Lambert Tallien, who was to be among the leaders who would overthrow Robespierre on 9 Thermidor (July 27, 1794), arrived to accompany her to the city gate. Tallien caught a glimpse of the endangered aristocrats hidden in the embassy, but he kept his promise to her that he would not give them away.

After Thermidor, when some thought the Revolution was over, and after meeting Germaine, Benjamin reported self-mockingly to Mme de Charrière in October 1794: "I have become a thorough Tallie-nist, and it is with pleasure that I see the moderate party firmly predominate over the Jacobins." He felt this might be construed as an unexpected reaction on the part of a "confirmed and fierce democrat such as I prided myself on being. I feel I am turning moderate."[26] At that time, the word "democrat" meant a person ardently devoted to the cause of the Revolution. Certainly, moderation had not always been his political position.

While Germaine experienced the Revolution firsthand, news of
the events in France often reached Benjamin in Brunswick, as he
admitted, in highly garbled form. He read the French gazettes when
they eventually arrived, though sometimes they failed to do so. French
émigrés there, keen on the restoration of the ancien regime, made
Brunswick a hotbed of conspiracy and rumor. Benjamin believed the
canard that, like the traitor Dumouriez, the leaders of the Girondin
party and Condorcet himself were in the pay of the Austrians. This
news was a great blow to Benjamin, as he had a very high opinion of
the Girondin minister, Jean-Marie Roland, whom he called his "idol,"
and the Girondins in general. In his hours of deep depression he said
that politics provided the only interest to arouse his curiosity—and
politics meant what was going on not in Switzerland, Germany, or
elsewhere but in France.

His position fluctuated. If, in 1792, he had hoped that Roland
would crush Jacobin vipers like Marat and Robespierre, by May 1794
he had adopted an extreme position closer to that of the Incorruptible
himself: if one was not for something one was against it. "To avoid
being ultra revolutionary I should not have to be among counterrevolutionaries," he told Belle. And in June 1794 he declaimed, "The
moderate parties are worthless, and at the present moment they are
worth less than ever." He had stood aghast at the proscriptions and
bloodletting of the Terror, yet later he began to accept Robespierre,
"tyrant" though he was, as a necessary evil that had to be transcended
to attain the desired end of a peaceful republic. "Whoever wants the
ends wants the means," he declared.[27] Germaine never adopted such an
extreme position. She never saw Robespierre or his regime as an inevitable means to a desirable end. This stance of Benjamin's appears as an
early aberration and yet also as a token of how he could be less moderate and conciliatory than she was. On the subject of the Jacobin Terror,
on terrorists and those she called reasoning assassins, on political

fanaticism in general, her judgment remained consistent. Her detestation of such excesses runs like a golden thread through her work.

By the time Benjamin moved into Germaine's orbit in the latter part of 1794 he had moderated his extreme opinions, which were due partly to his isolated position in Brunswick and partly also to the strain of contradictoriness in his character. He was, moreover, born a Swiss republican, as she was not; he had no taste for monarchy—after all, when in Edinburgh he had justified the execution of Charles I—and he detested aristocracy in the shape of the oppressive oligarchs of Berne. Parisian-born Germaine, whose beloved father served Louis XVI devotedly, favored then a constitutional monarchy and a liberal aristocracy. Benjamin was a republican before she was, but—through Ribbing—she had become a convinced republican by the time they met. This stance did not prevent her from remaining loyal to her aristocratic friends, a loyalty that would be held against her and would cost her dear.

Benjamin's Robespierrist inclinations were little more than political opinions. In 1794 he had no intention and no prospect of adopting a political career anywhere, least of all in France. Politics did not then occupy a vital place in his life as in Germaine's. With her, politics assumed the force of a passion and became enmeshed in the very fabric of her friendships and loves. If she was attached to a valued friend, and even more if she was in love with a person she admired, she did everything in her power to promote that person's political advancement. It was not just that she would be able to play a role through him; it was also that she could not love a man unless she admired his outstanding qualities that could be of service to the progress of the "new ideas."

As for Benjamin, he needed women, whether prostitutes for physical release or ladies of higher social standing to court and conquer. He looked to the passion of love to rouse him from depression and apathy. If it did not arrive he found some way to provoke it: "Besides, love is a feeling that one places, when one needs to do so, on the first person one sees. All the charms that it lends exist in the imagination of the one who feels it."[28] This Stendhalian remark, from his private diary in 1805, and others like it have made some think of him as a cynical seducer, rather in the style of Laclos's Valmont, a near contemporary since he appeared in *Les Liaisons dangereuses* in 1788. But unlike the fictional Valmont, Benjamin was in search of the feeling of passionate love; it is his cold eye that enables him to observe, as if from outside, the mechanism of his own sensations.

In some instances, this "feeling that one places" could give rise to violent passion, a passion that bore all the signs of genuine exquisite pain. Then, as with Mrs. Trevor, he would experience "a sort of fever that resembled the passion I had only wished to pretend in the beginning." In other circumstances, the suspicion of calculation—of somehow designing a show that is accepted and taken for the real thing—remains. This is what happens in *Adolphe,* Constant's novella, written in 1806–1807: Adolphe begins by feigning a love that Ellénore takes for true currency. As for killing oneself for love, Benjamin's strategy of threatening suicide with the aim of seducing a woman is made perfectly clear in *Le Cahier rouge* of 1811: "For a long time I had in my head the idea that to want to kill yourself for a woman was a way of pleasing her. This idea is not precisely true. When you already please a woman and she is only asking to yield, it is good to threaten suicide because she is being furnished with a decisive, swift, and honorable pretext. But when one is not loved at all, neither the threat nor the thing itself will have any effect."[29] For Benjamin, the physical consummation of love lay at the end of any strategy. It was a vital necessity in his life; he never contemplated love without it.

For Germaine it was different. She saw passionate love as an ideal state of feeling where the storms of passion prevail and should endure unchanged throughout life. How is one to know passionate love if it is not stormy? This passion, moreover, should foster in a woman pure devotion and self-sacrifice, of the kind Germaine proved for Narbonne, and should inspire a similar reaction in the ideal beloved. There should be, as it were, a quid pro quo in mutual devotion. Love, above all, is a union of souls. She once described her ideal man in a passage that she removed—perhaps wisely—from the published version of *De l'Allemagne:* "The idea occurred to me to depict the character of a man in all its perfection and strength." He is one who does not judge by following received ideas, but solely according to the "heart's impulses"; who is generous of soul "without any regard for human convention." He displays intrepid bravery combined with tender concern for the woman he loves, uniting force and gentleness; he is at once her protector and her slave. Most notably, he is endowed with a poetic imagination. The ideal man as she conceives him will judge men by "the warmth of their souls"; he will observe whether they betray "a spark of enthusiasm."[30] This is what she sought and what she saw at the beginning of her relationships with Narbonne and Ribbing, both of whom failed ultimately to live up to this demanding ideal. As she wrote to Narbonne in despair, "Apparently I have dreamed what I believed I was for you and the only thing that is real is my letters."[31] Benjamin, during the months of his "persecution" of her, was not subject to this veil of idealization.

Perhaps one of the strongest demands she makes of the ideal man of her dreams and desires is that he should not pay heed to social convention, and here, like the others, Benjamin would ultimately fail her. What is the great charge leveled against the heroes of her novels, comte Léonce de Mondoville in *Delphine* and Oswald, Lord Nelvil, in

Corinne? It is that they do not sacrifice all for love because they are subject to the views of parents or to the opinion of others in society.

Germaine braved her parents' disapproval of her relations with Narbonne; she threw personal reputation to the winds to rescue him. She never bowed to social convention: she despised it, denounced it, and defied it throughout her life. Nowhere did this become more apparent than in England, while she was staying at Juniper Hall. When Dr. Burney, esteemed musicologist and father of the celebrated forty-year-old novelist Fanny Burney, obliged Fanny, much against her will, to give up her friendship with a person of such dubious morality and revolutionary tendencies as Mme de Staël, Germaine inquired of Fanny's sister, Susan Phillips, "Is a woman under guardianship for life in this country? It seems to me that your sister is like a girl of fourteen."[32] And when her mother's onetime suitor, the historian Edward Gibbon, keen on the proprieties, ventured to question Germaine's public liaison with Narbonne, she cited indignantly the reasons for their being together, starting with the upheavals caused by the Revolution: "I do not get carried away in the least by romantic notions, and I believe everything reason has successfully held against them ever since the beginning of time. But when extraordinary circumstances, like the revolution that brought them about, have intermingled the hearts and minds of two people for five years, when these same circumstances have given rise to a mutual dependency that renders it impossible for one to live without the other, finally when everything called social convention, reputation, wordly advantage, no longer offers anything but absurdities and ashes, I do not know what would be the reason for living if we had to part."[33]

None of the men with whom she was passionately involved shared this view. Narbonne, for example, was reluctant to favor the marriage of his impecunious friend Alexandre d'Arblay to Fanny Burney:

"What about Society, and public opinion—and *what will people say?*" he asked Susan Phillips, who believed that he was pained at Germaine's disregard of the proprieties.[34] As for Benjamin Constant, he thought that reputation was "always useful and very often necessary." For example, in 1794 he deliberately went back to Brunswick to prove to everyone that he had not been dismissed.

"What is esteem?" Benjamin asked Mme de Charrière rhetorically. "The approbation of a number of individuals who, taken separately, do not seem to us to be worth the trouble of making an effort to please them: I agree, but these individuals are those among whom we have to live. Perhaps they should be despised, but they should be mastered, and for that it is necessary to join with those who most closely share our views, so long as you think as you like." He added, "We are living in an age of storms," and, thinking of La Fontaine's fable, he declared that although the role of the reed that bends in the wind is not pleasant, that of the isolated oak tree is not safe, "and besides, I am not an oak."[35] Better to bend and survive than to be alone, proud and uprooted. Indeed, he would follow this course in the future. This attitude is an example of the cool reasonableness to which Benjamin partly subscribed, far from the indifference to social reputation that Germaine would display, at no little cost to herself.

Both Germaine and Benjamin had experienced misery in their respective marriages and were pretty forthright on the subject. "Marriage! Marriage! Marriage! What a monster!" declared Benjamin, in response to his wife's contempt.[36] Germaine was no less scathing about matrimony when writing candidly to Ribbing from the woman's point of view: "Don't you think it bizarre that you must pay so high a price for the honor a man does you in spending a few detestable nights with you? Oh! How I loathe marriage!"—unless it was to Ribbing, she added, safe in the knowledge that they were both already married.[37]

Germaine and Benjamin, in their unequivocal detestation of matrimony as they had experienced it, saw eye to eye. But that was not the end of the matter, for they never abandoned the notion of an ideal marriage. Here, however, their views had little in common.

Germaine had before her the image of her parents' union, which—despite the strains mentioned by Mme Necker in her reflections—remained one of mutual devotion and fidelity. All the same, she regarded a good marriage as a rarity, verging on the miraculous. To experience love in marriage would be Germaine's ideal: she wrote in *Delphine* that "a woman's destiny is over if she has not married the man she loves," and she identified "the supreme good, love in marriage."[38] Yet at the same time she followed in the tradition of medieval courtly love poetry, where the fusion of souls, often without physical consummation, occurs with the lover rather than the husband. The idea that marriage results in the destruction of passionate love survived in poetry and fiction. In her book on the passions, which Germaine was still writing at the time she met Benjamin, she said that anyone seeking "the romantic happiness of the heart" was less likely to find it within marriage than outside it: marriage tended to promote "the pleasures of virtue" rather than "the delights of passion."[39] It was not, then, the quiet of the heart's affections that Germaine was seeking.

Despite his unpleasant, humiliating experience of matrimony, Benjamin never lost the idea of marriage as a desirable state, but, like many of his masculine contemporaries, he envisaged it as a union with a sweet girl of sixteen or thereabouts or, failing that, with some pliant and undemanding attractive woman who would satisfy him in bed, take care of his household, and not interfere with his work. Yet, he suspected that this paragon of a wife would soon be bored and would soon bore him as well. What he sought in an ideal marriage was really the quiet of the heart's affections that Germaine rejected in favor of stormy passion between great souls. He saw marriage not so much as a value in itself but as a solution to his problems, a refuge from the strains of society and the upheavals of the world.

Such differences did not surface in the early days as the two friends set out for Paris in 1795 to make their mark on the French Republic. A curious reversal in their positions on the political chessboard was about to take place. As yet, however, Benjamin was not Germaine's lover: he was simply a highly favored member of her court.

CHAPTER THREE

A Bold Throw

Nobody wanted Germaine de Staël to come to Paris in the spring of 1795. She was well aware of this unpromising state of affairs. So why did she embark on such a dangerous adventure, and what did she—as distinct from Benjamin Constant—gain from it?

It was only after much agitation, hesitation, and troubled reflection that she decided to leave Coppet, her beloved father, and her younger son, Albert, and make the risky journey to Paris. Accompanying her were her elder son, Auguste, aged four; her trusty valet de chambre and confidential man of all tasks, Joseph Uginet, known as Eugène, and other servants; and her friend Benjamin Constant, as yet untried and untested on the French public scene. Some members of her circle would never understand why she could not stay quietly and comfortably at home, surrounded by her family in Necker's charming château between lake and mountains, especially as Paris was in a state of disorder and unrest ever since the overthrow of Robespierre.

She had not received the authorization of the National Convention, established in September 1792, to enter France and reside in the capital, though she could reasonably claim to be following her duty in joining her husband at the Swedish embassy. Many of the men now in power felt no desire to welcome her, chiefly because they refused to believe any of her public declarations of republicanism and because they suspected her—quite wrongly—of intrigues on behalf of the ultraroyalists who wanted to restore the ancien regime. Not even her husband was looking forward to her arrival: he was engaged in delicate negotiations with the French Republic, which Sweden was the first to recognize, and he did not want his wife to come through like a tornado, disrupting his existence and his diplomatic mission by her presence. All the same, M. de Staël was not prepared to try to stop her himself, leaving it all to his zealous secretary, Jacobsson, who set out posthaste for the Franco-Swiss frontier with the intention of persuading her to turn back. The mission was in vain: Jacobsson missed her.

The fact was that Germaine did not want to live her life drop by drop, as it were. She was not one to stay still, even if her vivid imagination made her worry about possible outcomes—at any rate, if there were difficulties and obstacles, she felt that she would find some way to circumvent them. If there were a challenge, she would rise to meet it. She would defy fate. Endowed with so much energy, she was restless: she found life at Coppet lugubrious, dull, and dispiriting, with its old servants and patriarchal manners. Her mother had died after a long illness the previous year, and her beloved father, Germaine felt, had become lost in grief for his wife. Isolated, robed in his fame, he was the object of worship, "and one yawns in church," she was to tell her husband, declaring that she preferred the rue du Bac, where the Swedish embassy was situated.[1] She had good friends in Switzerland, among them her cousin, Albertine Necker de Saussure, but she missed Paris.

It had been nearly three years since her hurried exit from Paris at the outbreak of the September massacres of 1792. Paris had been the scene of the triumph of her salon, but it meant far more to her than that. It was her birthplace, and she loved its sparkling light and invigorating air. Moreover, important things went on there. She yearned for it as the center of literary and political life, and as the arena for stimulating intellectual discussion of the latest ideas, for enlightening or uplifting plays and concerts, and for brilliant social intercourse—it was the only place she really wanted to live. Had she not settled for Eric de Staël because marriage to him, as ambassador to the French court, meant that she could stay in the capital? Germaine incarnated that yearning for the ambience of Paris felt most deeply by those who find themselves deprived of it. Benjamin, however, felt no such attachment. For him, as Germaine's escort to the French capital, it seemed a place of opportunity.

From a purely practical point of view, even Germaine might not have risked traveling to Paris without Benjamin as the friend and "protector" she felt she needed. Endlessly obliging, he could protect her if they should happen to meet any of the brigands who notoriously infested the appalling roads. Moreover, Germaine now had in Benjamin a person on whom to lavish her pent-up energies. She saw in him the promise of a serious career in literature and republican politics, which she could launch and promote: he could then be as useful to her as she to him.

They arrived in Paris on May 25, the same day as the Prussian ambassador Gervinus, who related in a letter of May 29 how, on entering the city, the first thing he saw was two or three guillotines.[2] An hour later he observed a number of men in carts being hurried to execution. It was like a town under siege, he said, with troops everywhere and a military camp in the midst of the Tuileries. A few days before, on May 20, a mob had invaded the Tuileries palace, and demonstrators had burst into the Convention demanding "bread and the Constitution of 1793." One of the *députés*, Féraud, had been murdered and his head paraded on a pike—a barbaric custom popularized in 1789 that had not yet become outmoded. This was not the first uprising, for food was scarce, inflation was rampant, and the lower orders were starving. And so it would continue as the precarious National Convention, transformed into the Directoire on November 3, 1795, was buffeted in turn by the extreme Left and extreme Right, by Jacobins keen to return to a regime à la Robespierre, and by ultraroyalists eager to take advantage of the government's weakness and restore the monarchy. The Directoire's response would be simply to try to exclude whichever party was on the rise and to rule by frequent coups d'état.

Germaine and Benjamin thus entered Paris in the midst of one of the most confused and confusing periods in French history. It was also during this era that many of the complex elements that were to mark their lives, their association, and their writings began to take shape.

The men who governed in the Convention in the months after the fall of Robespierre and in the short-lived Directoire have not received a good press. Most were regicides, having voted for Louis XVI's execution, or had at least acquiesced in the Terror of 1793–1794. Those who deposed Robespierre and signed his death warrant on 9 Thermidor were former colleagues of his. A few of those responsible for atrocities under the Terror were guillotined or deported to Guiana as an example, but nothing could remove the stain on the reputation of those who survived to grasp power. It was to such men that Germaine and Benjamin would have to turn for support or protection. She already knew some of them: Jean-Lambert Tallien, for instance, had escorted her from Paris in September 1792.

After the end of the Terror everyone breathed a deep sigh of relief, and they lived in dread that it might return. Many had witnessed macabre scenes on the streets or in prison, which they now tried to expunge from their memory by indulging in pleasure, as if every moment might be their last. Others who had lost close members of their family remained traumatized or yearned in vain for *le repos*, for peace and tranquillity. Yet others devoted themselves to the acquisition of wealth, by supplying the armies or by speculating on the *assignats*, or paper money, issued by the impoverished government, which also encouraged people to invest in *biens nationaux*, properties confiscated from those who had been guillotined or who had emigrated.

The period after the Terror was also the age of the fashionable dandies of the anti-revolutionary *jeunesse dorée*, who wore huge cravats, fantastically exaggerated redingotes, and the tallest of top hats. Benjamin simply took more care about his attire, as he had done since meeting Germaine, and eventually he wore his hair cut à la Titus, in what was thought to be Roman style. Among the women there was the "Greek" fashion: revealingly diaphanous, high-waisted, white muslin gowns. Some, like Joséphine de Beauharnais, Creole mistress of the Director Barras and future Mme Bonaparte, Delphine de Custine, and Pulchérie de Valence, who was married to her aunt's lover and who attracted Ribbing, became notorious for their many love affairs. Germaine and Benjamin encountered free-living ladies à la mode in the Parisian *salons dorés* they frequented, where, as Germaine later reported, at Sunday soirées there was a strange mix of elegant, high-society survivors from the ancien regime and upwardly mobile members of the Convention who aspired to acquire the social veneer they lacked.

Characteristically, out of a generous desire to help her friends in exile, before even arriving in Paris Germaine committed an indiscretion that did nothing to help her political reputation with the new leaders. On her journey, she had stopped for two days near Yverdon. At an inn there she met her friends Mathieu de Montmorency, Narbonne, Mme de La Châtre, and Jaucourt, all former constitutional monarchists. They wanted her to deal with their family affairs and to do all she could to end their exile. During this time, however, Germaine was under surveillance by the French authorities. They made no nice distinctions between, on the one hand, the émigrés who had followed Louis XVI's two brothers into exile and had taken up arms against the Republic—these were the ultraroyalists proper of whom Germaine always disapproved and who hated her—and, on the other, those reformers among the aristocrats whom Benjamin called the "*fugitifs,*" who left France only when they were threatened with arrest, or worse. All were considered dangerous enemies seeking to overthrow the Republic. The French agent who spied on Mme de Staël qualified the private meetings as "political discussions." From this misunderstanding or deliberate misinterpretation, much trouble for Germaine would ensue. "My life belongs to my friends," she would say, "but my opinions are my own."[3] She could easily reconcile her attachment to the principles of 1789 and her faith in republicanism with her unswerving loyalty to her liberal-minded aristocratic friends in distress. Others could not. At first, however, little of this opprobrium seemed to have attached itself to Benjamin.

Germaine swept into the handsome Swedish embassy, and her masterstroke in silencing those who suspected her of reactionary intrigues and who wanted her out of Paris left her husband's secretary Jacobsson lost in admiration. Early in June she gave a grand dinner for the leading politicians of the hour. She instantly charmed her guests with her grace and subtle flattery, including the former Girondin, Jean-Baptiste Louvet, author of *Les Aventures du chevalier de Faublas,* who would later prove very helpful to Benjamin. Then, after dinner, she invited ten of them, one after the other, into a nearby room for a private discussion. In the end, all of them had to admit with some embarrassment that since Mme de Staël was now in Paris they could not very well insist on her leaving. For the moment her presence was tolerated, and she was safe from harassment.

Then, in February 1796, she wrote a letter to the editors of the *Nouvelles Politiques,* whose chief was a man both she and Benjamin knew well, Jean-Baptiste Suard. She denied that she had ever been engaged in "political discussions" with royalists and proclaimed her faith in a republic based on justice and harmony, because "in the present circumstances, republican government alone can give France peace and freedom."[4] She would maintain this view throughout the Directoire, and beyond. This act of self-defense received considerable publicity.

Around the same time came the release of the new Paris edition of Germaine's *Réflexions sur la paix adressées à M. Pitt et aux Français*, first published in Switzerland at the end of 1794. The sharp-tongued polemicist and political figure Pierre-Louis Roederer, who at that time could be counted among Germaine's friendly supporters, wrote a favorable review of the work, which contained a manifesto of her own opinions directed at the French leaders as well as her unsolicited advice for the British Prime Minister, William Pitt, whom she regarded as excessively influenced by reactionary royalist émigrés in London. In her view, Pitt and the Allies at war with France were pursuing a policy that served only the purposes of fanatical Jacobins. After proclaiming her loathing for Robespierre and the Terror she declared that it was the moderates who should be given support, with a view toward restoring order and liberty in France. The clock could not be turned back for it was vital to "go forward with one's era."[5] She argued that the French should be left to choose their own government and establish a constitution that would preserve the safety of property and of the individual. The leader of the Whigs, Charles James Fox, was sufficiently impressed to borrow from her essay in his famous antiwar speech to Parliament on May 24, 1795. Her call to the moderates of all parties to unite behind the Republic offered, she felt, the best way to defeat extremism. In a world where factions were fighting each other relentlessly, however, her stand must have appeared to many to be idealistic and out of touch.

At this point, Benjamin entered for the first time the political arena that he had hitherto observed, with exaltation or indignation, from afar. Enthusiastically, he had told his aunt, Mme de Nassau, about the victory of the Convention, the quelling of the insurrection, and the rebels brought to trial. He soon realized, though, that the situation was more uncertain, and the triumph insecure. There were no laws of libel, and he was struck by the extent of free speech and press, which enabled journalists and députés to make unsubstantiated allegations and personal attacks on others, and particularly on Germaine, with impunity. He wrote to his aunt about the unprecedented union of arbitrary power "with complete licence in every regard. The government can do everything and it fears everything."[6] He remarked that people said and did exactly as they liked, and that as a result a good deal of disorder ensued.

At the end of June 1795 Benjamin published three articles entitled *"Lettres à un député de la Convention"* in Suard's journal, the *Nouvelles politiques*. These articles, sometimes almost conversational in tone, were unsigned, but the author's name would eventually become known. With striking clarity he dealt with a burning issue of the moment: as a protective measure, in the forthcoming elections two-thirds of the existing députés were to remain in place. Benjamin, like Germaine, took a principled stand in opposition to this proposal. He quoted from Germaine's *Réflexions sur la paix adressées à M. Pitt et aux Français* without naming her, alluding to her as the most wise and eloquent author to write about the Revolution—a comment that might well apply to her later writings on the subject but was at present, perhaps, a little premature.

These *"Lettres,"* addressed to an unnamed député of the Convention, made a devil of a racket, Benjamin remembered many years afterward. He wrote confidently, as if he were a French citizen—which he was not. Some of his phrases invite comparison with his later writings: the use of the term "liberal principles," for instance. He wanted to avoid a return to the eleventh century and to act instead in

accordance with the approaching nineteenth century, with the resolutely modern, agreeing with Germaine's desire to "go forward with
one's era." Naturally, he met with severe criticism from those who, like
Louvet, supported the proposal he opposed, but in the salons, no doubt
largely through Germaine's advocacy, his dissection of current problems made him the darling of the hour. It was only when some royalists
invited him to cooperate in the restoration of the monarchy that he—
who like Germaine wanted a Republic on solid foundations—recognized that he had been mistaken in his approach. Evidently he would
have preferred free elections—insofar as they were free in an era when
illiteracy was widespread and suffrage was limited to property own-
ers—but he also realized that these could lead to the fall of the Convention, which, for all the moral taints and shortcomings of its leaders,
formed a "bulwark of mud and blood" against the return of the ancien
regime or the rise of another dictator like Robespierre.[7] Thus, Benjamin would soon reverse his opinion; it was the first reversal of a
number that were to mark his future career.

The controversy with Louvet led to a private exchange of ideas
and burgeoning friendship. Benjamin had much to talk about with the
former Girondin, who had managed to escape the fate of his associates
who died by the guillotine or by suicide. At one time, in Brunswick,
Benjamin had regarded Jean-Marie Roland, the Girondin minister, as
his "idol"; now, in Louvet, he met the close associate of the revolutionary heroine Mme Roland. Soon he was collaborating with Louvet,
writing a speech for him to deliver in the Convention. To be friendly
with one of the prominent leaders of the moment certainly could not
do Benjamin any harm. Moreover, an article he had written to please
Germaine, advocating the return of the "fugitives," was signed with
his initials, B.C. His foot was on the ladder.

Ever since childhood Benjamin had desired fame. Writing to his
cousin Rosalie de Constant when he was sixty years old, by then a

famous député and political leader himself, he would own, "I have preserved only one chimera, that of leaving a famous name after me, and before God I do not know why. But I have had it since I was a child."[8] Now, on arriving in Paris in 1795, he had jettisoned, for the time being at least, his longstanding project of writing a major learned work and had thrown himself into political action. Through Germaine's encouragement and influence, he had found at last a definite aim on which to focus: to play a role in and leave a mark on French politics.

He wrote about his attitude of 1795 many years afterward, in 1811, in his unfinished autobiographical novel, *Cécile*, which was never published in his lifetime. There, Germaine is depicted as the celebrated, brilliant, charismatic, but demanding Mme de Malbée. By his own admission Benjamin was not a highly imaginative writer of fiction, and so close are the novel's events to those known about his life that it is difficult to regard the work solely as a novel. The portrayal of Mme de Malbée / Germaine is determined less by the demands of the novel than by the author's intimate concerns in 1811. The narrator—Benjamin's alter ego—declares, "I followed her to France. With all the rashness of my character and of a head younger than my years, I committed myself to revolutionary views. Ambition seized hold of me, and I saw only two things to be desired: to be the citizen of a republic and the leader of a party." Mme de Malbée shared his opinions and his hopes, observes the narrator, but her indiscretion, her notoriety, her numerous and contradictory connections with people of different political persuasion, aroused suspicion. Moreover, these shortcomings of hers ran counter to his ambitions. The "violent and coarse leaders" did not trust her, and "their suspicions reflected on me. I suffered greatly from this: I would have given half my fortune and ten years of my life to proclaim my devotion to a cause of which I was perhaps the only partisan in good faith." This implies, unjustly, that Mme de Malbée / Germaine was not entirely in good faith as a republican. As the narrator suggests, her life before the Revolution had given her the elegant manners of the aristocracy—the very upper class, whether of Berne or Brunswick, that Benjamin claimed he had always detested. And then there follows a damning phrase: "I returned with her to Switzerland although the journey interrupted the work I had begun in order to play a role in France."⁹ In short, the narrator claims that he had to interrupt his career to continue to follow in her train.

Such is the limpidity of Benjamin's style and his skill in conveying elements of Mme de Malbée / Germaine's character—her irresistible charm and childlike qualities, for instance—that the reader may be tempted momentarily to overlook the fact that he is writing about 1795 from the standpoint of 1811 and is proposing how, despite their similar views, in certain ways she stood in the path of his advancement. To what extent can this be said to be true? She nurtured his talent: they discussed together the ideas they shared, and they often worked in tandem. Would he have ventured to post-Thermidorean Paris in 1795 if he had not been invited to accompany her? He had no other pressing reason to do so. Would he have had immediate access to the journalists she knew, who disseminated his ideas and whom she would chivy to give his writings prominent and favorable reviews? Would he have plunged so rapidly into polemical journalism and enjoyed such close contact with those he later called "violent and coarse leaders" if he had not met many of them either through M. de Staël, who vouched for his good character and republican integrity with members of the Convention, or in Germaine's Parisian salon?

Indeed, it was there, in Germaine's salon, that eminent men could be found seeking to formulate the Constitution of Year III, holding discussions in which Germaine and Benjamin were able to take part. In her brilliant salon Benjamin also encountered writers, diplomats, dé-putés, and men of all parties, including leading moderates like the dramatist and politician Marie-Joseph Chénier, brother of the ill-fated poet, as well as influential members of the constitutional committee such as Emmanuel-Joseph Sieyès, the eternal constitution maker, and François-Antoine Boissy d'Anglas, president of the Convention after Thermidor. At any time, as he told his aunt on July 7, 1795, he found the Constitution far too interesting to think of leaving Paris. By the beginning of August 1796 he was informing her, "I have recently had a great success in Paris, I am on very good terms with the majority in the Directoire and the Councils." In the spring of 1797 he told her about the success of his latest pamphlet, *Des effets de la Terreur:* "It has strengthened my ties with the men who are at the head of the Republic." As long as there was no counterrevolution, he said, "my situation here is exactly as I wish it to be: that of a man of independent principles, a lover of liberty, and esteemed for a certain talent."[10] No sign then, in the early years of his association with Germaine, that he found her an obstacle to his advancement, although the idea may have flashed through his mind.

Despite its praise of her in terms that recall his letters to Mme de Charrière, his portrait of Mme de Malbée / Germaine sins by omission. He notes her celebrity but does not mention its nature. He lauds her intelligence and her "writings," but he does not refer to their important political character or to the fact that these published writings of hers preceded his. Her *Essai sur les fictions,* for example, probably written in 1794, which explored the true psychological nature of the novel and the need to raise its standing, impressed Goethe so much that he translated it into German. Thus, what Benjamin says in 1811 must be compared with what actually happened in 1795, and his own status then must be taken into account. The one thing that comes across most forcefully in *Cécile* is the new and overwhelming nature of his republican ambition in 1795. In his letters from May 1795, Benjamin seems eager, fresh, and largely hopeful and positive. He spoke of Germaine then, at the end of May 1795, as "a person whose heart, mind, astonishing and sublime qualities draw me and bind me to her even more every day."[11] After all, his "conquest" of her had not yet been achieved. He still had a great deal to aim for, and he could not do without her as muse, Egeria, and in a great many ways the smoother of his path.

In the period that followed, both Germaine and Benjamin were preoccupied with vital matters on which their establishment in France depended. One was the question of their respective financial resources, and the other was the knotty subject of their nationality and citizenship, a problem that would pursue them for the rest of their lives.

As an inveterate gambler, Benjamin was rapidly caught up in the frenzy of speculation that seized many members of post-Thermidorean society. He told his aunt that living in Paris was fantastically cheap: his food, clothing, and lodging, which consisted of three fine rooms, cost very little. And the sale of confiscated property, or *biens nationaux*, promoted by the government, was "prodigious," he said. This type of commerce seems to have aroused no qualms among his contemporaries, as perhaps it does with the more tender consciences of today. It was by no means unusual for people to seek to prevent the confiscation of their own property while encouraging others to purchase mansions and landed estates that had been confiscated. One's high-minded political principles did not preclude the dedicated pursuit of self-interest.

Benjamin wrote excitedly to his aunt extoling the rich opportunities for investment in *biens nationaux*. He suggested to her that if she came to France with 15,000 francs she could buy "a magnificent estate" that would give her an income of 4,800 francs. He specified rates of interest and went into other details at considerable length. "I have just acquired an unimaginable bargain! I have bought land for 30,000 francs, which gives me 8,000 livres income. You will admit that it is difficult to make a better investment!"[12] Of course, he needed to

own property in France in order to be a citizen with the right to vote
and to hold local or, indeed, national office: so much the better if
said property were bought as "an unimaginable bargain." Sagely, his
aunt warned him not to put all his eggs in one basket. Benjamin
conceded that if the tide turned, a restored monarchy was likely to
boot out of the country any owner of *biens nationaux* and he would
have to flee. Still, he advised not only his aunt but also his uncle,
Samuel de Constant, to follow the same course of action as himself,
pointing out its benefits. No time must be wasted, he urged, because as
the Republic became more stable, the price of *biens nationaux* would
rise. Germaine clearly shared Benjamin's views on the property market: writing to Benjamin's father, Juste, who wanted news of his son,
she declared, "To reassure you in your fatherly feelings, I shall mention that Benjamin has just made a very fine purchase of *biens nationaux*
in France, and that he will have in all likelihood ten thousand livres in
solid money [as distinct from fluctuating paper *assignats*] for the price
of his house in Switzerland."[13]

In order to pay for his new investments in France, Benjamin had
sold the house on the rue de Bourg in Lausanne that he had inherited
from his mother's estate. He purchased three separate properties in
Normandy: the château de Vaux and its farmland, near Gisors; the
farm of Coqueréaumont, near Rouen; and the farm of Saint-Denis de
Moronval, near Dreux. These properties were dispersed: he had to
travel many miles to deal with his Norman tenant farmers, who could
be difficult when it came to paying the landlord. He was to sell these
farms in the ensuing few years—too soon, Germaine thought, to make
the vast profits he had expected.

In the autumn of 1796 he embarked on a major purchase in the
environs of Paris: the abbey of Hérivaux and its adjoining estate. Soon,
he had fifty men a day working for him, he reported to his aunt. They
were engaged in knocking down the abbey and other "improvements."

Benjamin loved Hérivaux, where he could approximate the life of an English country gentleman, a style he had admired during his youthful escapade in Great Britain years before. He loved the soft, green French countryside—a sharp contrast to his birthplace on Lake Geneva, where the strong light hurt his eyes. "I am still enjoying delightful solitude on my country estate," he told his aunt. It offered him a respite from Paris and the constant conspiracies. He delighted in walking in "my forests" with his beloved dogs. If his aunt were to pay him a visit, he wrote, she would find "a small house, all that remains of the vast building I have had pulled down, some young acacia trees that give no shade, some young fruit trees that yield no fruit, newly sown meadows where there is no grass, a pond that is not yet filled with water."[14] He was so comfortable there, he told her, that he did not want to leave his acacias. Part of his library was in place, the rest of his books were on their way, and studying had recovered some of its old attraction.

Nonetheless, the extensive "improvements" at Hérivaux consumed a great deal of money. Benjamin took to borrowing as he had in the past to deal with his debts, a course of action that inevitably added to his troubles. Germaine soon perceived that he was embroiled in financial difficulties. She was to help him later, when she could, with the sum of 2,400 livres. Eventually, Jacques Necker came to his (temporary) rescue with a large loan of 34,000 francs that Benjamin was inclined to regard as a gift.

Germaine and her father's delay in helping Benjamin is explained by the fact that during these years, 1795 to 1798, they were themselves experiencing some serious financial problems. It was hardly the moment for them to try to recover Necker's large personal loan to the royal treasury, and, adding to their problems, Necker's name had been placed on the list of émigrés, which meant that all his French properties and their valuable contents had been sequestrated. Yet, in spite of his high position as finance minister to Louis XVI, he had never become a

French citizen, and as a Genevan he could hardly be regarded as an émigré. Germaine would have to take formal steps to persuade the Directors that this was indeed the case. Otherwise, the two mansions that Necker owned in Paris and the château and estate at Saint-Ouen where she had played as a child would be confiscated. Germaine foresaw ruin. As a result of her long negotiations, however, Necker's name was at first provisionally and then finally removed from the list of émigrés in July 1798. He could now sell the houses in Paris, retaining the retreat at Saint-Ouen. As a result, he was in a position to lend Benjamin the considerable sum to help him at Hérivaux. Benjamin would keep this property until March 1802, when he sold it and bought Les Herbages.

Apart from financial problems, Germaine and Benjamin, in different ways, were faced with the question of their nationality and citizenship. In theory, both of them—Germaine on her mother's side—could claim descent from the Huguenots who had been forced to flee the country in 1685, when Louis XIV repealed the Edict of Nantes that granted religious toleration to Protestants. During the Revolution, descendants of such forced religious exiles were granted French citizenship and permitted to return. This approach had been successfully taken by Benjamin's father, who was now residing at Brevans, near Dôle. Benjamin chose to adopt the same argument: although it was not so readily accepted in his case, his petition would be granted in March 1797. His enemies would never forget that he was born in Lausanne; they saw him as a Swiss interloper who had no business participating in French affairs.

Germaine's position was unlike his: she was born in Paris, and it would seem evident, therefore, that she was a French citizen by birth. But matters were not so simple: they were complicated by her dependent legal status as a woman, a daughter, and a wife; by a good dose of misogyny; and by the tactics of the powers that be in their mission to be rid of her. There was no shortage of excuses. First, her parents were both Swiss, and Necker's devotion to the French crown meant nothing now that the monarch had been guillotined. Second, she was married to a foreigner and thus took her husband's Swedish nationality, which had indeed proved immensely useful to her at critical moments during the Revolution. When her husband died in 1802 she should have been able to revert to French nationality, but the authorities never concurred. So convoluted was the matter that at times even she herself was not sure what her nationality was. She would make use of the equivocation if the occasion arose, but she was also to suffer under it. The irony was that any foreigner who met her saw her as French to her fingertips.

In short, in spite of their great contribution to French literature and political life, both Germaine and Benjamin would remain outsiders. But it was she alone who would face persecution.

The few months of apparent security following Germaine's arrival in Paris, during which she presided over her influential salon, came to a sudden end on August 18. Her former butcher, the député Louis Legendre, who had been a close associate of the powerful revolutionary leader Georges-Jacques Danton, denounced Mme de Staël in the Convention. Legendre claimed that she was working for the return of the ultraroyalist émigrés. What seemed to him particularly appalling was that respectable members of the government had yielded to her powers of seduction and had even dined with her instead of staying at home with their families, as they should. M. de Staël, seated among the diplomats, was deeply offended, and he rose and left the chamber. The *Nouvelles politiques* hastened to Germaine's defense as "a person whose extraordinary union of intelligence, knowledge and talent honors the France of her birth," stressing her own and her husband's total devotion to the Republic and urging respect for her sex and her gifts.[15]

From the tone of these words and especially the allusion to her as French by birth, it sounds as if Benjamin could have written them. To be publicly—as well as wrongly and dangerously—attacked as a person engaged in maneuvers on behalf of the ultraroyalists was sufficient to convince Germaine that it would be sensible to leave Paris. Early in September she departed to a mansion on Mathieu de Montmorency's estate at Ormesson, near Enghien. Benjamin visited her there but returned to Paris regularly to deliver by hand her letters to notabilities, engage in negotiations on her behalf, defend her, and pursue his own affairs.

Two days after the royalist insurrection of 13 Vendémiaire (October 5, 1795), Benjamin was walking with Germaine's friend François de Pange in the Palais-Egalité, as the Palais-Royal was now called, when they were caught up in a brawl. Since the stirrings of the Revolution, the Palais-Royal, today one of the most peaceful and enchanting enclaves in the city, had been the center for often-incendiary speeches and rabble-rousing. From its noble arcades rose the sounds emanating from numerous cafés, brothels, and gambling dens. A drunken military man accused the two well-dressed friends of being royalists, a serious charge in the days following 13 Vendémiaire, and they were seized and hurried to prison. Nine years later, Benjamin still remembered the night he spent there with François de Pange, and how it gave him an idea of what the loss of freedom was like: "The noise from the street, the footsteps of the free as they walk beneath the windows, everything that recalls one's own situation and that of others, seemed to me the most unpleasant aspect of being imprisoned."[16] Fortunately the imprisonment did not last long; the following morning they were released. Two of their influential friends on the Comité du Salut Public, Louvet and Chénier, came to their rescue. Chénier vouched for them in the portentous style of the day: "I, representative of the people, declare that I know the citizens François de Pange and Benjamin Constant to be men of probity, enlightenment and civic duty."[17] According to Chénier, they had publicly condemned the rebels and upheld the Convention. On his release, Benjamin was annoyed that his name, unlike that of François de Pange, did not appear in the press reports of the incident. He set out at once to join Germaine at Ormesson.

Repressive measures followed the royalist uprising of 13 Vendémiaire, which had been suppressed by the man of the hour, vicomte Paul-Jean de Barras, and an as yet little-known Corsican general in his entourage named Napoleon Bonaparte. A number of Germaine's friends fled in fear of their lives to take refuge with her at Ormesson. This did not please the triumphant members of the Convention. Germaine might have looked for assistance from Barras, the new strong man: she had been in contact with him since the summer. Handsome, courageous, pleasure loving, and corrupt, he appears in her letters to him, where she flatters him outrageously, as her hero, savior, and protector. He helped her privately on various occasions, when it did not cause him too much trouble, but she could not count on his aid.

Germaine was actually accused of fomenting the uprising, and a decree was passed: she must leave France forthwith. M. de Staël protested at this treatment of his wife and Boissy d'Anglas, one of the leading politicians, intervened on her behalf, both citing the unlawful deprivation of her human rights. The order to leave was withdrawn, but Germaine thought it wise to depart "on grounds of health" for Forges-les-Eaux, a small watering place in Normandy, chosen perhaps for Benjamin's visits to his Norman farms. He duly joined her there. It was quiet and dull, just the place for reading, writing, and entertaining a few friends like sad Pauline de Beaumont—later inamorata of François-René de Chateaubriand—who had lost most of her family in the Revolution. No one seems to have inquired whether there was any truth to the charge of Germaine's participation in a royalist conspiracy. In that ambience of constant fear about plots and plotters, suspicions against her were deemed sufficient to condemn her.

By mid-December 1795 Germaine had had enough of Forges-les-Eaux. She visited Paris briefly, where she met Ribbing, then she left with Benjamin for Coppet. There she remained for a year, until December 1796, though Benjamin would return from time to time to the capital to pursue his ambitions and also serve her interests. The journey to Coppet was not an easy one in the depths of winter. Germaine, the inveterate traveler, wrote to François de Pange from Besançon: "You are quite right not to travel. What roads!" At the relays where they changed horses, she added, any attempt to pay with "republican" paper money was out of the question: people wanted only hard cash. On the very same day she confided to Ribbing how she had suffered being constantly shaken up in the carriage, and she still had before her the prospect of crossing the "terrible mountains" of the Jura, with their perilous precipices, dark fir trees, and dazzlingly white expanses of snow.[18]

Once safely ensconced at Coppet, where Necker did not share their great enthusiasm for the Republic, Germaine and Benjamin settled down to some serious writing. These were the years of their closest literary and political collaboration. Germaine was still at work finishing the first volume of her substantial study, *De l'influence des passions sur le bonheur des individus et des nations* (the second volume never appeared). Addressed to "passionate spirits," her book made a great impression on her contemporaries when it was published in the autumn of 1796. Already Fanny Burney, the author of *Evelina* and *Cecilia*, who had heard parts of it being read aloud when Germaine was staying with Narbonne and other friends at Juniper Hall in Surrey in 1793, was lost in admiration for this "profound politician and metaphysician." Stendhal found "very fine truths" in it and remarked wryly that he was "trying to translate her thoughts into French" so that he could make use of them, as indeed he did. At readings in Switzerland, Rosalie de Constant, no unconditional admirer, could not forbear criticizing Germaine's "metaphysical gobbledegook" but was nonetheless "astounded by the profundity of her ideas and delighted with the brilliance, the power or the novelty of her thoughts."[19]

As for Benjamin, he was engaged on his first important work, his political pamphlet *De la force du gouvernement actuel de la France et de la nécessité d'y rallier,* which made its appearance in the spring of 1796. The Directoire, with whose prominent figures he now had close ties, greeted the pamphlet with great approval. Indeed, so pleased were the members of the government that they decided to have it reprinted in *Le Moniteur,* the official journal. Yet such government approbation never extended to Germaine. Instead, she was being accused once again of conspiring against the state; the Directoire gave the order for her to be arrested at the frontier if she ventured to return to France. Instructions were precise: her carriage was to be thoroughly searched for cases with false bottoms, interior safes, and concealed shelves—even the axles were not to be overlooked. "The woman named Staël" figured on a list of thieves, forgers, and other criminals. Germaine's indignation at this offensive treatment knew no bounds: she was not one to keep silent.

With her uncle Necker de Germany she hastened to the office of Félix Desportes, the French representative in Geneva, to request a visa for her passport so that she could go to France when it suited her. Waving a letter from her husband who asserted that the minister of police denied any knowledge of the order to arrest her, she cried, "Do not think, sir, that the Directoire will not be pleased to see me: it knows that I am part author of Benjamin Constant's work; that this work was written entirely in my home and in my presence; consequently it is impossible for it [the Directoire] to doubt my devotion to its cause. M. Constant is very closely connected with all the members of the Directoire."[20] Thus, ironically, a year after her arrival in Paris with the unknown Benjamin Constant, the famous Mme de Staël had to rely on his ties with the Directoire, ties that she had originally instigated.

Meanwhile, Germaine, who was accustomed to drawing on her contacts to have her writings noticed, did all she could to publicize Benjamin's pamphlet, urging Roederer to review it favorably in his paper, *Le Journal de Paris*, and recommending it to another acquaintance for publication in England and Germany. Her claim to Desportes to be part author of *De la force du gouvernement actuel* is contradicted by her comments to Roederer, who, in her opinion, had not sufficiently appreciated Constant's pamphlet in *Le Journal de Paris:* "Benjamin's work is not mine," she declared. Admittedly, she wrote, there were places to criticize, but "see if it is possible to put more ideas and style in a pamphlet. I own that even I was surprised, despite the high opinion I have of his intellectual ability. . . . There are pages equal to what we most admire in French." Then, after praising his purely literary accomplishments, she offered her main political criticism: "I should never have justified the Jacobin appointments," that is, the important administrative positions given to men on the extreme Left rather than to moderates.[21] Benjamin, more responsive to the practical needs of the moment, had recognized the dilemma that customarily follows the total collapse of an arbitrary regime: after the death or exile of many distinguished public servants, the government is often obliged to employ any official with experience, whatever his credentials. Germaine could not agree: "This book and I make two," she insisted to Roederer, declaring her independence.[22]

All the same, *De la force du gouvernement actuel* was written while Benjamin was staying with her: they discussed it, they read their works in progress to each other, and they shared the same ideas. Germaine had stressed the need to reinforce the center in two essays of 1794, her *Réflexions sur la paix adressées à M. Pitt et aux Français* and her *Réflexions sur la paix intérieure*. And there is at least one reminiscence of her book on the passions in Benjamin's pamphlet. Germaine, who favored trenchant images, compared the powerful passion of love to "the burning wind of Africa" that desiccates and destroys everything in its path, a comparison so striking and novel that it would arouse much hilarity among Swiss wags of neoclassical taste. Benjamin, whose style usually tended to be more sober, alluded to an all-consuming feeling "like the burning winds of Africa" that cause all in their path to grow dry and wither.[23] Benjamin may have been so taken with the forceful image that he used it himself.

In *De la force du gouvernement actuel* Benjamin tried to show how to make the government strong and attractive. He developed an idea of Germaine's that he had already adumbrated in his *Lettres à un député de la Convention*, namely, that after the Revolution of 1789 there could be no going back. He also returned to a theme that he had worked on in Brunswick but had abandoned, a refutation of Edmund Burke's *Reflections on the French Revolution* (1790), much admired for the force of its counterrevolutionary arguments. For Benjamin, as for Germaine, the end of the ancien regime meant the end of heredity: a person's destiny no longer depended on birth but on merit. Humanity's forward drive toward the newly formed interests that arose from this great change was inevitable and unstoppable, and so there was no point in attempts by counterrevolutionaries to prevent it, like the British-sponsored royalist invasion of Quiberon that had failed the previous year. He saw the main threat coming from the Right, although the communist "Conspiracy of Equals" led by "Gracchus" Babeuf came to light in the winter of 1795–96. The Revolution was not all of a piece, permanently stained by the crimes of the Terror. The way to separate the valuable principles of 1789 from the Terror was to establish a strong republic based on law, with guarantees of order and liberty—a firmly grounded republic that would attract the support of reasonable people of all parties. Here, he and Germaine were agreed.

Whereas Germaine privately expressed her reservations about the pamphlet to Roederer, Benjamin made public his reservations about her *De l'influence des passions,* which he reviewed in *Le Moniteur Universel* on October 26, 1796. He discussed there its political, not personal, aspects. He remarked that unlike most women writers, Mme de Staël, "a Frenchwoman," dealt successfully with the most difficult political and moral subjects: "The principles are generally good; the political ideas are not free from error. . . . It becomes clear that the author is better acquainted with the theory of liberty than with practical knowledge of the Revolution."[24] Hence her prejudice against the estimable Condorcet, a note that "produces a painful effect." Leaving aside the reputation of that ill-fated revolutionary philosopher, Benjamin's comment sounds patronizing: after all, it was she, Necker's daughter, who had experienced the Revolution firsthand as he had not, and she had also been closely associated with many of the leading thinkers and participants. He hastened to add, however, that these small faults or errors of judgment did not detract from the merit of the work as a whole. He quoted her political views where they coincided with his own. It is at this point, a few months after they have become lovers, that Benjamin marked the connection between some of their ideas while at the same time seeking to demonstrate his intellectual independence vis à vis a woman who remains under a government cloud.

The long period of eighteen months that Benjamin had spent proving his passion, either in extravagant and violent displays of despair at having been rejected or in devoted attention to her every need, finally ended in success in the spring of 1796. Germaine's distress at being betrayed, first by Narbonne and then by Ribbing, had found expression in the bitter complaints of her ambitious book on the passions, but near the close of the book the author still preserved hopes of finding what she had always sought, lasting happiness in love: "Perhaps, at the very moment I am speaking, I believe, I still wish to be loved."[25] That touching phrase gives a hint, maybe, of the place that Benjamin was beginning to assume in her life.

Germaine might not have been physically attracted to Benjamin, he might not have had the aristocratic graces and the heroic virtues of her ideal, but gradually she grew convinced that his sensibility was different from that of his ungrateful predecessors. And perhaps that very sense of difference gave a disillusioned woman the illusion of a fresh start. She wrote in her book on the passions, in a passage that might apply to Benjamin, that it would be eminently desirable to be the sole love of a "man whose energy has not effaced his sensibility, who cannot bear the thought of another's misery, and places his honor in kindness, a man faithful to vows that public opinion does not guarantee."[26]

Proof of the existence of such a steadfast and solicitous man was to be found in an extraordinary document known as the Testament, a secret pledge or register of their commitment to each other. It begins with a mutual confession of faith, followed by Benjamin's declaration alone:

We promise to devote our lives to each other, we declare that we regard each other as indissolubly bound together, that in every way our fate lies in common forever, that we shall never contract another tie, and that we shall reinforce those which unite us as soon as we have the power to do so.

I declare that it is truly from the bottom of my heart that I undertake this commitment, that I know nothing on earth as kind and good as Mad. de Staël, that I have been the happiest of men

during the four months I have spent with her, and that I consider it
the greatest happiness of my life to be able to make her happy
while she is young, to grow old gracefully along with her and
to arrive at the end of all with the being who understands me
and without whom there would exist no interest, no feeling on
this earth.[27]

The Testament is signed by Benjamin, though not by Germaine,
and is undated.

None of his predecessors, who doubtless *uttered* protestations of
eternal love, had ever *written* such a declaration that formally promised
lifelong trust, faith, and fidelity. It needed two born *littérateurs* to
conceive or formulate it. The Testament is thought to date from March
or April 1796—after "four months" spent happily working together at
Coppet, from December onwards. Or it might date from July, "four
months" after the consummation of the liaison. Yet the actual date
seems less important than the nature and content of the document, an
extraordinary contract of unconventional spiritual marriage in which
the two "betrothed" affirm their intention to regularize their union as
soon as they are able—Germaine of course still being married to M. de
Staël (Benjamin had recently obtained a German divorce from his
wife, Minna). This document is surely intended to be as permanent as
the vows of marriage made in church. The first part of the contract is
written in the name of both of them, speaking as "we." Then, characteristically, Benjamin veers off to speak for himself, in a state of euphoria, as "I." He declares that he will devote his life to making her happy
and will never leave her as long as they live, that they will grow old
together: this was just the sort of thing that Germaine longed and
needed to hear.

Was the Testament composed by Benjamin alone, though inspired
by Germaine, with the intention of proving to her once and for all,

after so long a period of trial, the depth of his feelings? She could have
signed the first part. Why did she not do so? Was it because she did not
need to declare her commitment, since her "surrender" was sufficient?
Or was it because the second part of the document related primarily to
Benjamin's point of view, as he was borne aloft in his discovery of "the
being who understands me"? She, looking for lasting love, wanted
someone to support and protect her, in the manner that society proclaimed the norm for women. She had expressed the view that love is
the whole history of a woman's life; however, it was not the whole
history of hers, devoted as she was also to works of ideas and imagination. She knew she was a celebrated woman of independent means
whose talents were widely recognized. Thus she held in her mind two
images of womanhood: the delicate creature, weak by nature, who
needed to be supported and protected by an admired master, and the
daring, visionary, exceptional woman. She would never be able to
reconcile the two, either in her life or in her novels.

There were some, relatives and friends, who did not warm to the
idea of their liaison. Rosalie de Constant, always thinking of Benjamin's
interests, worried about her cousin and wondered where it would all
lead. Mathieu de Montmorency, ever concerned for Germaine, had
serious doubts about Benjamin's sincerity and told Albertine Necker de
Saussure how he had questioned Germaine several times, warned her
about Benjamin, and begged her not to land herself in "a misfortune
greater than any she could previously have known from experience."
He stated for Germaine's benefit what he thought about Benjamin's
"disturbed mind" and his wild "political outbursts"—the *grand seigneur*
did not share the ambitious Benjamin's republican ardor—utterances
"that seem not to be rooted in his heart or his beliefs."[28] In addition,
Mathieu listed among Benjamin's faults his unfortunate appearance, his
style of dress, his odd obsessive habits, his nervous mannerisms. All
of this left Mathieu astounded when trying to conceive the kind of

attachment this man could inspire. How could so much intelligence result in so unattractive a person? He discussed his misgivings with Adrien de Mun, elegant and cultivated grandson of Helvétius (the favored philosopher of Benjamin's youth), who shared his opinion. Justifying herself to Adrien, Germaine did not reject the criticism of Benjamin but said simply, "His defects are on the surface and his qualities lie deep down."[29] By this time she had come to count on what she now believed to be Benjamin's intrinsic virtues hidden behind an unfavorable exterior; besides, she had had enough of those whose outward grace concealed their inner failings.

If Germaine preserved any lingering doubts about her liaison with Benjamin, they were dispelled in July 1796 by an act of chivalry. An article appeared in the *Feuille du jour* that libeled Benjamin as a "terrorist," a member of the extreme Left actively opposed to the Directoire. Although he was in Paris on one of his periodic visits, Germaine sent him a cutting to make sure he saw it. She was expecting him to publish a rebuttal; instead, Benjamin challenged the author of the article, Bertin de Vaux, to a duel. When news of the challenge reached Germaine in Switzerland, she trembled in agony and apprehension about the outcome; she could not stop crying. She loved courage, but she also loved life. Here was the situation of countless novels she had read, where the hero bravely puts his life at risk and the heroine's love is revealed not only to herself but also for all to see.

The parties were in the Bois de Boulogne with pistols at the ready when a mutual friend, Honoré-Jean Riouffe—a former Girondin who had been in prison with Mme Roland but escaped her terrible fate—intervened and reconciled the duelists. Bertin de Vaux published a generous retraction, declaring that he had been misinformed: "Nobody is less like a terrorist than M. Constant."[30] Another journalist, however, took up the gauntlet: he spoke of Benjamin as "this adventurer who has arrived from Switzerland with the express purpose of teaching the government the secret of making use of terrorists to murder honest men" and accused him of cowardice, which was certainly not one of his faults. "Honor and glory to the *Constant Benjamin* of Mme de Staël!" sneered the scribbler.[31] Bertin de Vaux felt obliged to issue a further rebuttal, contradicting his colleague's fanciful account of the duel and proclaiming his newfound friendship with his honorable opponent.

Before setting out for the Bois de Boulogne, Benjamin had pondered on the likely effect that news of his death would have on Germaine, with her high emotionalism and acute sense of suffering. He drew up his will, leaving her the house and estate of La Chablière, all his papers, and a ring. He also penned a note to be sent to her in the event of the worst, announcing that he was seriously wounded. Such delicacy, when it became known to her, moved her deeply. "If you only knew what he means to me, what a letter I have just received from him again, what an angel of sensibility he is for me: it is on him alone that everything in my life depends," she told Rosalie de Constant. Germaine used the very same phrase—her whole life now hanging on the thread of Benjamin's love—that she had employed for Narbonne and Ribbing. "What I have suffered is beyond words," she informed Rosalie. "Oh! I have really felt that my life's destiny depended on him forever."[32] Germaine may have originally drifted into the liaison with Benjamin for consolation, but by July and August 1796 she was passionately in love with him, as he found when he returned to a joyous welcome at Coppet.

The question of divorce was mooted. If Germaine divorced Eric de Staël, she and Benjamin would be able to regularize their union and marry, as proposed in the Testament. Word of their intentions, if that is what they were, soon leaked out. Some friends were shocked at the idea. Although divorce had been legal in France since 1792, and despite the laxity and license of society under the Directoire, it carried a definite stigma in *le grand monde*. Pauline de Beaumont, speaking of Germaine's rumored plans for divorce and remarriage, told Charles de Constant that "you would need courage to see Mme de Staël if she does such a foolish thing."[33] But nothing came of their supposed plans. Necker was opposed to the idea, though he consented to her more or less formal separation from her husband when M. de Staël made a brief visit to Coppet in September 1796, on his way to take the waters at Aix-les-Bains. And Germaine was not going to make any move that might involve the loss of her children. Nonetheless, the last had not been heard of the question of marriage between Benjamin and herself.

The bold gamble of their venture to Paris and the two years spent amid the early chaotic upheavals and perils of the Directoire produced very different results for Germaine and Benjamin. He discovered his direction at last in the world of politics; made numerous invaluable personal and social contacts with leading literary figures, philosophers, and intellectuals; and began to establish his position—however much it might be challenged—as an active political thinker and writer at the center of political affairs. In short, he became known. He entered into negotiations with important men not only on Germaine's behalf but also for his own sake in order to claim French citizenship. He acquired property in France that would eventually allow him to take part in elections and stand for public office. On top of all that, his dogged pursuit of Germaine was crowned with success. In theory, he had what he wanted: (partial) satisfaction of his ambitions—he was still not the leader of a party—and fulfillment of the passion he had so long and ardently displayed.

Germaine, however, suffered a number of setbacks. Her Parisian salon, brilliant as it had appeared, was of brief duration. She did not succeed, as she had hoped, in establishing herself as a mover and shaker in republican politics. The men in power were not interested in her advice as they were in Benjamin's, though his differed little from hers. Her motives were questioned: she was still widely regarded as an *intrigante*, a woman who meddled in politics, in matters that were not part of her "sphere." Worse, she was accused of conspiring against the very Republic she wished to support, forbidden to set foot in her beloved Paris, and even threatened with arrest as a common felon if she did. As a result, she was obliged to spend months away from the capital. It cannot be said that she achieved anything like the political fulfillment that she engineered for Benjamin and that he sustained with the talent she had recognized and nurtured. On the positive side, however, she was able to do much to help her father and her friends in their various difficulties. She published to widespread acclaim the first of her major works, her book on the passions, whereas Benjamin so far had produced only articles and a political pamphlet, important as it was. Moreover, she entered into a new phase of her relationship with a companion as passionate as she was, an intellectual equal. And she had, surely, proof of his undying love.

CHAPTER FOUR

⤳ *Enter the Hero* ⤳

THROUGHOUT THE YEAR 1796, and throughout all the comings and goings between Coppet and Paris and the provinces, Germaine and Benjamin could hear the thundering reverberations of French victories. General Napoleon Bonaparte, appointed commander in chief of the French army in Italy in March of that year, entered Milan soon afterward, in May. From Montenotte to Castiglione, Roverdo and Bassano to Arcole and Rivoli, Napoleon's campaign against Austria looked like one long triumph up to the peace of Campo Formio (in October 1797). Other French generals, such as Moreau and Hoche, were also supremely successful in defeating the Austrians, but the young Bonaparte, already a master of propaganda, issued such eloquent proclamations and addresses to his soldiers that he captured the public imagination with his élan and bravura. Here, it seemed, was a grand and glorious accomplishment to counter the obscure machinations of plotters and extremists on the Left and Right and the devious maneuvers of disreputable politicians. There was no talk then of French exploitation and despoliation of Italy.

Benjamin could not help but to allude to the victorious armies in his articles, while Germaine—always attracted to feats of physical courage—saw Bonaparte as the incarnation of the hero she so much admired in literature. The echo of the army's exploits in Italy would serve as a ground bass to the experiences and thoughts of Germaine and Benjamin, though neither could foresee the path that the Corsican general would take only a few years later in 1799 when he seized power. During the drama of their further involvement in the upheavals of the Directoire, Bonaparte would appear twice in person, on his return from Italy after the peace of Campo Formio and again on his return from Egypt.

At Coppet in October 1796, Germaine was complaining about feeling ill—something she did extremely rarely. Usually she enjoyed such good health that she had trouble appreciating or sympathizing with the ailments of others. This time, she had the vapors, she had a fever, she felt at a very low ebb. Germaine, it turned out, was pregnant.

She was determined, however, not to allow her pregnancy to interfere with her intention to return to France. When a friend inquired about her "position" there, she said it was distinctly bad because of continuing accusations about her supposed connections with ultraroyalists, but she was determined to defy danger, just as she had in the spring of 1795. The Directoire still had not granted her permission to return to France, and when she set out from Coppet on December 19, 1796, she was indebted to Benjamin for his protection. Earlier, the only protection he could offer was his mere manly presence; now, it included his important and useful connections with the men in power.

With a view toward having a French country residence of her own (Saint-Ouen was still under sequestration), Germaine bought a house at Angervillers, but she disliked it and did not keep it long. Instead, she went to stay with Benjamin at Hérivaux from the beginning of 1797 until April, when she moved to Ormesson, where she was more comfortable and closer to her friends. Then, at the end of May, she moved to the Swedish embassy on the rue du Bac, where, on June 8, she gave birth to a daughter, Albertine. Two days later she was issuing invitations to dinner, then the main meal of the day, which was taken at around four o'clock in the afternoon. A steady stream of friends came to call, all soon engaged in discussing with her the events of the day. The more conservative among them expected her to be still abed and nursing the infant, like any other woman in her circumstances, though they acknowledged sourly that Germaine had enough servants to deal with any mundane tasks.

Much ink has been spilled about the parentage of Albertine de Staël, later duchesse de Broglie. As noted, M. de Staël paid a brief visit to Coppet in September 1796, and he also stayed there on his return from Aix-les-Bains. Despite his virtual separation from his wife, did he insist on his conjugal rights? Some have noted that, like Benjamin, Albertine had red hair—but that is hardly conclusive. More striking is the deep affection and attachment to Albertine that he always felt—and often confided to his diary—quite unlike his relationship with her brothers, Auguste and Albert, which was cordial enough but not close. They even went on writing letters to each other when Albertine was older. It looks as if he believed she was his daughter, although that bond did not involve any commitment on his part to her upbringing and education. In later years Germaine, short of funds, expected him to contribute to Albertine's dowry, which she could scarcely have done unless she believed him to be the girl's father. After her mother's death, the duchesse de Broglie destroyed all the letters in her possession between Germaine and Benjamin, which makes it likely that she was determined to eliminate any hint of her own illegitimacy as well as all the private and personal details of their convoluted relationship. The need to preserve her mother's reputation as well as her own would have been paramount. The few letters that survived tend to confirm this hypothesis. In any case, Albertine created an emotional tie between Germaine and Benjamin that would figure prominently throughout their lives.

No sooner was Germaine up and about than she was again busy not only with her own preoccupations and family concerns but also with the affairs of her many aristocratic friends. Most notable among these was Charles-Maurice de Talleyrand, the (unlikely) bishop of Autun, who was to occupy an important place in her life for the next few years. Along with many highborn young men under the ancien regime who found themselves condemned to be unwilling members of the clergy, he lived nonetheless a life of pleasure and self-indulgence. An accident in childhood had left him with a pronounced limp, but apparently this did nothing to detract from his charming elegance. Chateaubriand, who loathed him, asserted that he was good-looking in his youth. In her younger days, Germaine's friendship with Talleyrand was warm, to say the least. In London in 1793 he had formed part of her social circle and had associated with her and his close friend Narbonne while they resided at Juniper Hall. After leaving England for the United States, Talleyrand wrote desperate letters begging her to save him: "If I stay in this place another year I shall die here," he cried.[1] Imagining his imminent demise, she could not let such a plea go unheard. Enlisting the aid of Chénier, she succeeded in having all the charges against Talleyrand dropped and his name eliminated from the list of émigrés: the way was open for his return to France. She was overjoyed, and so was he: he wrote to her that she had achieved absolutely everything he desired.

Making his way via Hamburg, Talleyrand arrived in Paris in September 1796, not long after the birth of Albertine. But he soon faced a new problem: how was he going to live? Impecunious and unemployed, he complained to Germaine that he could barely manage without some post. Germaine provided him with funds and applied directly to Barras on his behalf, pointing out that by finding a place for such a gifted man the Director would have at his side someone he could trust implicitly. Finally, Barras yielded to her repeated entreaties. Talleyrand was appointed minister of foreign affairs on July 16, 1797.

The untried Talleyrand of 1797 who was obligated to Germaine was nothing like the famous (or infamously corrupt) wily diplomat and power broker of later years. He owed his entire career—and his immense fortune—to Germaine de Staël, and everyone knew it. The view of Mme de La Tour du Pin, who like Talleyrand had recently returned with her husband from the United States, was typical: "The intervention of Mme de Staël, all powerful at that time through Benjamin Constant, had made him a minister," she was to write in her memoirs, probably overstating Benjamin's power but not his status and influence.[2]

Germaine expressed her gratitude to Barras. She was soon engaging Talleyrand to intervene with Napoleon in Italy on behalf of an aristocratic widow in dire distress who was pursuing Italian compensation for her late husband's sufferings. One personal gain for Germaine from Talleyrand's appointment was that she was invited—with or without Benjamin—to dinners and soirées at the ministry of foreign affairs. At one of these functions she met Lucien Bonaparte, Napoleon's brother, whose improvisatory theatrical harangue to the guards during the coup d'état of 18 Brumaire 1799 was to turn the tide and consolidate Napoleon's success. Lucien, who eventually fell out with his brother, would remain a good friend to Germaine. For a while, too, there was talk of Benjamin becoming Talleyrand's secretary, but nothing came of it.

At first, Germaine had some reason to feel satisfied: for the moment, no more was heard of her being arrested, nor had she been ordered to leave the country. Not only had she obtained the provisional removal of her father's name from the list of émigrés, but also she had managed to raise her friend Talleyrand to high office. In addition she had witnessed with no little pleasure Benjamin's great success at the Club de Salm, later known as the Cercle Constitutionnel, where the leading *philosophes, idéologues,* men of science, and politicians forgathered to debate the future of the Republic. A second edition of his pamphlet, *Des réactions politiques,* together with his *Des effets de la Terreur,* appeared in June to much acclaim. His fears about the advance of the Right and the increasing activity of reactionary royalists were being confirmed.

Yet, while Benjamin was enjoying such great success as a journalist and a political thinker, Germaine became the target of many ultraroyalist hacks. The more polite resorted to ironic digs, but most did not mince their words. She was called a "hermaphrodite" (suggesting a man-woman, or even a bisexual), "a prostitute," "a spark of discord," "the most active and despicable *intrigante* in Europe," "Messalina-Staël" or a sink of sexual perversion, "a witch," "a dressed-up hag," and so on.[3] Since the Revolution similar insults, often with the innuendo of sexual license and perversion, had been leveled at any woman who was seen to play some role in public life, from Marie Antoinette to Manon Roland. This consequence of Germaine's fame could not have been pleasant for her, and she must have feared that such gross insults would seriously damage her, putting her at greater risk. The contrast between Benjamin's status in the public eye and her own was marked: while his was being affirmed daily, hers remained precarious. She carried on regardless.

On September 4, Germaine and Benjamin spent the evening with Barras. They knew that the Directoire was about to strike against the extreme Right, and they approved of this action as essential to save the Republic. Germaine, however, was afraid of what might happen to Benjamin and to Barras if anything went wrong. What followed was something she did not anticipate, and it forced her to differ from Benjamin.

Hearing the boom of cannons, Mme de La Tour du Pin and her friend Mme de Valence, curious to know what was going on, dressed inconspicuously and set out on foot through streets that they found either deserted or full of soldiery to call on Mme de Staël. "She was with Benjamin Constant," remembered Mme de La Tour du Pin, "arguing with him very heatedly because he maintained that the Directoire's coup d'état, in arresting the [royalist] députés, was indispensable."[4] Germaine was fearful about the treatment of royalists under government arrest, while Benjamin used the argument of necessity—a reminder of his earlier view in Brunswick when he regarded Robespierre's tyranny as necessary.

Unlike the events of 13 Vendémiaire 1795, the Directoire's coup of 18 Fructidor (September 4, 1797) was marked by the most severe repression: suspects were rounded up, imprisoned without trial, banished summarily, or deported to French Guiana, a punishment known as the "dry guillotine" because prisoners rarely survived the ordeal. Germaine was deeply shocked: what she had wanted was the strengthening of the Directoire and the victory of the Republic, not these draconian measures taken indiscriminately against people who were defeated, including those who were innocent. Some friends, like Suard and his wife, she had warned beforehand, and they had escaped in time. Others, like the economist Pierre-Samuel Dupont de Nemours, she saved from deportation by appealing to Chénier. A few days later she left for Ormesson, where she gave refuge to friends and acquaintances who were fleeing from proscription. Soon, she was being accused of showing far too much sympathy for the "*fructidorisés*," the royalist victims of 18 Fructidor.

Germaine could not forget her part in desiring the coup d'état, and she famously spoke of her profound remorse in *De la littérature* (1800) and again later in *Considérations sur les principaux événements de la Révolution française* (published posthumously in 1818). Benjamin would criticize the events of 18 Fructidor in *Souvenirs historiques* (1830), but in 1797 it was a different matter. Soon after the coup he enjoyed one of his most successful moments: the speech he delivered on September 16 at the newly reopened Cercle Constitutionnel was loudly applauded by an immense crowd that spilled out in front of the (former) Palais Bourbon close by. He was asked to repeat it from the balcony to cries of "*Vive la République!*" which presumably were not uttered by those who disapproved of the deportations. Several "citizenesses" were present, but it is unlikely that Germaine was among them. She was intending to go to Switzerland without Benjamin, she said, although in fact she did not leave France. She informed his uncle, Samuel de Constant: "Your nephew will not be accompanying me; my stay will be brief and his successes are very great in the party of which he approves. When the Cercle Constitutionnel reopened he gave a speech before two thousand people that was applauded as if he were Gracchus in Rome. You can imagine that he feels content in France. He has done everything he possibly could for me and for those who are dear to me: it is to him alone that I owe being able to stay in France. My principles would not suffice for me to be forgiven for my sympathies."[5]

Clearly, Benjamin was not aiming to leave Paris; he wanted to take advantage of his rising position with the victors and his success in reinforcing it through his networking, his speeches, and his writings. Talleyrand would be recommending him to Bonaparte in Italy, who was thinking of forming a group of *publicistes,* or journalists. Benjamin was doing well in his ambitious projects, as noted in Germaine's letter: "His successes are very great in the party of which he approves." She could have said "the party of which *we* approve," but she did not do so because she did not support what she regarded as punishment without trial and the vindictive pursuit of the vanquished. She made it plain that he felt "content"—though she did not. It would be surprising if by this time, in the autumn of 1797, given his personal success, Benjamin did not feel that, in spite of all Germaine had done for him, she was now proving a potential obstacle to the advancement of his political career. And Germaine, while acknowledging her debt to him and certainly not begrudging his success, could not refrain from obliquely separating herself from his stance on 18 Fructidor: "My principles would not suffice for me to be forgiven for my sympathies." These words suggest that her republican ideals, sincere as they were, did not serve to gain acceptance for her moderation and her humanitarian conduct; they also suggest that such humanitarianism was not Benjamin's prime concern at the moment.

In her memoirs Mme de La Tour du Pin, a moderate royalist, declared that she had seen Germaine almost every day during this period and that there was a difference of opinion between Germaine and Benjamin: "In spite of her more than intimate liaison with Benjamin Constant she was working for the royalist party, or rather, for a compromise."[6] Mme de La Tour du Pin's swift self-correction seems plausible, for Germaine, who could not bear extremism and sectarianism, was always seeking reconciliation and a compromise between the moderates of all parties. However, Mme de La Tour du Pin did not disguise her dislike of Benjamin, whom she thought a hypocrite. Doubtless Germaine and Benjamin disagreed in September 1797, but he was soon finding ways to stand up for her in the press. Ostensibly the difference formed merely a passing cloud over their relationship. Yet Benjamin had never really cared for Germaine's close involvement with members of the aristocracy, which he thought imprudent and impolitic—as indeed it was. Nor did he share her all-embracing compassion for those in trouble. Though much moved by the misfortunes of others, his compassion did not tend to be immediate and active like Germaine's. If you were in trouble she hurried to help you, regardless of what side you were on. For her, compassion meant self-sacrifice; it was an essential part of her religion and morality, and the enduring legacy of her mother's moral lessons.

It was through Talleyrand that Germaine met General Napoleon Bonaparte for the first time, on the morning of December 6, 1797. He had returned triumphant from Italy the previous day. In his presence, she, the renowned conversationalist, esteemed for her witty repartee, could scarcely speak. Her admiration and enthusiasm for the military genius, universally lauded as a hero in the press, overpowered her and rendered her tongue-tied. Here was the young Bonaparte, not yet thirty, sketched by Jacques-Louis David—without trappings, and with straight hair, a compelling gaze, and a romantic aura—the model of sober republican taste and simplicity itself. She had written letters to him in Italy, all of them lost today, doubtless expressing her boundless admiration in an excessively flattering tone, rather like her epistles to Barras. Bonaparte would profess to regard them as love letters sent by a woman who was not in her right mind. In all likelihood they were intended to obtain his intervention on behalf of General Lafayette, whom she knew well, and others who were still prisoners of the Austrians. She had adopted their cause long before and had tried to enlist the support of Belle de Charrière in her campaign—indeed, this was the chief object of her visit to Colombier some years earlier that had so aroused Belle's dislike of the writer she saw as a parvenue.

From the beginning, Germaine did not succeed in making as favorable an impression on Bonaparte as she wished. If she harbored any hopes of attracting him to her brilliant circle, she misread the man. At this time a friend to the *idéologues,* he might well be stressing his own intellectual pretensions, but viscerally he did not care for intellectual women, especially those who "meddled"—that is, took a serious interest—in politics. After December 6, she met him on several occasions at diplomatic and government receptions. At a dinner where she was seated between Bonaparte and Sieyès, people noticed that the general treated her coldly. She went to hear Talleyrand's address when Bonaparte was received as a member of the recently founded Institut. The plainness of the hero's garb contrasted with the elaborately adorned uniforms and plumed hats of the Directors, but he appeared gratified to join the distinguished *idéologues* and eminent men of science who made up its numbers. It was the image he cultivated and wished to project at that moment. Talleyrand invited Germaine to the dazzling ball that he gave for General and Mme Bonaparte on January 3, 1798. When word reached her that the French were planning to "liberate" Switzerland, she found a way to speak with him in a tête-à-tête on Swiss liberties, trying in vain to convince him to change his mind. She knew that invasion would be followed by exploitation. Bonaparte was less interested in Swiss freedom than in acquiring funds for his projected expedition to Egypt.

Germaine left for Switzerland with Benjamin, but he returned to Hérivaux at the end of the month while Germaine remained with her father at Coppet, trembling at the sound of gunfire as the French troops approached. Although they were treated with courtesy, others did not fare so well. She knew of the pillaging and the onerous cost of the French occupation borne by many of her Swiss friends, some of whom carried their complaints to the Directoire in Paris. Father and daughter were worried about how they would be affected by the legal and financial consequences of the invasion: when Geneva was annexed all Genevans became French citizens and thus were subject to French laws.

Germaine and Benjamin remained apart, and living in very different circumstances, from January to the summer of 1798. During this period, Germaine was lauding to the skies Benjamin's genius, reminding all that in Paris he was known as "the Burke of democracy" (unlike Edmund Burke himself, who had defended tradition and privilege).[7]

As for Benjamin in Paris, he was pursuing his career and seeing his friends. Ever since the summer of 1795, when he first met Julie Talma, possibly through his friend Louvet, he had enjoyed a close friendship with her. Perhaps this important association with Julie had begun with a brief affair but he had thought better of it. She fell deeply in love with him and teased him about his "indifference" in the letters she wrote to him—his replies have not been found. In an age of remarkable women Julie Talma was not to be overlooked. She was some years older than Benjamin, and although not strikingly beautiful, she possessed great charm and strong and long-suffering character.

At sixteen Julie Carreau, who was illegitimate, joined the corps de ballet of the Paris Opéra. She had—by different "protectors"—several sons, who tragically predeceased her. In 1791 she married the former Girondin and soon-to-be-famous tragedian François-Joseph Talma, Napoleon's favorite actor. She and Talma would be divorced ten years later, in 1801. An ardent republican, she shared Benjamin's political opinions, regarding him with admiration as "the voice and the mind of the Republic."[8] Notable republicans as well as leading *idéologues* such as the distinguished doctor Cabanis frequented her salon on the rue Matignon. Benjamin became very attached to her over the years, so much so that he would stay by her side when she lay dying in 1805, and he was deeply affected by her death, calling her "the most disinterested woman friend."[9] Was not Germaine disinterested? Or did he come to regard her courageous actions on behalf of himself and others as a form of power play? And what, if anything, did Germaine know of Benjamin's *amitié amoureuse* with Julie Talma, his confidante, which lasted some ten years?

It was also during the first months of 1798 that Benjamin suffered the first real disappointment in his meteoric rise in French politics. For some time his attempt to be elected to the municipal assembly of Luzarches had been frustrated because he had not resided there a sufficient length of time, as the law required. Somehow, this obstacle was eventually overcome. More serious by far was his failure to be elected député to the legislative Council. After everything Benjamin had done for the Republic, he expected success as his due. But on April 14, 1798, he received formal confirmation that this was not to be—his place was taken instead by Talleyrand. At the same time he was attacked in the press and fought another duel in the Bois de Boulogne to clear his name: once again, the journalist in question, Georges Sibuet, issued a retraction.

When Germaine heard of the duel with Sibuet she was very upset at this disregard of her feelings. Why could he not have responded to the man in writing? As for herself, as a woman she could not reply by word or deed to calumny without further dishonor. *She* could not fight a duel every time she was insulted in the press, and no chivalric swordsman sprang to defend her honor when she was called a prostitute or a Messalina. But as Burke had famously said, "The age of chivalry is gone," speaking of those who did not arise at once, sword in hand, to save Marie Antoinette from insult—and worse.[10] In Germaine's eyes Benjamin was prideful, impulsive, and violent. "He never stops mixing republican violence with chivalric spirit. He will kill us, but for myself I wish it were done," she commented with no little bitterness, thinking that he would be the death of her.[11]

She was also extremely worried about the dire state of Benjamin's finances: his funds were not sufficient to pay for all the building work at Hérivaux, and she feared that he might turn to moneylenders. On April 30, 1798, she rashly appealed to his father—whose financial expertise, it must be said, was not at all evident—to take charge of Benjamin's affairs to prevent the ruin that was looming on the horizon.

"With me he does not need money," she added.[12] She meant well, but her decision to involve Juste de Constant was a great mistake. Relations between the father and son were always delicate, as she well knew, but perhaps more so than she could really appreciate, given her close rapport with her own father. According to Rosalie de Constant, Juste and Benjamin usually argued about money whenever they met. Germaine asked Juste not to tell Benjamin what she had ventured to advise. His pride would have been wounded by her indiscretion.

The following month, on May 15, 1798, while Germaine was still at Coppet with her father and children in the midst of the depredations caused by the French occupation of Switzerland, Benjamin wrote a very long, breathless, revealing, dreadful letter from Hérivaux to his aunt, Mme de Nassau. He wanted his aunt to find him a wife.

I am writing to you, my dear Aunt, from the depths of the most complete solitude, in the midst of my forests, and feeling that I lack only stability in my situation to be tolerably happy. I am writing to you to ask you if you can possibly help me to give this situation what it lacks. An emotional tie, to which I am bound by duty, or if you will, by weakness, but to which I feel I shall hold firm as long as a duty that is more real does not set me free, and which I cannot break without admitting that I am frightfully weary of it, something I am too polite to admit, a tie which, in casting me into a world I no longer care for, and in detaching me from the countryside I love, makes me deeply unhappy, and threatens with the utmost confusion a fortune that, in the midst of my wanderings, I have preserved only by a miracle, a tie, in fine, that cannot be broken without a shock that cannot come from me, has kept me in chains for the last two years. I am on my own without being independent. I am subjugated without being in a union. I see the last years of my youth drifting by without enjoying the tranquillity of solitude or the legitimacy of gentle domestic affections. I have tried in vain to break it. Given my character, it is impossible for me to withstand the laments of another person when all I have to oppose them is my will, when in consequence I can postpone my liberation from one moment and from one day to another, without any obvious inconvenience, and I wear myself out in a situation that goes against my tastes, my favorite pursuits, and the peace and quiet of my life. Besides, once this tie is broken, I shall be on my own in a manner that will add to the image of the suffering, whether true or false, that people will say I have caused. To console me for this, I need to give someone a little happiness.

Can you guess, my dear Aunt, what I am driving at? I am asking for something I have considered for the last year, about which I have written to you twenty letters that I have torn up, it is for you to find me a wife. I need one to be free, to be happy."[13]

There follows some account of his finances. He declares that, among other advantages, he can bring to the marriage the properties of La Chablière and Hérivaux. He also describes the sort of person he has in mind: the bride should be Genevan (that is, newly French, like himself), sixteen years old "at the most," presentable, of simple orderly habits, and ready to live in the country at Hérivaux, with only occasional visits to Paris. "As to her character," he wrote, "I leave it to you. Where intellect is concerned, I have had it up to here."

He reaffirms that he has been thinking of all this for a long time but has been distracted by the elections. Now that he knows he has failed to be elected député, "I am keen to be surrounded by my books, to settle far from revolutionary storms," to be forgotten by the newspapers where he has been under attack. "I shall no longer be the satellite of a burning Meteor, condemned to find once more through another the miserable fame that I should like to be rid of. At last I shall no longer live, as I have lived far longer than people realize, doing out of compliance to another what looks like madness, and praying every day for solitude for myself and a lover for my Mistress." Ready to leave the choice of bride to his aunt, Benjamin makes it plain that he wants neither a servant nor a prodigy. Above all, he wants someone whose name is not to be found in the newspapers: "For two years I have been breathlessly following the chariot of a famous woman." As to whether his "Revolutionary career" will shock the parents of the bride, he insists that "I have really left this career behind me, and chance offering me the possibility to withdraw without quarreling with my companions in arms, I am tempted not to let slip this fortunate opportunity." He has been planning this approach to his aunt for more than six months. In this "serious and great negotiation" he urges her to secrecy. "It is a sort of conspiracy against my Master, and merely formulating it makes me feel afraid. But you know how cowards when pushed to the limit become courageous," he concludes, not without irony.[14]

Doubtless the cause of this extraordinary letter—extraordinary in view of all that has gone before and all that is left unsaid or simply fudged—lies in his deep, bitter disappointment at his failure to be elected député, his fury at being attacked in the press by his political opponents, his serious worries about his financial troubles, and his resentment at Germaine's well meant but unfortunate interference in appealing to his father to take charge of his affairs. The letter attests to his volatile nature—did not Belle de Charrière call him a chameleon? After just one important setback following two years of remarkable and scarcely interrupted success, he is prepared to cast his political career to the winds. Indeed, most significantly, he stresses that in actuality his political activity runs counter to his true nature and especially to his love of solitude, a pleasure he had so enjoyed during his youthful English escapade. It takes him away from the quiet life he really wants to lead, one "far from revolutionary storms," in the country, among his books. He also dares to affirm that in pursuing his ambitious political career he has acted out of "compliance" to a famous woman in a way that now looks to him like "madness," as though he had not thrown himself at once into politics with heady republican ardor, as he later describes so vividly through the experience of the narrator in *Cécile*. Was Mathieu de Montmorency right to doubt Benjamin's political sincerity and integrity?

Benjamin then passes to the nature of his association with Germaine, whose name is never mentioned in the letter. The word *lien*, or "tie," is repeated at intervals three times in one long breathless sentence. The word appears again further on. He tells his aunt that he has been in chains for the "last two years," which leads back to April 1796, and the very beginning of their intimate liaison, as distinct from their association since the autumn of 1794. For a whole year (that is, since April 1797), he has been thinking of remarrying and has even written many letters to his aunt that he has torn up. Later on, after all this beating around the bush, he says that for more than six months (that is, since November 1797) he has been contemplating the idea of asking his aunt's help in finding him a wife. Thus, for six months, a year, two years, he has been trying to be free, he claims. He sees himself as a prisoner, the satellite of a meteor, attached like a slave to the chariot of a celebrated woman, subordinate to a "master"—in short, as a wretched man who can be freed from Germaine's chains only by a higher duty, marriage to another, the sole pretext that would prevent Germaine from having any possible claim upon him. Mindful of the opinion of others, he believes that this marriage would also stop anyone from blaming him. Marriage is not desired for its own sake: paradoxically, it is intended to free Benjamin once and for all from everything, including his burgeoning political career, without upsetting his associates, so that he can return, like Cincinnatus or Washington, to private life on his country estate.

It seems clear that Mme de Nassau—along with the other members of the extended Constant family—had no idea of Benjamin's debt to Germaine, and not only for his elegant lifestyle at Mézery or Coppet. His family presumably knew nothing of the extent to which he owed his contacts with the powerful French leaders principally to her. The idea that he had preserved his wealth "only by a miracle" overlooks the fact that by accompanying Germaine to Paris in 1795 he discovered the prospect of "an unimaginable bargain," began to speculate in *biens nationaux,* and acquired property in France—which it is unlikely that he would have done if he had returned to Brunswick or remained in Lausanne.

The devotion to Germaine that he had displayed during those first eighteen months of violent unrequited passion appeared to have vanished into oblivion. The extravagant acts that Germaine had once regarded as a form of persecution, such as banging his head on the chimneypiece and attempting to commit suicide, had culminated in his ultimate triumph over her resistance. Yet, if the phrase "the last two years" has any meaning, from the very instant of Germaine's "surrender," his wild passion was transformed as if by magic into a "tie." How genuine, then, was this passion? Was he passionately in love only in his imagination? Was his passion genuine only so long as it was frustrated? Was he faithful only to the sincerity of the moment?

When he drew up his will at the time of the duel with Bertin de Vaux he left his Swiss property, La Chablière, to Germaine; now he was offering it to his new bride, whoever she might be, as part of the marriage settlement. In the famous Testament of April 1796, he had promised Germaine lifelong devotion and fidelity, with the prospect of matrimony as soon as they were both free to marry. Yet now all he could see in their relationship was his subordinate position, chained to the chariot of a celebrated woman—a position he had assumed eagerly enough and with full knowledge of her celebrity. He blamed Germaine entirely for the "tie" under which he suffered. But what exactly is this "tie"? It is, above all, the disagreeable state that inevitably follows upon a woman's "surrender."

According to Constant in his *Lettre sur Julie*, not published until 1829 though written long before, Julie Talma was unlike other women because she was a realist: she recognized the true state of relations between the sexes. She "understood and admitted that women who have given themselves and men who have gained what they wanted are in a precisely contrary position." He elaborates on this theme: "It is only at the moment of what is called their defeat that women begin to have a definite aim, that of preserving the lover for whom they have made what must seem to them to be a great sacrifice. Men, on the contrary, at this very same moment, no longer have an aim; what was one for them turns into a tie. It is not surprising that two individuals in such an unequal relationship, quickly come to misunderstand one another." That is why marriage, he maintains, is such a good thing—it gives the man and woman common interests. The same opinion on love affairs is reiterated in his novel *Adolphe*, where the eponymous antihero, speaking of his long liaison with the luckless Ellénore, declares that "she was no longer an aim: she had become a tie."[15] Benjamin's view was doubtless shared by many of his masculine contemporaries.

Apparently, Mme de Nassau did not take her nephew's request for a wife too seriously; she suggested that it would be better for him to remain single. "Your will be done," replied Benjamin sardonically from Hérivaux on June 28, 1798, shortly after Germaine left Coppet for Saint-Ouen, where she arrived after five or six days. "I am all the more easily resigned to it because my legitimate sovereign has returned and all attempts at revolt have been abandoned. To speak more seriously I must tell you that I have received new and such kind tokens of devotion from the person I believed for a moment it would be better for her and myself to appear less closely connected, that I could not without the darkest ingratitude and future bitter regrets, contemplate doing anything whatsoever to cause her pain. So I beg you, my dear Aunt, to forget the part of my letter relating to all that, above all, to show it to no one. . . . The arrival of my dear friend changes nothing in my habits, I am staying either on her country estate [Saint-Ouen] or my own [Hérivaux]." Solitude is a necessary help in time of trouble: "I am going to try to add to it the life of study I have neglected for some time. The Revolution devours all one's faculties." His aunt must have felt relieved that she had not engaged in a lengthy search for a bride. From Paris on July 16, 1798, there followed a further letter of excuse to reassure her: "I felt rather ashamed at changing my mind so suddenly about what I had written to you. I had some regrets at having wanted to loosen a tie with a person who gives me proof of her utmost devotion every day, and all of that must have given my style a certain awkwardness that you noticed."[16] It is not surprising that he felt awkward about such a sudden volte-face.

What were these new tokens of devotion that Germaine had given him? On May 12 she had written to her Paris bankers requesting payment to Benjamin Constant of 2,400 livres in order to settle an outstanding debt to him. Doubtless this formula was to protect Benjamin's reputation since it is highly unlikely that she owed him any money; the opposite is more credible. This gift, arranged only three days before his intemperate letter to his aunt, is assumed to be one of the "kind tokens of devotion." Sometime after July there would be Necker's loan to Benjamin of 34,000 francs, probably at Germaine's urging. All this made up a considerable sum. Germaine, meanwhile, had no inkling of Benjamin's abortive attempt to break free. That did not undo the fact, however, that in May 1798 he had formulated in his mind and had put into words on paper his self-justification and his desire for freedom. Moreover, he had communicated those words to another.

In October Germaine left for Coppet with Benjamin, and she stayed on in Switzerland when he returned to France in February 1799. From then until April she was actively engaged in the elections, moving between Coppet and the city of Geneva, working tirelessly to have Benjamin elected député for the newly created French département du Léman and, when that failed, commissioner or representative of the Directoire for the Geneva region, which also failed. His uncle Samuel reported that she "moved heaven and earth" on Benjamin's behalf and scarcely drank, ate, or slept: "Her life is entirely devoted to that end."[17]

During the long periods when Germaine and Benjamin were together, either at Saint-Ouen in the summer of 1798 or at Coppet from the autumn of 1798 to the summer of 1799, among all their other activities they were busily engaged in writing. This was a period of close collaboration, and it is often difficult to separate the contribution of one from the other. Benjamin was at work on his pamphlet *Des suites de la contre-révolution en Angleterre en 1660*, published in July 1799, in which he again opposed the return of the ancien regime, aiming to reveal the disadvantages of the restoration of Charles II and pointing especially to the reprisals that followed his accession. The very same thing, he argued, would happen under a Bourbon restoration. Germaine praised Benjamin's courage in attacking the Jacobins as well as his talent in showing how the reactionary regime that Louis XVIII would impose would be dependent on the foreign armies that placed him on the throne. It has been suggested that this pamphlet was written to support the policies of Director Sieyès, who could count Benjamin among his sympathizers. Benjamin was also working on a translation and commentary of the libertarian William Godwin's *Enquiry Concerning Political Justice and Its Influence on General Virtue and Happiness*, a work that Germaine praised highly. Benjamin agreed. "The author is very daring in his ideas, and above all he has the fairly rare gift of not shirking any difficulty," said Benjamin, who admired Godwin's original turn of mind.[18] The translation was never published in Benjamin's lifetime.

Meanwhile, Germaine was writing a comprehensive overview and examination of the situation in France under the Directoire, *Des circonstances actuelles qui peuvent terminer la Révolution et des principes qui doivent fonder la République en France.* There was nothing else quite like it. Many spoke of "the present circumstances"; this was a sort of catchphrase. Many brooded over how to bring the Revolution to an end and how to establish the Republic on firm foundations. But none had probed the current state of the parties and factions or had analyzed the problems and possibilities for liberty with order in such a disciplined way. Benjamin collaborated very closely with her on the manuscript, as can be judged from the numerous cuts and changes that he made. Had *Des circonstances actuelles* been published in 1799—it did not appear in a masterly edition until nearly two centuries later, in 1979—it would surely have established Germaine as an important political thinker who sought to put political science on solid footing, an assessment that would have to wait two decades until the publication of her *Considérations sur les principaux événements de la Révolution française.* Presumably, Germaine decided not to publish *Des circonstances actuelles* because by the time she finished it the circumstances had indeed changed. With the armies and their generals becoming ever more powerful and the Directoire ever more dependent on them, it seemed hardly the moment for criticizing the military spirit as being contrary to liberty, as she did in *Des circonstances actuelles,* declaring her firm faith in amelioration through enlightenment, not through armies. Doubtless she judged, too, that the book might damage Benjamin's political career.

During this period, Germaine and Benjamin felt particularly close to abbé Sieyès, who has been called the key to the Revolution. She had long admired him—in June 1799 she spoke to him of her ten-year homage—for she thought of him as the Newton of French politics, someone who had completely changed the way of looking at things and had inspired a new era. The taciturn political theorist had written a famous pamphlet, "What Is the Third Estate?" with its reply, "Everything," that had galvanized the liberal-minded public in 1789. He had also been associated with the making of the various constitutions since that date, an activity that always fascinated Germaine. His interest in German culture, which preceded his stint as ambassador to the Prussian court in Berlin, likely appealed to Benjamin, who was so well versed in the subject. He saw Citizen Director Sieyès then as a man of principle, "the last hope of the Republic," the guarantor of the ideals of the Revolution and of a regime where individual liberty would be preserved. "You are my hope and I believe in the Revolution because I believe in you," he told Sieyès when sending him a copy of his pamphlet on the restoration of Charles II or "counter-revolution" of 1660.[19] For both Germaine and Benjamin, as they worried constantly about where the country was heading, it was as if the mere presence of Sieyès at the seat of power reassured them.

What neither of them knew was that Sieyès, using the pretext of a Jacobin plot, was actively conspiring with General Bonaparte and others to bring about a coup d'état that would put an end to the disputes of the weakly fluctuating Directoire. Bonaparte was the very "sword" he had been seeking for this purpose. It so happened that Germaine, who had been planning to return to France for some time, left Switzerland mere days before the coup. Benjamin met her en route, and together they reached the staging post at Charenton, where they stopped to change horses, on the afternoon of 18 Brumaire (November 9), when the coup took place. They were told that a party of dragoons had just passed by: it was escorting Barras, who had been overthrown, to Grosbois, his country estate. In the evening the couple arrived in the capital, which was buzzing with rumors and where nobody knew what was really afoot.

The next morning, 19 Brumaire, Benjamin hurried to the palace of Saint-Cloud, whither the députés had been led to transfer the seat of their deliberations. He sent hourly reports by courier to Germaine: the outcome was far from certain. Dreading a Jacobin victory that would doubtless result in her being persecuted or even executed, in a panic Germaine collected from her business agents all the money she had available so that she could flee the country with Benjamin and Mathieu de Montmorency. Even Bonaparte seemed preferable to the return of the Jacobin Terror.

Much was bungled in what the historian and liberal political thinker Alexis de Tocqueville would later claim was one of "the worst conceived and worst executed coups d'état imaginable."[20] But Bonaparte triumphed because people were weary and wanted peace and quiet, and the army stood with him. It was easy enough to be taken in by Bonaparte's fine declarations, for on 19 Brumaire he swore a solemn oath, designed to reassure anyone who doubted his republican ideals and intentions: "We desire a Republic founded on true liberty, on civil liberty, on representative government; we shall have it, I swear; I swear in my name and that of my companions in arms." On 20 Brumaire, he—with Sieyès and Roger Ducos, the newly installed three Consuls at the head of the government—swore to remain "faithful to the *République une et indivisible*, to liberty, equality, representative government" and was greeted with cries of "*Vive la République!*"[21] To many it seemed that Bonaparte, the First Consul, widely seen as the incarnation of the Revolution, had saved the Republic. Moreover, Sieyès was entrusted with the new constitution of Year VIII—surely proof that the ideals and principles of 1789 would be preserved.

At first, in the general confusion, Germaine did not know what to think; certainly she disapproved of what she called the military spirit. Soon after the coup she published an extract from Necker's writings, believing them to be pertinent, and in her preface she expressed her opposition to despotism. But, after all, the Republic was saved. All one had to do was put one's trust in Bonaparte's solemn oaths and regard him as the savior and as a truly republican hero. She conveyed her enthusiasm for the man of the hour to her father, but Necker, the constitutional monarchist, had his doubts. "You portray in bright colors the delight of Paris and your pleasure in the *gloire* and power of your hero," he wrote to her. Your hero, not mine, he was suggesting here, stressing with heavy irony his reservations about the forthcoming "perfect" constitution. "I hope and pray that your satisfaction will continue, and like you I think that Sieyès . . . will provide a constitution without any faults, a perfect one perhaps, as you say in advance." In Necker's (correct) view of the situation, it was Sieyès who had eased Bonaparte's path to power. When, a month later, her father saw from Coppet that the institutions of representative government in France were being dismantled one by one, he cried ironically, "Long live the Republic! Is that still what people say?"[22]

From the beginning Benjamin, too, had similar doubts and was less sanguine than Germaine. That Sieyès had kept his own counsel and had not taken Benjamin into his confidence about the plot is evident. Had he known about the leading role that the constitution maker had played in the planning and execution of the coup of 18 Brumaire, it is unlikely that Benjamin would have ventured to warn him about Bonaparte as he did on the following morning. In an urgent note to be delivered to Sieyès personally, Benjamin wrote, "Citizen Director, After the first feeling of joy at the news of our deliverance, I have had second thoughts. . . . I believe that this is a decisive moment for liberty. People are speaking about the move to adjourn the Councils [the legislative body], a measure that I regard as a disaster for it destroys the only barrier to stand against a man you have joined to yesterday's events but who because of this is only all the more threatening for the republic; his proclamations, where he either speaks only of himself, or else he declares that his return [from Egypt] has encouraged hopes that he will put an end to France's ills, have convinced me that in everything he does he looks only to his own rise to power." However bad representative government might be, Benjamin argued, it was still a bulwark against the ambitions of an individual and could alone act "against any attempt at usurpation." (The word *usurpation* meant dictatorship and despotism to Benjamin and would figure in his important later writings on the subject of tyranny.) He begged Sieyès, as protector of the Republic, to save the legislative body that would be of such help to him "in the struggle in which you and the Republic will probably soon have to engage." Fully aware that by writing this way he might appear ridiculous, he declared that he was nonetheless ready to risk ridicule to serve Sieyès and liberty, for perhaps the time would come when it would be necessary to "defend it against B. and . . . to fight against a person like B. it is needful to have the support of a [legislative] body."[23] Benjamin's fears were soon to be fulfilled.

All the same, perspicacious enough to see through Bonaparte's designs at once, Benjamin decided not to play the hero but, while he had the chance, to try to satisfy his ambition and pursue the political career he had been ready to jettison so cavalierly not long before. Only a few days after his proud and passionate defense of liberty against the looming threat of Bonaparte's dictatorship, he was addressing Sieyès again, this time as "Citizen Consul." On November 15, the day that the constitution of Year VIII was promulgated, he boldly asked for a position. He would have preferred to be a député, he said, "because I believe I would have served liberty in that role," but he was ready to settle for the next best thing available: "To-day, when the destinies of the Republic are linked to your name, I should find it most agreeable to serve it, under this very name that invites Europe to remember the first principles of liberty."[24] A little flattery, learned from Germaine, would not be amiss when applying for a post to the man who had inspired the Revolution.

It was through Sieyès, and during the month that he remained Second Consul, that Benjamin was promoted to the newly formed Tribunate. After a few short years, and despite the longstanding query over his nationality, Benjamin had reached the pinnacle: a place in the high councils of the French government. True, it was not quite as good as being a député, for although he and his fellow tribunes were permitted to discuss the laws and express their approval or disapproval, they could not vote on them. As for Sieyès, his desire for safeguards did not suit the First Consul, who had deceived him. Sieyès and the lesser known Ducos were soon replaced by Cambacérès and Lebrun, men who were more closely attached to Bonaparte. Showered with honors and rewarded for his services to the nation, abbé Sieyès was to be found a few years later living in state and entertaining royally.

Power was now rapidly accumulating in the hands of the First Consul, who had no particular reason to favor Germaine and Benjamin. They would find themselves in a new role in a new era, and in a position that was going to have serious repercussions on their relationship.

CHAPTER FIVE

❧ *A New Order* ☙

THE WORLD WAS CHANGING FAST, but in the beginning Germaine and Benjamin did not fully apprehend the nature of that change. How could they, when they were being challenged by a number of contradictory messages? The First Consul had solemnly sworn to uphold the liberties of the Republic and representative government. Yet the two companions would see him whittle away these liberties one by one in his gradual advance to dictatorship—and he would be a very different kind of dictator from those of the past: a ruler who had his eye on the minutest details in the lives of his subjects. There might be a Tribunate and a Senate, but Bonaparte soon let their members know how he expected them to behave.

Meanwhile, the partners could scarcely fail to note certain similarities to the ancien regime, the very outcome they had dreaded and energetically opposed under the Directoire: Bonaparte resided in the Tuileries, the palace of the Bourbon kings; his court, with its chamberlains and strict etiquette, was modeled on the style of his royal predecessors. There were signs that Catholicism would again become the official religion, a move particularly unwelcome not only to Protestants (as Germaine and Benjamin were by tradition) with long memories of persecution but also to deists and freethinkers. By rallying to the new regime, ultraroyalists along with former Jacobin extremists were rewarded with offices at court, in the administration, or in the army. Soon, the number of newspapers was drastically reduced, and those that remained mostly followed the official line. The companions felt the sharp thrusts of Bonaparte's paid hacks. They grew aware that their private correspondence was under surveillance; they had to resort to subterfuge, such as using the addresses of trusted servants. In a few brief years they would watch aghast as General Bonaparte, the savior of the Republic, moved from First Consul to Consul for Life in August 1802 and then, in December 1804, crowned himself emperor. Long before that consummation, however, they could have no doubts about his true aim.

The two responded in distinctive ways to the new order according to their deepest natures and instincts. Although Benjamin had foreseen, in his warning to Sieyès, the danger to liberty in the advent of Napoleon Bonaparte, he seems at first—with Germaine and some of their friends among the republican *idéologues*—to have been under the delusion that a kind of respected parliamentary opposition could function, just as it did in England. After all, he had been appointed to the Tribunate to discuss the laws: that must mean something. He soon discovered that he was expected to discuss them in a manner that did not offend the First Consul or appear to frustrate the great man's designs for order, as he understood it. How would Benjamin, the ardent republican, react? Would he take a stand?

As for Germaine, there was no question: she had been talking openly on diverse subjects ever since, as an adolescent, she had conversed precociously with many of the prominent figures of the Enlightenment. She was used to what she called "an agreeable and independent society," where there existed free and witty expression of views by people of different ideas and outlook, such as she had culti-

vated in her own salon at all times under various regimes.[1] Such
freedom and exchange were vital to her way of life. When, keen to
attract adherents of all parties, Bonaparte sent her friend, his elder
brother Joseph, to find out what exactly she wanted, appealing to her
self-interest by offering to repay the famous two million livres that
Necker had lent to the royal treasury, she replied: "My God, it is not a
matter of what I want but of what I think."[2] This declaration of the
independence of the intellectual deserves to stand alongside Voltaire's
better known defense of the right of one's opponents to express their
views without hindrance. She saw herself and her closest friends as
representing "the party of liberty": they were the upholders and de-
fenders of the true ideals of the Revolution and of the civil rights won
in the early days, "the rights of man," individual liberty, toleration,
freedom of worship, and the rest. Prudence was not one of her virtues;
speaking her mind had cost her dearly in the past and would do
so again.

The Tribunate met for the first time on January 1, 1800, and thenceforward sessions were held twice a month in the Palais-Royal, in a
small, insignificant room described as looking rather like an old chapel.
Only a few days after the first meeting there was trouble over a
question of procedure. The government was introducing a law that
would give it the right to name the date and length of debates in the
Tribunate: if within three days the tribunes had not come to a decision,
their "silence" would be regarded as agreement. Benjamin considered
making a speech in defense of an independent Tribunate. As Germaine
remembered it many years later, he consulted her beforehand. They
had both read Montesquieu and firmly held that the legislative power
should be separate from the executive. Benjamin pointed out to her
that if he went ahead with his speech, her salon—at that moment
graced by many eminent people she liked, including Talleyrand, the

minister of foreign affairs; the esteemed lawyer and influential publicist Pierre-Louis Roederer; and Bonaparte's brothers Joseph and Lucien— would be deserted in an instant.

In effect Benjamin was offering her a way out, but despite her fears, she encouraged him. Although her father had advised caution her response was immediate. She said to Benjamin that one must act in accordance with one's beliefs. Would he have refrained from making his speech if that was what she wanted, if she had not supported and inspired him? On January 5, Benjamin gave his eloquent address with its resounding prophesy: without a free and independent legislature there would be "only servitude and silence; a silence that all of Europe would hear and judge."[3] Germaine was expecting guests that day; by five o'clock all of them had sent excuses. The cultivated Joseph Bonaparte, publicly reprimanded by the First Consul for associating with her, did not reappear for three months. Talleyrand, who owed her so much, never contacted her again during Napoleon's supremacy. Roederer was to be seen no more in her company.

According to one newspaper, *Le Surveillant* on January 7, the First Consul did not conceal his annoyance; indeed, Bonaparte was known for his sudden bursts of anger, whether genuine or feigned for reasons of policy, which could be thoroughly intimidating. A campaign against the pair, often threatening in tone, was launched in the press. It was claimed that Benjamin's appointment to the Tribunate was unconstitutional. Moreover, the "French people" gave Germaine some useful advice: "It is not your fault if you are ugly, but it is your fault if you are an intriguer. Change your ways at once, if you don't want something bad to happen to you. . . . Take your Benjamin away. Let him go and try out his talents in the Swiss Senate. Let him avoid coming here to disturb a people that is tired of his maneuvers and yours." Other papers joined in the chorus "against these pygmies who want to fight Hercules."[4] Benjamin tended to be more sensitive than she was to such attacks; by now she was fairly used to them, distressing as they were. Rather, she was hurt by the social ostracism and the betrayal not only by Talleyrand, whom she regarded as one of her intimates, but also by Roederer, whom she valued as a distinguished colleague or friendly associate. Even more wounding than social ostracism, perhaps, and far more dangerous, was the fact that Roederer had conveyed to Bonaparte some incautious words uttered in her salon. Ironically, it was through Germaine and Benjamin that Roederer had been introduced to Sieyès and was thus able to take an active part in the preparations for the coup of 18 Brumaire. He rocketed to favor, becoming one of the most prominent and most ardent supporters of Bonaparte's regime.

In total disarray at the impact of Benjamin's speech, Germaine addressed Roederer on January 9, 1800: "Explain to me, I beg you, Roederer, what has been going on for the last three days, this outpouring of hatred against Benjamin, this *Journal des Hommes libres* unleashed against me simply because I am the friend of a man who has made an independent speech on a matter of procedure! . . . Is a mere opinion a crime committed not only by Benjamin but also by myself? I certainly had nothing to do with his speech, for devoted as I am to him I do not tell him what to do. I am more astonished, more astounded than I have ever been. Is this your way of keeping your promise to me?" She hastened to remind him that she had helped him when he faced persecution at the time of the coup of 18 Fructidor 1797 and had supported him religiously ever since. She did not expect to be persecuted when the friends she had assisted were now in influential positions. "*I was counting on you as my defender, and I learn that it is you whom Bonaparte has quoted as having told him what people claim is being said in my home* [Her emphasis]. All this persecution is utterly crazy! Where will you find anyone more concerned than ourselves in excluding Jacobins from government? What woman has proved herself *at all times* to be more enthusiastic about Bonaparte than myself? What is the purpose of all this persecution because of a few independent remarks . . . ? Is it the aim of government to propel its friends into the ranks of its enemies, when it is obvious that nothing is more contrary to their aims, interests, and inclinations?" This suggested outcome was hardly diplomatic. She continued: "Have I ceased to be the woman who befriended and defended you for two years? Is not Benjamin the one who, first among Sieyès's friends, brought you together? . . . Has all morality in friendship, society, kindness come to an end? . . . I do not hide from you the fact that for the last three days I have been suffering more than I have ever suffered in my life."[5] This last phrase she often used to mean she was suffering exceedingly. Indeed, she was in despair.

Benjamin's confidante, Julie Talma, asked him, "What is this despair of one of your women friends who spends her nights weeping, because the talent and courage you have shown has made you some powerful enemies?"[6] Julie did not understand as Benjamin did the nature and cause of Germaine's distress: the sudden loss of her foothold in society and of her trust in the quid pro quo of loyalty; the ease with which she lapsed into deep melancholy and mental suffering; the lack of control over her emotions, which her mother, for all her efforts, had never been able to instill. And how did Julie Talma know that Germaine cried every night if Benjamin did not tell her? Here was surely a more intimate betrayal of Germaine than that of Talleyrand or Roederer—one that fortunately was unknown to her.

The wily minister of police, Joseph Fouché, summoned Germaine to his office. Though notorious for his zeal in carrying out executions during the Terror, he was on her extensive guest list and was by no means ill-disposed toward her. He informed her that the First Consul suspected her of having inspired Benjamin to make the offending speech. Proudly, she denied it: her friend was not the sort of man who needed a woman's encouragement, and besides, there should be free expression in the legislature. Apparently some members of Bonaparte's entourage wanted her thrown out of the country. Fouché was not so extreme. He advised her to leave Paris for a while until the brouhaha subsided. There was nothing for Germaine to do but obey and depart for Saint-Ouen. Her father urged her to be prudent: she should live quietly in the country, keep silent on political affairs, and try not to dwell on her misfortune. She should be patient and devote herself to writing her book on the nature, function, and importance of literature in modern societies, *De la littérature considérée dans ses rapports avec les conditions sociales*, which she had begun the previous year. By early February she was allowed to return to Paris, where she hoped to restore her reputation through literary fame.

Why was it not Benjamin Constant who was summoned to police headquarters and advised to go quietly into the country for a while and mind his tongue? It was Benjamin, after all, who had made the offending speech in the Tribunate. Yet the First Consul chose to blame and punish Germaine de Staël for it. So what if she had inspired or encouraged Benjamin? The eloquent words were his. The imputation that he was a mere ventriloquist's dummy could not have been pleasant for a proud man. Misogyny was certainly a factor in Bonaparte's sharp response to Germaine. It is also possible that although Benjamin had made his mark under the Directoire, he was not yet tiresome enough in the eyes of the First Consul to warrant punishment other than through the press. Bonaparte would not forget him, however, and later he was to say forcefully to Cambacérès when urging surveillance on Germaine, "Keep an eye as well on Benjamin Constant: and at the slightest thing he meddles with, I shall send him back to Brunswick to his wife!"[7] As for Germaine de Staël, Bonaparte once remarked that people always left her salon feeling less favorably inclined toward him. "*La fille de M. Necker*" had the fame, the connections, the reputation for "meddling" in politics as no woman should. It was clear to him that she would not be actively supporting his regime, and those who were not for him were against him. He also knew that she could not keep silent. It was sufficient for the moment, as a warning shot over the bows, to give her a good fright.

In spite of all her troubles, Germaine went on with completing her book. Her creative energies were unstoppable; she rarely allowed anything to interfere with her literary endeavors. In April 1800, *De la littérature* was published to singular acclaim and controversy. The extraordinary forward-looking work struck her readers as being unlike anything else from the hand of a woman, most of her feminine predecessors or contemporaries having devoted themselves largely to novels, stories, poetry, memoirs, history, or works on education. Whatever its shortcomings in matters of detail, it was a grandly ambitious work of synthesis that ranged widely over the whole field of European literature. It was full of new and striking ideas; its tone was elevated and generous; its hopes for liberty of thought and expression, for "torrents of enlightenment" in dark places, were eloquent and stirring. She knew where her originality lay: the relationship between literature and social and political institutions in each age and each country had not been treated before. She stressed "the importance of literature in its widest sense, that is, including philosophical writings as well as works of the imagination; indeed, everything that concerns the exercise of thought in writing, except the physical sciences." As a politically committed writer, she held that in the modern era literature is "a weapon for the human spirit," inseparable from the advance of liberty.[8]

Such arguments did not appeal to the First Consul or his entourage. The idea that authors in northern Europe had a particular sensibility of their own, distinct from that of Greece and Rome, and had a great deal to offer to new writers in France was anathema to proponents of the superiority of French classicism and grandeur—a political notion cultivated under Napoleon. Similarly, the association of the new literature of the fledgling nineteenth century with governments that promoted freedom of thought and expression did not suit the powers that be. Whereas later writers like Sainte-Beuve saw the book as the manifesto for a future Romanticism, much of the contemporary criticism of *De la littérature,* a paean to the values of the Enlightenment and the ideals of 1789, was political. Critics concentrated on the notion of perfectibility, a notion that was not new but that Germaine believed she was the first to apply to literature. Passions ran high: the counter-revolutionary writers who were opposed on principle to the philosophy of the Enlightenment, which they held responsible for the Revolution and all the ills that followed, took issue with Germaine's views. In the preface to the second edition she cogently answered blinkered critics of the Enlightenment in terms as valid now as in her own day: "What is there that men have not misused? They employ air and fire to kill each other, and the whole of nature becomes a means of destruction in their hands. Does that mean that what is good should not occupy the rank it justly deserves? You could say that prejudice, baseness and lying have done no harm to humankind, such is the severity towards philosophy, freedom and reason."[9]

Chateaubriand, at work on *Le Génie du Christianisme,* was greatly put out to find that his thesis of advancement through Christianity had been developed in *De la littérature.* His friend, the poet and critic Louis de Fontanes, who had the extraordinary idea that Voltaire had introduced Shakespeare to the English, made a personal attack on Germaine in *Le Mercure de France:* "When a woman appears on a stage where she does not belong, the members of the audience, in shock at this contrast, judge severely the very lady they would have surrounded with favor and homage if she had not changed her place and purpose."[10] In a note to the preface of the second edition Germaine replied to Fontanes without naming him: "I know there is a kind of attack that can always be repeated; these are all the innuendos whose aim is to condemn me as a woman for writing and thinking." With telling understatement, she called all such long-lived misogynistic pleasantries "a little tired." But Germaine privately complained to the *idéologue* Pierre Daunou, a moderate member of the Tribunate, about having to reply to Fontanes and others indirectly and in general terms. She wished it were otherwise: "If I could transform myself into a little man, however little he might be," Germaine reflected, then she would be able to mount a serious attack.[11]

Among the favorable notices there was a contribution by Benjamin. It was then the custom to publish "extracts" from the work under discussion, passages favored by the critic, accompanied by a few comments that conveyed a tone of approbation or disapproval, as the case might be. Benjamin's "extracts"—they are hardly reviews in the modern sense—appeared in *Le Publiciste* on May 26 and May 31, 1800. He alluded to her real talent, brilliant imagination, and energy of expression. He referred his readers to her deeply personal and moving words on the unfortunate position of gifted women writers who exercise their minds, suffer discrimination, and are accused incorrectly of exerting boundless and baleful political influence. Most strikingly he singled out the book's libertarian aspects, those that ran counter to the spirit of the times under the First Consul. For instance, he quoted such words as "liberty gives the strength for its defense" and mentioned her stress on the need for independent judgment. In the chapter on eloquence he cited her reference to "the cause abandoned by favor" and her defiance of servitude.[12] Benjamin chose to emphasize the book's thrust for liberty rather than its purely literary aspects, which were to prove so influential in the coming years.

All this time Benjamin was busily engaged with writings of his own. Perhaps he was trying to put the finishing touches on *De la possibilité d'une constitution républicaine dans un grand pays*, in which he challenged the long-held opinion of Montesquieu and Rousseau that a republic was a suitable form of government only in small countries. This unfinished study was not published until 1991. He was probably also busy with his magnum opus on religion and his important work on the principles of politics. He told his cousin Rosalie in October 1800 that he was writing a hundred pages a day and that "two thick tomes" were about to be published.[13] He made a similar announcement to his friend, the *idéologue* and historian Claude Fauriel, who at that time was one of Fouché's secretaries, but no such work appeared.

After the painful consequences for Germaine that resulted from his speech in the Tribunate on January 5, Benjamin soon realized that there was really no future for him as a tribune, though he continued to participate in the discussions. By August 1800 he was telling his cousin Rosalie how "ideas of liberty grow fainter every day." By October, he was complaining to her about the Tribunate and his role there: "I don't know how to speak when there is nothing to say." He further complained that he had to spend "two sessions a month treading water."[14] The euphoria of his arrival in Paris with Germaine in 1795 was long gone, as was the novelty of her encouragement and fostering of his political career. His militant republican ardor had abated in the unforgiving light of the Consulate. He knew that Bonaparte's allusions every now and then to his credentials derived from the Revolution and the Republic were just window dressing. The only way Benjamin could have pursued a political career was to follow many of his contemporaries in finding some way of placating and serving the First Consul, and thus reaping the honors and financial rewards that would ensue. To his credit, he did not do so—at least not before twelve years had passed—but he was not happy about his life with Germaine, and this unhappiness was augmented by her disgrace. She could do nothing for him anymore, yet he found himself having to do a great deal for her in running her errands. That sort of effort had been fine when he was courting her, but it seemed less attractive now.

Already, in May 1798, at the first serious failure of his political ambitions under the Directoire, he had spoken to his aunt, Mme de Nassau, about settling down in marriage with some malleable young girl, about his political activity not being in accord with his true nature, and about giving up politics to return to a simple life in the country where he could devote himself to his studies. The twice monthly sessions of the Tribunate allowed him to spend some time on his estate at Hérivaux, where he could enjoy the pleasures of the countryside and country life: talking with a few rural neighbors of similar outlook, taking solitary walks with his dogs, contemplating his pond and his acacia trees, engaging in quiet communion with his books, reading, writing—all far away from the heady social round so necessary to Germaine. His tendency was to veer between frenetic activity and quiet and solitude, whereas she was a constant whirlwind of energy and sociability.

The end of his association with the Tribunate came soon. In 1801 he, together with dissident republican colleagues, fought against the establishment of special tribunals for political crimes, and Bonaparte was mightily displeased. A year later, on February 10, 1802, Benjamin and his friends were expelled from the Tribunate (which, emasculated, lingered on until 1807). Germaine could not resist saying that, rather than being purged, the cream had been "skimmed" off it.[15] Bonaparte, in a fury, made clear what he thought of the independent-minded intellectuals in the Tribunate: "There are twelve or fifteen metaphysicians in that place fit for drowning. They are vermin on my clothes. I am a soldier, son of the Revolution, I won't be insulted like a king."[16] So much for Bonaparte's onetime high regard for the *idéologues* of the

Institut! Benjamin's expulsion from the Tribunate in 1802 marked the end of his political career for over a decade.

Germaine was not entirely happy either: she was torn between Paris, where she was accustomed to spending the winter season, and Coppet, where she passed her summers with her father. True, since the publication of *De la littérature*, she had largely recovered her social standing in Paris, and the capital offered her dazzling distractions from ennui and melancholy, but she felt that things were not the same, partly because people were more cautious about expressing their views. According to Benjamin, she sometimes dragged him along with her on her social round, but he would escape as soon as he could. Her Parisian salon on the rue de Grenelle drew a varied gathering of high-ranking officials, military men, ambassadors, former émigrés, former members of the Convention, writers, and savants. One foreigner called it a veritable Vauxhall, comparing the variegated company of Germaine's salon to that of the famous London pleasure garden. Guests included Fouché, the Consuls Cambacérès and Lebrun, leading generals, her former lover Narbonne, various English noblemen, and the famous beauty Juliette Récamier, who had become a cherished friend. Apart from the semipublic gatherings and formal dinners, Germaine gave private suppers for intimates where opinions could be expressed more freely.

After the signing of the peace treaty of Amiens in 1802, the capital was inundated with visitors from England, Germany, and elsewhere. It was not just the hospitality of the salons that drew them but also the plays, vaudevilles, operas, concerts, musical soirées in private mansions, lectures, exhibitions, visits to the major painters, balls, dances, dinners, receptions. There was something going on all the time; one hardly had a moment to oneself. The Prussian composer and diplomat Johann Friedrich von Reichardt related in his memoir of the winter of 1802–1803, spent in Paris under the Consulate, how he went from one entertainment to another, relishing the cultural feast, commenting on the growing authoritarianism as well as on all the generals, nouveaux riches, thinkers, and artists that he encountered.

That was at one pole of Germaine's life. At the other was the quiet repose of Coppet—dull in comparison, for both she and Benjamin were bored by Swiss society with its commonplace tittle-tattle about possible or forthcoming marriages. Yet at Coppet resided her beloved father. For a while she harbored the delusion that Necker would come to live with her in Paris or its environs. She tried to persuade him to join her, but he did not want to leave the tomb of his wife in the grounds at Coppet. In addition, he was a sick man, so bloated he could scarcely walk. Moreover, he was wise enough to know that he had no place now in Paris. The partings between Germaine and her father were painful. He would watch to catch a last glimpse of her in her carriage as she departed, and she would be overcome by agonies of conscience: What if this were indeed to be the last occasion when she would see him? Depart she must, though, impelled by some inner demon, despite the immense disillusion she felt at the course her life had taken, so movingly expressed in the final pages of *De la littérature:* "Oh! How happy one was ten years ago when . . . life had not yet belied its promises."[17] Now, during these early years of the Consulate, she would often bemoan how Parisian society had changed for the worse, how it had become boring now that people did not venture to speak openly, how she grew tired of the society she had once loved. Nonetheless, she did not change the pattern of her life but continued to move between Paris and Coppet despite all the upheavals and discomforts of travel.

There was only one person on earth, she felt, who truly loved her, and that was Necker. "You are my only support on earth," she assured her father. She used the word *appui*, implying someone to lean on and rely on, to trust implicitly, someone who was lastingly there for her, someone for whom she came first. Of this she could be certain. No other man had ever fulfilled this role as the great figure endowed with *gloire*, the ideal husband she had wanted as a girl and could not have. "I have affectionate relationships elsewhere," she told him, "but I have no support (*appui*) and never has a creature had greater need of another. I must therefore hope for the same lifespan as you and from the bottom of my heart I wish that mine will be more brief so as to bring us together with greater certainty."[18] The strength of her father's love, however, could not fill her vast need for affection of another sort, for passionate love. And it would seem that Benjamin did not provide the *appui* she needed. Her companion now belonged with the "affectionate relationships" (not the grand passions) to be distinguished from the solidity of Necker's support. She had often thought that she loved more deeply and truly than she was loved, until she met Benjamin, who had proved his unique devotion through his long courtship. But there was a subtle difference now. When Benjamin was about to leave Coppet for Hérivaux she remarked that he was carrying away with him "a large part of the charm of my existence"—not all of it.[19]

In October 1800, she confided to a friend, Joseph-Marie de Gerando, that the three men she had most loved in the past were N, T, and M—Narbonne, Talleyrand, and Mathieu de Montmorency. Ribbing is a notable omission. Then she went on, alluding to Benjamin without revealing his name even by an initial: "I have new friends who are very dear to me, but the past seems above all made to shatter the imagination and the heart. The present, which would inspire even more bitter regrets than this past, cannot erase the trace of it."[20] These words suggest that while the bitterness resulting from the failure of her past loves cannot be effaced, her present relationship with Benjamin would cause her even greater sorrow if it were to founder in a similar way. Such a statement is clearly the the admission of a woman who does not feel secure. As she was to write to her father after leaving for Paris a year later: "Goodbye, my own dearest, you who love me more than the others and whom I love more than everything else in the world."[21] Did she sense a change in Benjamin, or had she learned that his affections were engaged elsewhere?

By mid-November 1800, Benjamin was lightly turning to thoughts of love. He suddenly recalled a mistress from his Brunswick years, Charlotte von Marenholz (née von Hardenberg), whom he had dropped and completely forgotten after meeting Germaine for the first time at Montchoisi. He had not had a high regard for Charlotte's intelligence—he made that clear to Belle de Charrière—but she had been in love with him. The news that his cousin Victor, Rosalie's half-brother, was stationed in Berlin, prompted Benjamin to ask Rosalie, "What has happened to Mme de Marenholz?" He wondered if Victor, then in the service of the King of Prussia, had seen her and whether "she spoke of me."[22] Shortly afterward, on learning of her marriage to a French émigré, Alexandre du Tertre, he commented wryly on "a Lady who interested me a great deal in the past. I find it very inconsiderate of her to marry another after having loved me." Fancy being forgotten after the passage of "a mere seven years"![23] His thoughts did not linger too long on Charlotte, however, because he had just met someone else.

In mid-November Julie Talma introduced him to her friend Anna Lindsay, who had recently arrived in France, along with many other returning émigrés, after having spent some ten years in exile in Brussels and then in London. Anna was the eldest child of the large brood of a Calais tavern keeper. Her youth, charm, and Irish beauty had caught the eye of the Duke of Fitzjames; his duchess, in whose salon the girl acquired the essential social graces, took her under her wing and then showed her the door. A secret "marriage" to a British aristocrat produced a son, but he then properly married another woman. Anna also had two children with her "protector," Alexandre de Lamoignon. According to Chateaubriand, who met her when he was in exile in England, she was "the last of the Ninons," a reference to Ninon de l'Enclos, the brilliant seventeenth-century courtesan so admired by Belle de Charrière. To Benjamin, Anna gave a proud but pitiful self-description: "Déclassée through an unfortunate fate, and cast into a sad career, I have struggled desperately to win what little position I was entitled to expect." But, she claimed, she had never met with anything but egoism, narrow-mindedness, and ingratitude.[24] In her late thirties, she was looking for love and security.

Benjamin fell passionately in love with her—or so his ardent letters to her suggest. With him, love always implied a considerable degree of extravagance and frenzy: "I love you like a madman, as neither my age, my long experience of life, nor my heart, sorely wounded by suffering and closed firmly shut against any deep feeling, should still allow me to love. I am writing to you with a trembling hand, scarcely able to breathe, my brow covered in perspiration. You have seized, entwined, consumed my existence; you are the sole thought, the sole feeling, the sole breath that still gives me life." He conveys to her the image of the sensitive soul, wounded and solitary, an image partly derived from Jean-Jacques Rousseau with added elements of unbridled passion. "Whatever the cost, I am happy to have met a woman who is just as I had imagined, such a one as I had given up hope of ever finding, and without whom I was wandering in this wide world, alone, discouraged. . . . I shall love you forever. Another thought will never seize hold of me. What have I not found in you? Strength, dignity, sublime pride, heavenly beauty, a dazzling and generous mind, love perhaps, a love that resembles mine, without constraint, all-consuming, passionate, tremendous! . . . Why did I not know you earlier? I should have seen all my youthful illusions fulfilled! I alone was made for you."[25] And on he continues, bringing to mind the passion he once displayed for Germaine: the banging of his head against the chimneypiece and his attempted suicide during his courtship of her, or his declarations of lifelong fidelity in the famous Testament.

In later letters to Anna, having presumably achieved his object, he inquired: "When will those delightful hours return that passed by so quickly? . . . Never have I felt what I feel for you . . . Never have I been overcome by so violent a passion. . . . You are the sole being who satisfies my heart and my imagination. . . . I, too, have journeyed through life *alone* because of my character, in the midst of struggles. . . . I shall devote my entire life to you. Lean yours upon me. Be assured that nothing will ever separate us." The news that Germaine was about to arrive from Coppet did not interrupt the flow: "Remember that in a few months we shall be united forever."[26] Apparently, he was already contemplating marriage to Anna, whom he had just met the previous month.

The arrival of Germaine in December brought Benjamin rapidly down to earth. He sent Anna a note the next day: "I shall not see you when you are alone this evening, I must grant *her* an entire evening in order to have an example to put forward against her everlasting complaints."[27] While Germaine was complaining that he no longer seemed as assiduous as in the past, Anna was insisting that he make a clean break with Germaine. Benjamin was compelled to admit to Anna that such behavior would leave him open to a charge of ingratitude and hard-heartedness; moreover, it would attract attention, and the scandal would give ammunition to his numerous enemies. At the time he was still a member of the Tribunate, and in that position he had to fulfill certain duties and protect his reputation. "As a result," he told Anna, "I need to defend my ideas, to handle carefully a type of connection that has nothing in common with my feelings for you."[28] The distinction he makes between his tie to Germaine, regarded as a sort of political arrangement, and his physical passion for Anna is clear.

What he wanted was to live with Anna: "You are my ideal woman, I have often told you this, and I do not think I could ever love another after you." In short, he was hoping to have it all, without causing tongues to wag. When he left for Coppet in the spring of 1801, Anna drew her own conclusion about him: "The coldest heart made a mockery of mine. . . . He is still with her and he thinks me cowardly enough to wait for him and forgive him. . . . What a cruel wretch! . . . What skill in deceit! . . . I despise him and adore him." Benjamin told Julie Talma candidly that although he loved and desired Anna he was not prepared to make any sacrifice for her and did not want her to sacrifice herself for him. "I only want her to love me madly and keep from plaguing me."[29] The affair appears to have lingered on until the summer of 1802. That was not quite the end, though, because some years later, when she met Benjamin again in Paris, Anna would try to rekindle the old flame. Whatever his masculine contemporaries might say about his unprepossessing appearance and his odd mannerisms, there were enough women who found him very attractive.

After being purged from the Tribunate with his like-minded colleagues, Constant seems to have concluded—no doubt sensibly enough, given the circumstances—that discretion was the better part of valor. In what was a form of withdrawal from public life, he worked at his desk to develop his ideas in a great work. He had sold Hérivaux, the symbol of his high aspirations and ambitions, which had swallowed up so much in effort and money. In its place he bought Les Herbages, a charming little country house with a garden, a stream, a wood, and a meadow. It was near Maffliers and the forest of Montmorency. He could be in Paris in four hours. At Les Herbages he aimed to live far from *le monde* and from the Parisian high society so essential to Germaine. Silence, repose, and perfect quietude—you would think you were in the depths of the forests of America, he remarked. All that was needed to make this place a real paradise, he said later, was a woman with whom one was passionately in love. It was not that he had abandoned his belief in civil liberty and republicanism—far from it—it was just that at the time he could see no likelihood of success in open defiance.

Germaine's response took a different form. Each further step toward authoritarianism and one-man rule, each diminution of individual freedom, each sign of abasement and servility in others, each loss of the "generous ideas" she treasured aroused her wrath, indignation, and defiance. She continued with her vocal criticisms of the regime, not always taking note of the sympathies of others, especially those concerned for their official position. She tried to be more cautious, but caution was beyond her: she had to say what she thought, often in the form of sarcastic witticisms. Later on, when she was visiting Lausanne with Benjamin, Rosalie de Constant observed, "The entire visit was spent in explosions against Buonaparte. It is her dominating passion these days."[30] She did not say whether Benjamin joined in Germaine's "explosions" or even favored them.

The spring of 1802 had seen a momentous change in Germaine's circumstances. Eric de Staël became partially paralyzed after a stroke, and although Germaine was now officially separated from her husband, she felt it her wifely duty to set out with him for Coppet, hoping that the cure-all waters of Aix-les-Bains might help him. Benjamin told his friend Claude Fauriel how he followed reluctantly at a discreet distance, ready to ride forward at Germaine's request if his presence were needed. At an inn en route her husband suffered a second attack that proved fatal. His death reawakened the morbid dread of impermanence and mortality she inherited from her mother, a dread she and Benjamin shared. It was never far below the surface of her glittering social life. Whatever difficulties she had experienced with her husband, he had been an important figure in her life. Then, only a few days later, she heard news of the death of Christian Guillaume Gerlach, the devoted tutor of her sons, a sensitive young man who gave her German lessons. It would be difficult to find a replacement for someone so gifted and musical—music being for her the great restorative in hours of loneliness. The fearful image of her father's death came ever closer with the loss of her husband and of Gerlach.

With Eric de Staël's death, the way was finally open for Germaine and Benjamin to fulfill the claim of the Testament, that they would regularize their position as soon as they could. Rosalie, the inveterate matchmaker, was convinced that the marriage was a sure thing. In spite of all Germaine's efforts to charm her, Rosalie did not really care for "*la trop célèbre,*" but she would certainly approve if they were to marry and settle down in respectable connubial bliss. She soon realized, however, that it was not to be. Germaine, despite her constant desire for a recognized protector, had no intention of settling at once for matrimony, having just escaped at last from an unhappy union. She let it be known that there was no question of marriage during her father's lifetime. But Necker thought highly of Benjamin and treated him as a virtual son-in-law: would he really have disapproved of the match after a decent interval? Benjamin, for his part, appears to have been in no hurry to marry Germaine either—a sign, perhaps, of the strains in their relationship. They knew each other too well.

That summer proved very hard for those who sympathized with Germaine's opinions. Among the developments that caused great concern was the promulgation of the Concordat with the Papacy that restored Catholicism as the state religion. It was purely a pragmatic measure: Bonaparte had not suddenly become devout. It countermanded, however, the separation of church and state, adopted by decree in 1795, and it was widely regarded as marking the end of the line for the republican spirit and individual freedom of conscience. Both Germaine and Benjamin, moreover, conceived Protestantism to be the religion most closely associated with freedom. The Concordat added to the disaffection of some high-ranking officers like General Moreau and General Bernadotte. Germaine later recalled that she had met Bernadotte often at this time, although it is unlikely that she was involved in any conspiracy: her aim was to influence public opinion through the spoken or written word.

Germaine also inspired her friend Camille Jordan, formerly a député under the Directoire, to write "in such a way as to make yourself known" as a friend of liberty, one to be included in the party of those who love freedom and hate despotism, the party "that will always recognize talent and courage."[31] His pamphlet on the true significance of the plebiscite to confirm Bonaparte as Consul for Life (*Vrai sens du vote national sur le Consulat à vie*), which proposed guarantees for freedom as well as proper elections, was published anonymously in the summer of 1802. It was seized immediately, and the friend who took it to the printer was imprisoned. Honorably, Jordan hastened to inform Bonaparte that he was the author, but because he had begun his pamphlet by admitting that he had voted for the Life Consulship, he escaped retribution. Germaine communicated her admiration for the pamphlet and its author to all her friends. Benjamin remarked to Claude Fauriel that the praise it received was deserved: "It is an act of courage and a talented piece of writing: the way it has been read clandestinely seems to me to indicate a new era in public opinion."[32] Yet Benjamin, who had been prolific in publishing articles and pamphlets under the Directoire, did not emulate Camille Jordan. Presumably Germaine would have encouraged him also to produce something in a similar vein for the party of liberty, yet he abstained. Or perhaps she was disappointed by his inaction and was looking elsewhere for consolation.

She warmed tenderly and flirtatiously to the new thirty-year-old hero, Jordan, valuing his talent, naturally *after* her father's, as "the last voice of virtue on earth"—a title that surely should have been Benjamin's.[33] And now Necker himself was about to venture into the fray, giving the public his last thoughts on political and financial matters (*Dernières vues de politique et de finance*), which he declared he was submitting first to Bonaparte in order to give him proof of his deference. In Germaine's opinion, the work was measured; it kept to the middle ground while being "bold in conception and feeling."[34] Expressing grave reservations about proposals for the Constitution of Year X, promulgated in August 1802, Necker preserved his perennial stance on the merits of constitutional monarchy—the road not taken. Bonaparte, who did not like criticism of any kind and who did not care for the advice Necker proffered, was not at all gratified: he chose to blame Germaine de Staël and directed his severe displeasure at her.

From a friend in the Senate, the *idéologue* Dominique-Joseph Garat, she learned that in government circles there was serious talk of dire measures being put into force against her. Germaine defended herself: "I am to be harassed in Paris for my father's work: it is claimed that this could disturb my peaceful existence in France. I do not believe it. Bonaparte, however you judge him, is too great a man to make a daughter responsible for the deeds of a father who was writing before she was born and who has been concerned with public affairs for the last thirty-five years."[35] Besides, her own views had long differed from those of her father, who never deviated from constitutional monarchy and who never shared her enthusiasm for the Republic. It seemed to her thoroughly unjust for Bonaparte to be angry with her: "I shall defy that ill humor," she told Camille Jordan bravely.[36] Germaine underestimated Bonaparte. She did not deny his greatness, but she could not conceive that a great man would be capable of baseness or deaf to Necker's wisdom. She failed to realize that Bonaparte did not give a fig for her father, the failed statesman and relic of the past, and that she herself was becoming something more than a minor annoyance in his eyes. Benjamin did not want to be part of the fallout: as much as he respected and esteemed Necker, he disassociated himself from *Dernières vues*. "What have I in common with this work?" he asked Fauriel rhetorically.[37]

For a while Germaine thought of going abroad instead of returning to Paris: the Italian patriot and statesman Francesco Melzi, whom she had entertained in the capital, urged her to visit his country. She invited Camille Jordan to accompany her to Florence and Rome. Benjamin would not be with them, for he was intending to spend the winter in Paris, and, she said, he would send them the latest news. She advised Camille to keep silent about the proposed journey. He declined to join her, however, and nothing came of it. Around this time Germaine and Benjamin decided that if they had any dealings with the government it would be wiser to act separately: they might then have a better chance of success. Moreover, they should not return to Paris at the same time. People were to think that they were not as close as before—and, in essence, they no longer were.

Then, in December 1802, came *Delphine*, Germaine's first major work of fiction, published in Geneva and Paris. It caused a sensation—everyone has read it or wants to read it, said Benjamin. Her former associate Roederer reported sardonically that theaters and churches were empty because the whole of Paris was behind closed doors reading Mme de Staël's new novel. People could talk of little else. Ever since June 1800, when she announced to her friend Mme Pastoret that she was finished with "odious politics" and was writing a novel, she had been steadily at work, through all the private and public vicissitudes of those two years.[38] She consulted a number of friends, including Mathieu de Montmorency, about various details in the plot, as well as her father, who advised her to change the denouement. Doubtless, she also spoke with Benjamin about the novel while she was composing it, though there is no evidence for this owing to the loss of their correspondence.

Just before the book's release, she said to Jean-Baptiste Suard (who would later review *Delphine* favorably) that it would be somewhat anti-Catholic in tone, placing "the religion of the heart" or natural religion above ritual and dogma, but it would not be political at all.[39] It is, however, obliquely if not directly concerned with the politics of the hour, that is, the Concordat with the Papacy and the Catholic revival in France. *Delphine* tells the story of a well-to-do, impetuous, generous, warm-hearted, independent-minded young widow—a lover of liberty not unlike Germaine herself but with the added gifts of youth and ravishing beauty—whose life is thwarted not only by her own rare qualities of heart and mind but also by a mean-minded, hypocritical society that prefers the slavery of convention and base self-interest to open-minded curiosity, élan, emulation, and, above all, "enthusiasm"—the deep and exalted passionate feeling that she would define later in her book on Germany.

The novel is set in a period of recent history during the Revolution, from the spring of 1790 to the autumn of 1792 and the beginnings of the Terror. Delphine falls in love with Léonce de Mondoville, a nobleman much concerned with his honor in the manner of Narbonne. Léonce reciprocates her love, but he is deceived by the lies he is told about her. He is also fiery and quick to resort to fighting duels like Benjamin. The readers of the day found much pleasure in looking for contemporary models in the characters—they saw Benjamin Constant, for instance, in M. de Lebensei, whose libertarian ideas have much in common with the author's. Lebensei defied opinion, though, and Benjamin did not. "Liberty . . . is the chief happiness, the sole glory of the social order," opines Lebensei.[40] The book owed its colossal success not only to the novelist's skill in manipulating many voices and points of view but also to its allusions to current controversies, not least those relating to divorce and suicide. Its treatment of varieties of female experience—what Germaine called "the destiny of women" in diverse happy or unhappy relationships—proved fascinating to her contemporaries. While using a form, the novel in letters, that was nearing its end after Richardson, Rousseau, and Laclos, she transformed it into something complex, many-faceted, rich, new, and vibrant.

Delphine may have a complicated plot and its moralizing may appear verbose to modern tastes, but it offers a large imaginative fresco of the conflicting emotions and ideas that surfaced in troubled, violent times. The novel is also intensely personal, for instance, as regards what the heroine calls "ingratitude in friendship," the betrayal of the trusting Delphine by a false friend, Mme de Vernon, in scenes that reveal how deeply Germaine was shaken by the way the now-powerful Talleyrand rejected her and failed to help her in her difficulties with Bonaparte. It is deeply personal, too, in its allusions to regret and terror, "the dread of the dark and icy state called death . . . the horror of nothingness" that both Germaine and Benjamin felt.[41] They shared also the religion of suffering that permeates the novel: it obliged delicate spirits to do their utmost to avoid causing suffering in others. Happiness, it cautioned, cannot be established on the suffering of another.

The book's epigraph is taken from the writings of Mme Necker: "A man should know how to defy opinion, a woman should submit to it." Germaine's argument, it seems, is with her mother and with her mother's dictum. Léonce weakly does not defy opinion, nor does Delphine conform. They are both "punished" as Mme Necker might have wished: in the first of the novel's two denouements, Léonce meets his death by firing squad and Delphine, unable to face life without him, takes poison. While it is evident from the tale that Léonce should have defied the opinion of society, it is not at all evident that Delphine should have yielded to it. True, she pays a heavy price for her independent spirit, but her daring defiance of social convention is nonetheless shown as deserving of admiration. That was how the author of a favorable review in *Le Citoyen Français* interpreted it, speaking of "the injustice of this tyranny of opinion, the worst form of servitude": there could be no political freedom as long as this kind of slavery persisted.[42] This review of *Delphine* is attributed to Benjamin because, although it is unsigned, it bears all the marks of his biting irony.

Loud and violent criticism of the novel was unleashed from on high and from the same counterrevolutionary and counter-Enlightenment lobby that had savaged *De la littérature*. Much of it was in bad faith and malicious, taking issue with the personal attributes of the author, her gender, her family, and her supposed immorality and impiety, as Benjamin hastened to point out. "All that, as you see," he commented ironically, "is very respectable, very charitable, and above all extremely Christian."[43] He took aim at the new revivalist Catholic party of Chateaubriand who wept and believed: in particular Benjamin singled out the truly religious spirit of the novel, which proposes a religion of the heart rather than of clergy and dogma, echoing Germaine's own words to Suard.

Such subtleties were of no interest to Bonaparte: he called them sentimental speculations by an insufferable woman. He did not like the novel's discussion of divorce for he was about to repeal the law of 1792 that allowed it; he also did not care for the author's depiction of bigotry and fanaticism among Catholics when he had just signed the Concordat with the Pope. The whole trend of the book, with its praise of Protestantism and of English respect for law and its stress on liberty of spirit and conscience, did not appeal to him. Here was a voice that was seducing readers who should have been siding with his policies.

Bonaparte, who had his spies everywhere, had been told about all that was being said in Germaine's influential salon, which was frequented, much to his annoyance, by members of his own family as well as by his officials and generals; he knew all about her scathing bons mots. Besides, he was sure that she had encouraged Camille Jordan to write his pamphlet and Necker to publish his *Dernières vues*. And after her freedom-loving *De la littérature*, now came *Delphine*, with its defiant preface in which, possibly remembering Benjamin's famous speech with its allusion to a silence in France that all of Europe would hear and judge, she scorned her mediocre critics and addressed her novel to "France, silent but enlightened, to the future rather than the present."[44] Bonaparte had had enough. On February 10, 1803, exactly a year after he had dismissed Benjamin and his friends from the Tribunate, he ordered her into exile: if she approached Paris she would be sent back immediately to the frontier.

What punishment could he have devised that would have been more exquisite than to banish her from her beloved birthplace, from her customary style of life and the company of her friends? Word reached Germaine in Geneva: despite the warnings she had been given, she was shattered and confused. She considered staying silent—but then, she thought, her celebrity was her defense. What if she were to write to the First Consul, she asked Claude Hochet, giving her word of honor that she would renounce writing "and submit completely to a life of obscurity, what effect do you think this would have on him? Is it reasonable for him not to prefer having me within his grasp than to drive me to London with my intelligence and resentment?" And she assured Joseph Bonaparte that she was grateful for his efforts on her behalf, but she found his advice, to wait six months, "cruel."[45] She gave him her word that if she were allowed to return to Paris she would neither write nor say anything to displease his brother. The First Consul would not hear a sound from her on political matters. Her father, unable to bear her distress, appealed to Consul Lebrun—even offering to come to Paris to speak for her—and received a flea in his ear. Among Bonaparte's objections, quoted by Lebrun, was "the excessively indiscreet demarches made by those who are known to be her closest confidants."[46] It had become an offense, in Bonaparte's view, to go to her aid. Benjamin felt that he was implicated. From the country he wrote to the First Consul: he could not bear the idea that any "demarches" attributed to him were the cause of his friend's misfortunes. But the plain fact remained that nobody was going to change Bonaparte's mind once it was made up. The Corsican vendetta he would pursue consistently against Germaine de Staël had begun.

The situation between Germaine and Benjamin changed with her banishment. Benjamin, having lost his role in politics, found his position reduced to that of a *cavaliere servente,* an escort attendant on a famous woman, and this role did not appeal to him at all. Yet he could hardly abandon her now that she was the victim of persecution and in such distress: to do such a thing would not enhance his reputation. Besides, he could not bear to cause her suffering. He was caught in a trap.

Germaine needed him, and Benjamin no longer needed her. She expressed her ideal of harmony between lovers through Léonce's words in *Delphine:* "Once, in many thousands of accidental encounters, two beings are in accord in all their faculties of heart and soul; only together are they happy, only alive when they speak to each other, nature has granted one half only to each of them, and the thought of one is completed only by the thought of the other."[47] Léonce is not describing mad passion but the union of souls, perfect amity and companionship, where the emphasis is on two persons being at one in thought and speech. They come alive when they are together, as eyewitnesses remarked after observing Germaine and Benjamin engaged in their brilliant conversational jousts. Perhaps she had him in mind when she gave these words to Léonce. She clung to this ideal of true companionship—just as she clung in principle to the ideal of happiness in marriage such as she depicted in *Delphine*—long after disillusion had taken hold.

Her disillusionment, first revealed in her book on the passions, was further evident in the essay she wrote in response to her critics and their charge of immorality, *Quelques réflexions sur le but moral de Delphine:* "Women reign supreme in the early days of love, and you cannot exaggerate, even in novels, all that passion inspires in a man who fears he is not loved; but when the tender heart of a woman has been won, . . . it is certain that the heart to cool first is man's."[48] Germaine's words invite comparison with Benjamin's cynical (but perhaps realistic) remarks in his *Lettre sur Julie,* where he acknowledges the distinctive attitudes of men and women in love—the man losing his purpose when he has triumphed, the woman finding hers in seeking to retain her lover. Germaine was not ready to let go.

Certainly, their ideas on political affairs had not changed, but Benjamin the realist saw as imprudence Germaine's bold acts of defiance. Foolhardy they might be, but they were also a form of resistance against the odds that posterity is inclined to interpret as phenomenal courage. Benjamin wanted to change the course of his life, return to his youthful literary ambitions, withdraw sensibly and pleasurably into his study in the country, continue his research, and wait to publish his thoughts another day. Germaine, meanwhile, went on writing and publishing her work. "*La fille de M. Necker*" could not abandon the public arena.

CHAPTER SIX

◈ *Journey into the Unknown* ◈

BENJAMIN DECIDED TO DO his disgraced friend a great favor—after considerable initial reluctance. In spite of his desire to enjoy the peace and quiet of Les Herbages, his new estate not far from Paris, he would disregard his own plans and accompany her on a risky journey in the direction of Germany. Risky, because it was a journey into the unknown—she had no friends in that country, nor did she know how she would be received. "I am scared of the new, the unknown," she admitted to her father, but this fear did not prevent her from setting out.[1] Benjamin had no high expectations of this undertaking. He was, he said later, impelled by empathy for her deep distress, which he felt could be fully understood only by someone like himself who really penetrated her nature. He let Germaine know that he was making an immense sacrifice for her—though, as it transpired, he was to be amply compensated. She deeply appreciated this signal act of kindness, yet at the same time, as she told her father, she was not at all grateful to find herself placed in the position of being obligated to Benjamin as the generous dispenser of benevolence. This, however, was the very position in which she had placed her previous lovers, friends, and countless

protégés, all of whom were indebted to her for personal favors, benefits, or "services," as indeed was Benjamin himself.

Since her banishment from Paris on February 10, 1803, Germaine had
been residing with her father and children at Coppet or in its environs,
but in September she ventured to return to France and settled at
Maffliers, some six and a half *lieues* (approximately twenty-eight kilo-
meters) from Paris, a distance that would prove to be important.
Friends of hers had homes or estates in the region: Juliette Récamier at
Saint-Brice and Joseph Bonaparte at Mortfontaine. Germaine thoroughly disliked the house at Maffliers because it proved to be damp and
depressing. No way could she spend the winter in such a place, where
six-year-old Albertine's fragile health might suffer. As it happened,
Benjamin's new home, Les Herbages, was near Maffliers: why was she
not staying there? Possibly she did not wish to implicate him further in
her troubles. Or perhaps his house was simply too small to accommo-
date her and her entourage, which consisted of two of her children,
Auguste and Albertine (her younger son Albert stayed with his grandfather at Coppet); her trusty factotum Eugène (Joseph Uginet) and his
wife, Olive, her femme de chambre; as well as various other atten-
dants. Benjamin had an entourage of his own at Les Herbages: as a
young man he had been accompanied by a personal servant, but now
he had, by his own report, a staff that included an excellent cook and a
concierge (men and women). Not surprisingly, he found the upkeep of
Les Herbages devilishly expensive.

From Maffliers, Germaine fired off letters to all those who might
conceivably help her to have Napoleon's decision reversed. Chief
among them was her friend and protector Joseph Bonaparte, who as
usual did his best to intervene with his brother but again to no avail.
When Napoleon heard from some woman well-wisher that Maffliers
was six and a half *lieues* from Paris and not ten as he had stipulated, he

flew into one of his frequent rages. He demanded that Germaine remove herself forthwith, or four gendarmes would escort her to the frontier. She was informed that henceforward she must not come closer to the capital than forty *lieues*. There was nothing for Germaine to do but to depart, after being allowed to visit her Parisian residence to collect what she needed for the journey. At that time Napoleon was busy with the long and quite public preparations at Boulogne for the invasion of England. He made it clear that while he was out of Paris Mme de Staël was on no account to be found in the capital, a pronouncement that dangled before her the prospect that when he returned to Paris and could keep an eye on her, he might rescind the order of banishment. She fed on this hope of returning to Paris after peace was signed. The abandonment of the invasion plans in 1804 and Napoleon's return to Paris would not, however, produce the desired result.

While Germaine was seeking aid from all her friends, Benjamin went to see that astute survivor of numerous regimes, Fouché, who was usually well disposed to her. No longer minister of police, he claimed that all this would not have happened if he had been in office. "And as for you, haven't you received an order [of banishment]?" Fouché asked Benjamin. "No," he replied. "Why should I?" To which Fouché rejoined, "Why, why? That's a good question: does anyone ever ask why in this country? Besides, I haven't heard anyone speak of you." Fouché added: "If there was anything against you, you can be sure I would warn you." "I beg you to do nothing of the kind," retorted Benjamin. "I want to wait steadfastly and peaceably for anything that could happen to me."[2] Germaine, who heard about this interchange from Benjamin and retold it to her father, was very impressed by this "Roman" reply. Yet privately Benjamin worried about his awkward position vis-à-vis the government, which he attributed to her and to her "imprudent" behavior. He regarded himself as "virtually proscribed" for his views: through his libertarian and republican stance he had acquired a considerable number of enemies during his short-lived political career, and he was intent on keeping as low a profile as possible rather than striking the noble pose of an ancient Roman, as he had done under the Directoire.[3] All the same, the fact remains that he was not proscribed: he could come and go as he pleased in Paris—participating when it suited him in the social round that she loved and that he claimed to despise—as she could not. She does not appear to have commented on this considerable difference in their situation, though the irony of it surely could not have been lost on her.

Around this time it becomes possible to follow closely in tandem what Germaine and Benjamin are thinking and feeling. In quest of an elusive happiness and deeply dissatisfied, veering between euphoria and melancholy, both of them appear highly sensitive, kind and thoughtful, vain, egotistical, ambitious for *gloire*, coolly reasonable and rational, wildly passionate and emotional—in short, full of contradictions. Both of them know each other and themselves, and both, in their worst moments, can be unjust to each other. The sources for this information are, on the one hand, Germaine's intimate letters to her father, in which she candidly reveals to the person she loves best her hopes and fears, her disappointments and her shortcomings; and, on the other hand, Benjamin's extraordinary diary, in which he probes his motives, exposes his faults and weaknesses, investigates his rapidly changing reactions, and examines the past, present, and future conduct of his life.

Benjamin's diary was composed strictly for its author's private pleasure as a record of his experiences. In the beginning he made it a rule to write down everything he felt. As he wrote in 1804, "I kept this rule as best I could, and yet such is the influence of the tendency to address the gallery that sometimes I have not obeyed it completely. Weird human nature! . . . This diary, this sort of secret unknown to everyone else, this very discreet listener that I am sure of finding every evening, has become for me a feeling for which I have a kind of need; all the same I do not entrust everything to it, but I write in it enough to find my impressions once again. . . . So this diary is a sort of story and I need my story like that of another so as not to keep forgetting and failing to know myself."[4] He was fascinated by his own sensations, doings, and prospects, and despite always apologizing in his letters for talking so much about himself, he could not stop: he had a great deal to say, much of it enlightening.

Some months before Germaine arrived at Maffliers in the autumn of 1803, Benjamin confided to his diary the already well-pondered matter that he had discussed at length with his aunt, Mme de Nassau, in 1798—namely, how to break free from Germaine once and for all without causing her the chagrin, pain, and suffering to which she was prone. At the same time he weighed up the putative cost to himself. The basic elements of the 1798 letter to Mme de Nassau, in which he had suddenly asked her to find him a wife, remain, but with fresh nuances born of changed political circumstances and the addition of certain crucial factors, including those concerning his intimate relations with Germaine, details that he could in no way communicate to his aunt.

Already, in the months they were apart, before Germaine's arrival in Maffliers, tensions in their relationship had been growing. In addition to the fallout from Benjamin's liaison with Anna Lindsay, Germaine, at Coppet, had been entertaining Robert Robertson, a hardy Scot, doctor and companion to Lord John Campbell, the son of the Duke of Argyll, taking them on excursions to the local points of interest. Her attraction to Dr. Robertson had turned into one of her more serious and risqué flirtations, those "*coquetteries de femmes*" as she called them when speaking to her disapproving father, claiming that they were of no importance and that they did nothing to interfere with her attachment to Benjamin.[5] These flirtatious or amorous episodes—of which there would be many more in her life—were significant to her in that they offered a token of her independence as a woman, a sign that she could choose for herself, not being bound by a lord and master or by rigid convention; perhaps, too, they gave her in her thirties—when women were supposed to have passed their sexual peak—the illusion of youthfulness. She would later admit to her father more than once that Benjamin's affection did not satisfy her: his feelings and character were, she maintained, too incomplete. Besides, she could scarcely overlook the subtle and not-so-subtle changes in his manner since the early, heady days, but she was anxious not to lose him because, as he well knew, she loved him in her way.

At the same time that Germaine was flirting with Robertson, Benjamin was toying half-heartedly with the idea of marrying Amélie Fabri, who was neither young nor beautiful but was well-to-do. He was being egged on by his aunt, his cousin Rosalie, and the rest of his family in Lausanne who wanted him to put an end to his equivocal situation: that of being attached to a woman who was free to marry him but did not wish to do so. He held to the notion that only the fait accompli of marriage to another could legitimately set him free from his convoluted involvement with Germaine. Naturally, he had grave doubts about entering into this new arrangement. It was freedom from Germaine that he wanted—or wanted whenever their temperaments clashed—and yet in order to attain it he was contemplating marriage to a woman whose conversation he found commonplace and whom he considered thoroughly insipid and "a complete nullity."[6] He envisaged mutual boredom. Still, if she was good in bed she would not need to give proof of her intelligence.

Germaine had learned of his plan to marry Amélie. Benjamin recorded in his diary that Germaine commented "with a certain amount of truth that no sooner would I be bound to Amélie than my imagination would go into reverse: instead of seeing as I do now the disadvantages of a woman of intelligence who is too famous, I should see those of a mediocre woman who would be no less demanding or at least full of complaints."[7] He was to confide gratefully to his diary that Germaine had saved him from the egregious blunder of committing himself to Anna Lindsay at a moment when he was ready to take on the burden of this woman and her children. If he had done so, he would have caused havoc in his life and would have felt obliged to look after her; fortune, independence, everything would have been lost. Yet he had experienced the most marvelous sexual fulfillment with Anna, "the complete delirium of physical love," and now he was contemplating marriage with Amélie, a woman he did not love, whom he was unlikely to change for the better, and who did not seem to have the wit to fancy him.[8]

He set out his enduring problems on the first page of his *Journal intime,* as the diary is known today, dated January 6, 1803. "I am over thirty-five, I no longer have many years before me. . . . Fear of boredom is my dominating impulse and the great danger in changing my situation is, precisely, boredom. My present situation is obviously false but it has its brilliant aspects. If I put up with the drawbacks of a liaison that drags me into the midst of storms and where I fulfill only a secondary role, I find in it more notable connections than I could elsewhere."[9] It was playing second fiddle, the "secondary role," that rankled so much: Benjamin did not like it that Germaine was independent and he was not. He wrote harshly on the subject of the independence of women, which he considered harmful both to men and to themselves. A wife should be subordinate, he insisted. If he were to break with Germaine, however, he realized that he might well lose many of the important contacts that he had made through her, contacts with the good and the great. He would no longer feel the weariness of being swallowed up in her celebrity (is there a hint of envy here, in a proud man equally avid for *gloire?*), "but I should have far fewer connections in France, where I want to live, and I should lose the pleasure in that swift and broad mind [of hers] and that fundamentally true heart, as well as that matchless devotion at my disposal now."[10]

Then comes a vital clue to the heart of the matter, which is, evidently, sexual, although the word *sex* is never used, being replaced by euphemism in the style of the day. "For a long time I no longer feel any love for Germaine," he writes. "My great vivacity enables me to compensate for this without bad faith. Great rapports of intellect draw us both closer together. But can this last? My heart, my imagination and *mes sens* [my physical and sensual urges] need love."[11] He needs a woman equally endowed with *sens*, or sexual drive, he declares. Women are necessary to him for his health, as necessary as the air he breathes: he feels better disposed toward the world after a sexual encounter. Above all, among the numerous reasons for a break, there is one that in his eyes proves insurmountable: "*Germaine n'a point de sens*," he claims with emphasis, which could be interpreted as lacking sexual drive and not being at all good in bed.[12] She no longer means anything to him in this regard: their relations are platonic. He could simply observe abstinence at Coppet and visit the resources (or brothels) of Geneva, but he dislikes hearing talk of libertinage à la Sade from his boon companions during suppers with prostitutes. Nor does he fancy the idea of taking a lower-class mistress or seducing married women in succession. Thus, the answer to this problem is a wife, someone who, unlike Germaine, is going to be a good bedfellow, compliant and subordinate. And yet, after pinpointing the lack of physical rapport and declaring, "I no longer feel any love for Germaine," he says later on, "I still truly love her," and later still, "I love her with all my heart."[13] Indeed, he declares, her kindness makes it impossible not to love her. He appears to be speaking of two kinds of love: one that suits him, gives him pleasure, and grants physical release, and one that by now rests on esteem, affection, and shared memories. Another factor in this second variety of love is doubtless charming little Albertine, who delights him and has the same kind of wit as his own. He is able to hold two contradictory notions—loving and not loving—more or less simultaneously. Or rather, as he once expressed it to his aunt, "Each individual has within himself a coalition, that is to say, a civil war. Death is the great peacemaker."[14] Another conviction of his was that there are not two sides to every question but thousands. No wonder he was in a perpetual state of indecision.

A further clue to his state of mind is undoubtedly political. Once, when they were quarreling, Germaine accused him of planning to marry Amélie out of fear of proscription. "We are governed by the same opinions," he wrote, "but as these are assigned two different characters, we do each other harm instead of supporting each other. I can be silent under despotism, but I do not desire reconciliation with it. She would be reconciled with it, but she cannot keep silent."[15] If Germaine offered to keep quiet, and at times would have liked an accommodation with the government, it was in order to be allowed to pursue her old style of life in Paris, not to abandon her ideals and convictions. And would Benjamin not be ready to write to Cambacérès, the second Consul, to assure him that he would be taking no part in political affairs and was withdrawing to the country to live quietly with his future wife?

Benjamin was in search of *le repos*, a peaceable existence. Later, at Fulda, on the way from Frankfurt to Weimar, Germaine, full of gratitude for what she called his incomparable support and his invaluable company during her current misfortunes, actually wrote and signed an extraordinarily submissive note promising to do nothing to disturb his peace and quiet: "I beg Benjamin to remind me, if I ever find myself in Paris once more, that I give him the absolute right to prevent me from taking any step, from the slightest to the most important, which could compromise my peaceable existence (*repos*) and above all that of my generous friend."[16] (It seemed that such vows between them were useless unless they were consigned to paper, to be produced at some later date.) Benjamin felt he was always in the public eye because of Germaine's position while never firmly holding on to "the helm" of the vessel of his life. Once free from her, he wrote, "I shall see clearly on my own . . . what are my means, my resources, above all what is my will, without this influence that long enduring memories make it impossible to destroy. Then I shall know what remains to me both for my freedom and my *gloire*. And I shall no longer be weakened by the political imprudence of Germaine nor pulled this way and that by demands that trouble my mind and overturn my plans. She will no longer be responsible for a [political] conviction that is less publicized, but more unshakable than hers. I must get married. But to whom?"[17] Time would tell whether Benjamin's political stance would prove to be more solid than that of Germaine.

And so, in the months before their departure, they had quarreled, hurling accusations, reproaches, and complaints at each other in furious scenes. Then there would be a lull, some marvellous tête-à-tête in which all the fury would be forgotten and forgiven. Benjamin confided to his diary that he alone valued Germaine at her true worth, that no one was as intelligent as she was, that nobody had as high an esteem for his intellectual powers. No one was as warm-hearted, kind, and devoted as she, he repeated at intervals like a mantra. Germaine might well be demanding, but any woman who had a mind of her own could be accused of making excessive demands: Benjamin had leveled the same charge at Belle de Charrière also. And did he not make demands of his own in his long struggle to break free?

Having dismissed the notion of lingering forty *lieues* from Paris in what *le monde* regarded as the desert of the provinces, Germaine faced two choices: either to travel abroad in search of the new and in quest of fresh triumphs or to slink back to Coppet. The idea of going to Germany, then divided into many small states, was not adopted lightly or on impulse. She was hoping against hope to meet Dr. Robertson in Berlin, whither he was due to travel with Lord John Campbell. Benjamin, moreover, had influenced her: from his stay in Brunswick he had come to believe that German thinkers were far more advanced than their French and English colleagues, and he had aroused her ever-vigilant curiosity about what was going on in German literary and intellectual circles, then little known in France. The late lamented tutor to her children, Gerlach, had given her German lessons, so that she had acquired a reading knowledge of the language and could usually manage to make herself understood. Besides, not only had the multitalented Goethe shown an interest in her writings and translated her essay on the novel into German, but she too was full of enthusiasm for his *Sorrows of Young Werther,* which she had read in French translation, and she had written to tell him so. She was also particularly eager to meet a French scholar with whom she had been corresponding: Charles de Villers, an authority on the philosophy of Kant, resided in Metz, and she hoped to stay awhile and converse with him on this subject. The encounter between herself, Constant, and Villers would prove especially stimulating.

Thus it was that Germaine, utterly distraught, left with Benjamin in the third week of October 1803 for the eastern frontier via Metz. The weather was inclement, the roads bad. He felt deeply sorry for her and tried to cheer her. It was his birthday on October 25, and that evening at the inn in Chalons he ordered champagne to celebrate and diverted her with his dazzling talk. Gradually, her spirits revived somewhat. Young Auguste later told his grandfather how Benjamin had helped his mother to regain her composure.

Despite her extreme agitation, Germaine had set out with a definite literary project in mind: the idea of writing a book about German literature, thought, and culture, and she began by taking notes and keeping a diary that she intended for publication. The proposed book would develop over the following years into *De l'Allemagne,* a work that would color the French public's image of Germany and serve as a source book for generations. And to this ambitious project she would soon add a novel, after seeing an opera about a water nymph in love with a knight who abandons her for a mortal. Here was an extraordinary female figure betrayed by a lover who prefers to settle for a commonplace union, a theme that definitely struck a chord with Germaine and would evolve into her novel *Corinne,* long the bible of gifted and aspiring women everywhere.

Benjamin had some writing in progress, but he had no new literary projects in view. Besides, he had his doubts about the whole journey to Germany. He could recall his own experiences as a chamberlain at the court of Brunswick years before, when he was thoroughly bored and had managed to offend the Dowager Duchess and many of those he encountered with his supercilious airs, cutting cynical remarks, and radical views. He had made few friends and his departure was not widely mourned. Only a few rare scholars like Jacob Mauvillon and Ludwig Ferdinand Huber, together with the remarkably rich libraries he discovered, left a deep impression on him. After his failed marriage to Minna, moreover, he could hardly have regarded his time in Brunswick as a great success. Consequently, he had no reason to suppose that liberal-minded Germaine would fare any better in the retrograde feudal dukedoms of Germany.

Was this assumption one of the reasons for his surprising decision to travel incognito after crossing the frontier? Presumably, he would have preferred it to be known that he was not part of her retinue. Germaine found his disguise as a private tutor amusing, but she urged him to present himself openly. Originally, he had intended to leave her and the children at Frankfurt, but circumstances intervened: Albertine suddenly grew ill, and Germaine was at her wit's end with worry. Benjamin proved to be a great help during this time; for instance, he coped with the doctor whom she could barely understand and wrongly suspected of incompetence. Germaine was deeply grateful to Benjamin, and as soon as Albertine recovered they were able to continue their journey.

Germaine did not exactly need to travel to Germany: she had a fine home in Switzerland, and she could have stayed with her beloved father at Coppet. But then she would have appeared to be "defeated" by the dictator, and she wanted the whole world to know about her banishment and how cruelly Napoleon had treated her. However tremulous she might seem, she was a fighter. She told Necker that she needed what she called "a success": clearly, its purpose was to let the autocrat know that there was a world elsewhere and that one did not send "*la fille de M. Necker*" into exile without some noise being made about it. She was not sure whether such a resounding success, if she attained it, would prove better or worse for her own position in France. But noise was just what Benjamin did not want: all he desired was to get on with his studies and his writing while hoping that the powers that be had forgotten about him.

Germaine's attitude toward her celebrity and its uses could be quite clearheaded. She had come to understand how, almost without realizing it, she had been seduced by fame in her youth, and how once she had attained it she had aroused envy and enmity, and had been forced to fight against her attackers. Describing her feelings of trepidation as she waited to cross the Rhine, she wrote in her travel diary, "You must not give your enemies the joy of having laid you low, and the only noble vengeance a magnanimous heart can allow is to carry on regardless and go forward, in spite of being weakened by deep wounds."[18] In assessing the limitations of fame and its concomitant amour propre, she perceived that they did not exactly yield pleasure but served rather as a kind of compensation. As she explained later to her father, "Pleasure means love, Paris, or power. One of these three things is needful to fulfill one's heart, mind or energy: all the rest is *métaphysique* [mere abstraction] where enjoyment is concerned, but real enough to cause distress if it is lacking. What do you say to this faithful portrait of my intimate self?"[19]

All the time she was away she wrote frequently to her fragile elderly father, sending him long informative letters full of political news and gossip, hoping to entertain him and distract him, as far as she could, from missing her as she missed him. She continued to worry about Necker's health; she would never have left him without being sure that his condition was stable, and she constantly needed him to tell her that, really, he was quite well. All the same, her Calvinist conscience nagged her. Later, there would come frightening news that he had been taken ill, but fortunately the illness turned out to be short-lived. Benjamin behaved toward her then as a brother and a veritable son to Necker, she was to tell her father. She spent three days in a torment of self-reproach. Her cousin, Albertine Necker de Saussure, was urged to send word immediately by a special courier if her father took a turn for the worse: even so, it would take a week for a messenger from Geneva to arrive. What if Necker were to die in her absence? She was convinced that she could not go on living without him.

Her arrival in the small city of Weimar on December 14, 1803, after a difficult journey through the snowy landscapes of northern Germany, was an event. No sooner had she settled at the inn than the ruling Duke Karl August of Saxe-Weimar himself came to call on her. As a young man he had visited Paris in 1775 and had enjoyed such kind treatment at the hands of M. and Mme Necker that he had never forgotten it. She found that her father was highly esteemed in the duchy. In addition, everyone had read *Delphine* and was curious to meet its author. The duke's wife, Duchess Louise, together with the

Dowager Duchess Anna Amalia, known as the protector of writers, behaved most graciously toward her, and she was immediately swept up into life at court, with its round of soirées, card parties, dinners, receptions, and balls. The duke even arranged for plays to be performed in the court theater especially for her. She could scarcely have imagined a more favorable welcome.

She quickly discovered that Weimar deserved its reputation as the Athens of Germany: a multitude of poets, dramatists, and thinkers resided in the small city, making it ideal ground for her projected book on German culture. She was soon issuing invitations to tea or supper to such eminent figures as Wieland, Schiller, and Goethe, learning all she could from them and from the numerous distinguished men of letters and philosophers she encountered. Upon meeting Goethe, she judged at once that he was the major figure, although like many others she found his personality and character to be less attractive than his great talent. She conversed with the famously reclusive Schiller notwithstanding his difficulty in speaking French; his wife, Charlotte, accompanied her to court or to the theater.

Frau Charlotte von Schiller remarked on the noteworthy fact that Mme de Staël had no male escort. Constant, evidently, had preserved his strange incognito and still did not present himself openly at this time. Otherwise, he could surely have helped translate for Germaine. Instead, he departed on a brief tour of the region. In his unfinished autobiographical novel *Cécile,* whose idealized heroine is based on Charlotte von Hardenberg, his former mistress in Brunswick, there is no mention of Weimar at all. According to the novel, the narrator/ Benjamin received a letter from Cécile/Charlotte on August 7, 1803, and he replied to it, asking for information about her life. The narrator also wrote to her from various German towns on his little tour, hoping to see her. However, because the story offers a disconcerting and even modern conflation of fact and fiction, verisimilitude and caricature, it is difficult to know what parts are to be believed. There are only two entries for Charlotte in his diary at this time, recording his letters to her, but unfortunately pages are missing for the whole period from April 10, 1803, to January 6, 1804. Was his quest for Charlotte another reason for his incognito?

On his return to Weimar after his excursion, Benjamin finally decided to abandon his curious disguise: he made his official entry into the city on January 4, 1804. By then, Germaine's triumph, accomplished entirely on her own, was complete. Through her, he was immediately caught up in the intellectual life of Weimar and the social whirl of court receptions and balls. She introduced him to Friedrich von Schiller, Johann Wolfgang von Goethe, and many others in the literary world, where the noble "von" was much in evidence, as M. Constant or the more aristocratic-sounding M. *de* Constant. He was presented at court and "everything went off well," Germaine reported to her father. "He is having a great success here," she informed her cousin Albertine. "He could not be received more favorably."[20] No one bothered about his reputation for radical political views "because people have opinions but no allegiance to a party." Twice a day he was to be found at court. He enjoyed the esteem and conversation of many leading men of letters. Benjamin noted in his diary for February 16, 1804, that with Germaine he attended "a very remarkable supper" at Goethe's home, commenting particularly on the great man's "profundity and new ideas."[21]

Benjamin owned to having profited a great deal from his stay in Weimar. He was very impressed by what he found there, especially "the impartiality and the love of truth, so pleasing and useful to me." He was sorry to leave a place where he had worked and lived "in safety." To his cousin Rosalie he admitted, on February 27, "I have been delighted, in some respects, with my journey in Germany. There, I have seen men occupied solely with literature and finding real happiness in it. If . . . certain circumstances [that is, Napoleon's dictatorship] last longer, perhaps it is in Germany that one should seek a new homeland."[22] The idea of settling in Germany to study and write, encouraged by his experiences in Weimar, presented an alternative to the life he had been living and a way of escaping from what he regarded as bondage. To his friend Fauriel he wrote from Leipzig on March 9 that during the winter he had been most usefully employed: he had discovered the treasures of German literature and for more than two months had been working eight hours a day. Never in his life had he spent more time at his studies, he informed his aunt.

Meetings with liberal-minded writers in Weimar, where originally he had not wanted to go, had not only further stimulated his own literary ambitions but also opened new horizons. In December 1804, reflecting on his journey to Weimar with Germaine, Benjamin confided to his diary, "I believed I was making a great sacrifice for her, and indeed I was. Yet the result of it for me was the advantage of discovering that a great part of Europe lay open to me, and that, far from Paris, I would still find keen interests in literature, study, philosophy."[23]

Germaine had prolonged her stay in Weimar in the hope of keeping Benjamin with her. She settled the extra expenses he had incurred by accompanying her and, as a token of her gratitude, provided him with a carriage for his own use. They had arranged to go their separate ways on leaving Weimar, and to part in Leipzig. The moment that she so dreaded and he so keenly anticipated—their forthcoming separation at Leipzig—soon arrived. In February, they set out together, encountering such deep snow that they were forced to turn back twice. Eventually, on March 3, they arrived in Leipzig, where they stayed for two days. According to the equivocal source *Cécile*, it was there that Mme de Malbée / Germaine extracted a promise from the narrator that he would never marry anyone else. There is, however, no allusion to this promise in the diary for March 3 to 5, when they were in Leipzig together. On the contrary, two months later, in May, Benjamin promised himself that he would never marry another: "What a sad thing is marriage and what good fortune to have escaped from it after being stupid enough to contract it. I hereby declare that if I do not marry Minette (which is something other than a marriage) I shall never marry." Meanwhile, on March 6, Benjamin had noted, "She has left," and repeated his mantra that no one was as good, loving, intelligent, and devoted as Germaine. This was followed by the cry, "And Albertine."[24] He declared that he found himself alone, in a cold bath of solitude, and that he felt very sad. He certainly does not sound like a man annoyed at having had a promise wrenched from him by a domineering woman.

Separation did not mean that Germaine and Benjamin lost touch with each other. The whole time they were apart they corresponded frequently: the letters are lost, but their existence is known from the record of his correspondence that Benjamin kept in his diary. While Germaine continued her journey to Berlin with the children and her retinue, having sent Olive, her femme de chambre, in advance to arrange their accommodation, Benjamin returned to Weimar before setting out for Switzerland, where he intended to see Necker and tell him in detail all that had happened. He walked and talked further with Goethe, with whom he attended the first performance of Schiller's *William Tell;* he dined afterward with the Dowager Duchess and the playwright; and he took his formal leave of the Duke of Saxe-Weimar and the court. "The position of prince is so contrary to nature that it renders mediocre men stupid and distinguished men insane," he observed curtly—a view unlikely to be shared by Germaine, who favored princes and aristocrats, accustomed as she was since her youth to dispensing the requisite flattery.[25]

Why did Benjamin not accompany Germaine to Berlin, a place of considerable importance? He does not say in his diary, but in his abortive novel *Cécile*, written a few years afterward and in a very different frame of mind, the narrator gives some explanation, omitting all reference to the shared triumph in Weimar and leaving the impression that Mme de Malbée / Germaine made up her mind to go to Berlin on the spur of the moment. In actuality Germaine was contemplating going there long before, privately because she hoped to meet Dr. Robertson again and also because it seemed to her folly not to seize the opportunity. As Benjamin wrote, "Mme de Malbée decided to visit Berlin. Having left France without a proper passport, and being on bad terms with the Consular Government, I did not want to expose myself to its malevolence by visiting a court where there was a French ambassador."[26] The narrator, it seems, was afraid of French reprisals and ready to leave his female companion to face alone the consequences of her recklessness.

Germaine, however, did not reach Berlin unprepared: she was carrying letters of introduction to prominent personages from the Duke and Duchess of Saxe-Weimar and the Dowager Duchess Anna Amalia, and from Goethe and Schiller. She even carried a missive from her friend Joseph Bonaparte to Laforest, the French ambassador whom the narrator of *Cécile* seems to fear so much. A few years earlier when Laforest was at the ministry of foreign affairs, he had served Joseph well during diplomatic negotiations, and he was pleased to comply with his superior's wishes. Far from making life difficult for her, as Benjamin may have anticipated, Laforest showed her the greatest kindness and consideration. On March 10, two days after her arrival, she was presented at court. King Frederick William III was most gracious, and Queen Louise treated her with especial favor in the friendliest manner. Germaine danced with the king's brothers; met savants and men of letters, including the philosopher of the ego, Fichte, while pursuing inquiries for her book; visited high-thinking women in their salons; attended dinners and suppers; played whist; and entertained at tea on Fridays. It was another triumph for her, again won entirely on her own.

Among the men of letters she encountered, she enthused to Necker, there was one remarkable fellow who knew more about literature than almost anyone of her acquaintance, spoke French and English fluently, and was only thirty-six. Far too distinguished to be employed as a tutor, August Wilhelm Schlegel could nonetheless give young Albert lessons while staying at Coppet, Germaine proposed, adding that "I myself would gain a great deal for the book I have in mind." He was not much to look at, short and fairly ugly, she thought, but he had expressive eyes. "As regards literature," she wrote, "Benjamin and I are not more intelligent than he, and even Benjamin is not so learned. You can have no idea what these Germans know when they put their minds to it. Their secret is never to move in society. That particular secret does not suit me at all, and yet literary merit depends on it."[27] It was indeed a mystery to her friends how she managed to reconcile her intense social life and her writing.

All the same, the grandeur of high life in the capital of Prussia, which she recognized as a pale imitation of Parisian manners and style, made less of an impression on her than the more intimate pleasures of Weimar, and she was inclined to attribute this to the absence of Benjamin. She worried constantly about his safety, hoping that he would not cross into France in the course of his return journey to Switzerland. The arrest of so distinguished a figure as General Moreau—whom she knew personally—for alleged involvement in conspiracy had upset them both; now came shocking news of the abduction on foreign soil and the immediate execution of the duc d'Enghien at Vincennes, a crime that inspired fear and outrage throughout Europe. She had learned that travelers were being kept under close surveillance in France. What if Benjamin were to fall into the hands of the tyrant?

Who knew what might happen to him? She longed to hear that he had arrived safely at Coppet where he was due on April 4 or 5. With Benjamin on his way, "it is rather as if I am coming home myself," she assured her father, for "Benjamin knows my thoughts as well as I do."[28] She went so far as to suggest that Necker would find Benjamin's lively company even better than her own.

With Benjamin on his unhurried way from Weimar to Coppet, stopping from time to time to visit friends and acquaintances, Germaine continued her literary and philosophical inquiries in Berlin, much occupied also with the diversions that, she agreed with him, did not really conform to her true and deepest sensibility. On April 6, a month after they parted in Leipzig, he arrived in Lausanne to see his family. He found two letters from Geneva informing him that on March 30 Necker had become seriously ill in his Genevan apartment and that his condition was causing grave concern. Germaine's cousin and close friend Albertine was with him.

Benjamin was profoundly shaken. His first thoughts were of Germaine, completely unaware of this crisis: "I shudder at the idea of what could interrupt the fairly happy life of poor Minette and cast her into the deepest despair."[29] (Whenever his deeper sympathies for her were aroused he reverted to her pet name, Minette, in his diary.) Then, on April 9, at two in the afternoon, Necker died. Benjamin recorded the news in his diary: "He is dead! What will become of her? What despair for the present, what isolation in the future! I am going to her, to console her, or at the least to support her. Poor unfortunate soul! When I recall her suffering, her disquiet, two months ago [at the false alarm over Necker's indisposition], and her lively delight, which was to be short-lived! Poor unfortunate soul, it would be better to die than to suffer what you are going to suffer. And how sorry I feel for his loss, a being so kind, so pure, so noble; he loved me. Who now will guide his daughter's existence?"[30] That very night, April 9, Benjamin slept at Coppet. Benjamin was overcome with compassion when he thought of Germaine and the appalling suffering she would soon experience. He felt for others more than for himself, he believed. Yet he seemed to find a sort of enjoyment in the idea of suffering. With Necker's death he saw Germaine, hitherto the dominating partner he had charged with leaving him the secondary role, as an object of pity, alone, isolated, vulnerable, having lost her protector and guide. The blow was going to overturn not only her life but also his own, for clearly there would be an opening now for him to replace her father—as her husband. It would seem to him that there was no further obstacle to their union, and that she would feel the need for it. None of this prevented him from judging her severely, however. He knew well enough that she would be overcome by self-reproach at having left her father to go to Germany, although Necker had encouraged her to travel there. In Benjamin's view she was being punished for not having strictly adhered to her duty as he had done in his youth by helping his father during those long years of litigation. Poor Minette! He feared for her safety, even for her sanity.

He decided that she should be informed of her father's grave illness, not of his demise. He would tell her the awful news in person, in the way least likely to bring about her suicide, for she had repeatedly said that her father's death would be followed by her own. The decision to spare Germaine the facts of Necker's death was due to an awareness of her violently passionate nature as well as the particular character of her relationship with her father, which she was to describe as "not that of daughter to father; it was fraternity, love, religion, my whole moral being."[31] Consequently, letters were sent to two friends of hers in Berlin: one from Albertine Necker de Saussure to Princess Radziwill, niece of Frederick the Great, and the other from Benjamin to Carl Gustav von Brinkman, whom Germaine knew very well from the time when he served in the Swedish embassy in Paris. Each letter contained a double message, one for Germaine telling of Necker's illness, the other for the recipient reporting his death, which they were to keep to themselves. A special courier, François Uginet, Necker's valet de chambre and brother of Germaine's factotum, delivered them. On her return from Berlin to Coppet she was to be retained in Weimar, where she would be surrounded by caring friends until he, Benjamin, could rejoin her, "the person I love best in this world."[32]

Meanwhile, in Berlin, Germaine wrote to Necker on April 10 to tell him that she had not received any letters from him and recounted for his entertainment the latest political doings; further letters to her father followed on April 14 and again on April 17. By then eight days had passed since his death. In the early nineteenth century the mail took nine days between Coppet and Weimar and left twice a week. People did not expect to hear news at once.

Benjamin left in haste for Weimar, covering the same route he had traveled earlier but in a very different state of mind, his thoughts revolving all the time around her despair, the dreadful moment when she would finally learn from him the truth about her father's death. He felt like a man on his way to execution, yet at the same time he was satisfied with the course he was taking. The moment was approaching when he would be able to arrange the rest of his life, which would include leaving his mark and acquiring a literary reputation. Benjamin concluded that the time had come to take command: "Certainly, I do not want to abandon you, my dear unfortunate friend, but I must for your own sake seize the helm of our life together. There is no longer any duty on your side to oppose it. My resolve is irrevocable."[33] In his own view, Benjamin was the only real friend Germaine now had who was capable of "guiding" her. Whether she would want him—or indeed, anyone else—for a guide was another matter entirely, one that he did not take into consideration as he recorded his thoughts in his diary during his journey.

For much of the way he traveled night and day. He had little sleep. The carriage wheels broke—a common occurrence—and he was forced to stop. Then a few days later they broke again. He changed his carriage for another, only to have it suffer the same fate twice. By April 22 he was in Weimar, weary with fatigue. When he told Germaine of her father's death, she fell into convulsions. Nothing could comfort or console her; she was carried to her room. She arose the next day in a state of blankness to face the rest of her life—like a shade on the bank of the Styx waiting to be ferried to Hades.

Yet the grim image of poor Minette that Benjamin had retained in his mind ever since learning of her father's grave condition and death was only partly accurate. The weakness of our nature is such that, once the initial shock wears off, few human beings are capable of remaining totally immersed in grief for twenty-four hours a day. Undiluted grief is what Benjamin, with his cult of pity and suffering, expected—and he was mortified when he did not find it. For, somehow, the life force exerts its demands. Germaine said she was virtually dead, that she could expect no further happiness in her life, and she meant it. But gradually she found much to occupy her.

Schlegel had accompanied her from Berlin to Weimar, and he continued to do his best to console her. Benjamin, who did not have as high an opinion of Schlegel's scholarly intellect and philosophy of life as Germaine, said he was not jealous of the time she spent with him, but he was. Perhaps she preferred Schlegel's attempt to divert her to Benjamin's all-pervasive pity, which might even seem humiliating. The two escorts both shared in Germaine's sad return to Coppet where, denied future happiness and existing henceforward in a tomb, Germaine took refuge in work. She soon undertook to write her study of the life and principles of her beloved father, *Du caractère de M. Necker et de sa vie privée,* published with his manuscripts. Many years later, Benjamin judged the work to be among her finest. She was also faced at once with matters arising from Necker's legacy: she felt it was her sacred duty to preserve it intact for her children. Germaine had dealt most competently with the financial morass left by her husband. Necker's affairs were in order, but she had an extensive and complicated network of details with which to acquaint herself and which demanded her decision and action, from changes in currency to interest rates, from mortgaged property in Paris to investments in land in Louisiana and New York. Much of her correspondence would be with her father's notaries and men of business.

Whatever she might say to her friends about everything being over, it was a woman of independence who gradually recovered her forces and took charge of her own destiny and that of her children. Germaine did not need any other guide or helmsman than the one beyond the grave.

CHAPTER SEVEN

⤳ *Corinne and Adolphe* ⤶

CORINNE AND ADOLPHE: these two charismatic fictional characters were indelibly associated with their respective creators from the moment that they became known to the public, in 1807 and 1816 respectively. Corinne *is* Mme de Staël, and Adolphe *is* Benjamin Constant, people said. Yet in essence each one is a somewhat distorted imaginative projection of its author's self-image. The independent, multitalented Corinne, stunningly beautiful, ardently passionate, adored and admired in Italy as a poet, enthusiastic lover of the arts and music and all that is highest and noblest in humanity, represents the best qualities of Germaine, whose shortcomings can be glimpsed only in the final pages; just as Adolphe, calculating, self-justifying, and embittered, incarnates mostly the worst aspects of his inventor's nature. True, Benjamin claimed that his novel was not a work of the imagination, but then he affected to think little of the book: fiction necessarily implies imaginative invention, as he well knew.

When these self-referential works were being composed the relationship between Germaine and Benjamin was virtually in tatters. She poured out her heart and soul in a long, slow, expansive, lyrical, wide-ranging novel, *Corinne ou l'Italie,* a work of keen psychological insights and broad cultural and political aims that gathers momentum only in the second part of the book. His responses were distilled into *Adolphe*, a subtly cruel, penetrating, concentrated, short novel of loathing and self-loathing. Evidently, both works are rooted in elements of the respective lives of their creators, but the two writers went beyond these autobiographical aspects to launch into betrayed dreams and aspirations on Germaine's side and self-deprecation and unsparing self-probing on Benjamin's. She was finishing *Corinne* when he embarked on *Adolphe;* they read parts of their writings in progress to select friends as well as to each other. He seems to have set out with the intention of writing something more succinct, less all embracing, than her novel.

How did they reach the desperate state that is variously depicted and implied through the trajectories of Corinne and Oswald, of Adolphe and Ellénore, in the course of these two vital fictional works?

In the months and years after Necker's death, the pressures exerted by Napoleon's rule weighed ever more heavily on their liaison. Declared "Emperor of the French" in May 1804 and self-crowned in December of that year, Napoleon said that the French had to be ruled by an iron hand in a velvet glove, but Germaine remarked that he removed his glove when dealing with recalcitrant women, for she was not his only female victim. Her patron, his elder brother Joseph, now named Imperial Highness and heir to the throne, assured Germaine that he was still her very good friend, but he was soon to be out of the country, as King of Naples and later King of Spain. She thought that the emperor, as a perfectly reasonable man, intended to relax the harsh measures taken against her, or so some of his associates suggested privately, but time and again her hopes were dashed. It would take her many years to realize that her exile was final and that the orders against her and the persecution she endured were the direct result of policy from on high.

Indeed, it was hard enough for her when an officer—however courteous—arrived at her current residence in the provinces with orders that she must remove herself and her children within forty-eight hours to a place forty *lieues* from Paris or be escorted to the frontier. She did not give up trying to test the emperor's intentions toward her. Always the great charmer, she did not comprehend the degree of Napoleon's visceral antipathy toward a woman who saw herself as endowed with "superior" intelligence and talent, who dared to claim the freedom to question his decisions, and who declined to indulge in the blatant sycophancy to which he had grown accustomed.

Her grief and sense of guilt over her father's death and her unhappiness at her enduring exile, as she flitted from unprepossessing town to town and from château to château, governed her volatile behavior. Benjamin, in turn, felt he could not abandon her when she was being misjudged and misunderstood. Nor could he leave her to her deep melancholy and misery, her mental suffering, her distress and sorrow, the intensity of which, said her cousin Albertine Necker de Saussure, could be "terrible." Inevitably, Germaine sometimes struck out at the person nearest to hand, who happened to be Benjamin; he replied in kind—and then wished he had not.

He blamed her for discounting his true sensibility; he blamed her for her vanity, coquetry, and what he called her weak character because it lacked stoicism and the capacity to stand alone, to find inner strength; he blamed her for being self-centered—a case of the pot calling the kettle black. Germaine had enough talent for ten or twelve distinguished men, he acknowledged, but it did not serve. "It is politics, it is the demands of love as if eighteen years old, the need for society, the need for *gloire,* melancholy as in a wilderness, the need to be appreciated, the need to shine, everything contradictory and complicated," he had complained in his diary.[1] It was all her fault, not least the parlous situation without issue in which he found himself.

Shortly after Necker's death and the return to Coppet, he was still on the same theme: "What can others do against the agitation of your life, your contradictory wishes, your need for a brilliant place . . . your coquetry in fear of old age . . . while your character is not strong enough to defy the enemies you always provoke by putting yourself forward?" He went on, first with the vivid image of a struggling bird, and then that of a ship under sail: "You do not want to suffer," he addressed her in his diary, "and you spread your wings in the open and fly in defiance of the winds, colliding against the trees, hurting yourself against the rocks. I can do nothing about it. As long as you do not furl your sails, as long as you do not see that one must first create a settled situation . . . as long as you do not realize *that,* I can do nothing for you. And everything I say applies doubly to you as a woman. A man has a career; he bestirs himself for a fixed aim. You bestir yourself to shine in a salon. Can this type of success, which leaves nothing behind, ever compensate for its cost?"[2] The injustice of this comment, leveled by a man who holds no position and has no career and who claims elsewhere that he alone knows her true value, is a token of his frustration and bitterness, and his fundamental reluctance to accept her genius as a woman. What of her famous writings, what of her book on the passions, what of *Delphine?* Had they left no mark?

He could not bear her misery, yet he feared to do anything to make it worse. He found temporary relief in the form of ladies he met in the social whirl of Paris. She, meanwhile, found refuge in the diversions offered by foreign travel, which at least offered something fresh and different, and in meeting new friends and immersing herself in the life of court and society abroad. In these milieux she undertook the research necessary for her writings. She also engaged in flirtations with younger men that usually ended in more distress and disappointment, while all the time trying to keep hold of Benjamin.

Yet throughout all the storms, the accusations, the quarrels, and the recriminations, the business of writing continued. Nobody knew when Germaine found time to write, but she did—sometimes in bed in the morning or, indeed, anywhere at all feasible, for her father had not wished to see her with pen in hand at her desk. She consulted friends and scholars; she revised; she promoted her books. Benjamin, however, had great difficulty getting started: he would embark on a plan and write with high enthusiasm, but after a while he would change his mind and begin again, altering his plan umpteen times. He had to remind himself that he did not want to produce a work of pure erudition. Germaine would be busy writing plays, her novel *Corinne,* and her letters on Germany that would develop into *De l'Allemagne,* while Benjamin would put aside his manuscript on polytheism for the writings that would later form the basis of his powerful and still resonant liberal treatise, *Principes de politique.* To take his mind off his troubles he also composed a play in verse, *Wallstein,* an abbreviated adaptation of Schiller's lengthy and equivocal drama *Wallenstein.* It was Germaine who persuaded him to write the important preface to *Wallstein* that contributed to the new movement in French drama. The first version of *Adolphe,* known as the *Épisode d'Ellénore,* pages that Germaine considered original and touching, also took shape at this time. Thus, the stormy upheavals in Germaine and Benjamin's relationship not only formed the backdrop to their literary activity but were also, in effect, an essential part of it.

In the months after Necker's death the question of marriage to Germaine moved to the center of Benjamin's preoccupations, but it was by no means at the center of hers. Why was he so keen? Plainly, it was because if they were to marry all the advantages would be on his side.

In accounts of their association it is widely assumed that Benjamin was weak and vacillating and that Germaine—despite her own weaknesses—was the dominating force, largely because of the revelations of his diary; his letters to his cousin Rosalie and others, like Claude Hochet, where he gives his side of the story or the part he wants them to know for his purpose; his depiction of the tyrannical Mme de Malbée in *Cécile;* and his portrayal of the enslaved protagonist in *Adolphe,* anxious to free himself from his burdensome liaison with Ellénore. Germaine left no intimate private diary of this period. In her letters to friends such as Juliette Récamier she may be expansive but she is also secretive and evasive: she tells them far from everything. Consequently, evidence is weighted on Benjamin's side and on his viewpoint. But to what extent did he provoke her with his world-weary remarks and cynicism?

Certainly, she was no saint: an only child, overly controlled by her mother, she had been indulged by her father, and she was used to having her own way and being the center of attention, surrounded as she was by a court of admirers who to some degree counterbalanced any public opprobrium. Her friend Catherine Huber, the well-brought-up and right-thinking companion of her youth, gave some sense of Germaine's faults as well as her virtues, her inexhaustible kindness and her fascinating charm, when she declared to her parents in 1789 that Germaine could be both adorable and detestable: "Given her astonishing intelligence, if Mme de Staël was less frivolous she would be the most heavenly creature, because along with superior wit she has a perfect heart but she often reveals a bad head. I, who know her better than anyone else and better than she knows herself, often find her unique, adorable, sometimes also detestable, but always singularly charming, and her intimate friendship, which allows me to enjoy all the treasures of her wit and all the good qualities of her heart, provides one of the delights of my life."[3] Others offered a similarly mixed testimonial to her diversity.

Though generous in the extreme, Germaine had undeniably high expectations of her lovers—from Narbonne onward—for whom she was prepared to disregard her reputation and even risk her life; she could also show herself to be a banker's daughter in insisting on a return when they reneged on their contract. She could use her distress, her mental suffering, and the threat of suicide as a form of moral blackmail, just as Benjamin had done when he first tried to win her with dramatic displays of self-harm. There is a curious moment in *Corinne*, where Oswald's mistress, the despotic and deceitful Mme d'Arbigny, determined to hold on to him at all costs, manipulates him with her despair, an act that is thoroughly condemned in the novel as despicable. It is as if, in the role of detached and dispassionate author, Germaine can see into the shortcomings of her own conduct. As her alter ego Corinne says, "Sometimes I look into myself as a stranger could do."[4]

While Benjamin saw Germaine as domineering, he was secretly determined—as his diary reveals—to dominate *her*, something he thought he could do only if he married her. The extraordinary, dazzling creature who had fascinated him at Montchoisi, whose voice, with its "supernatural influence," he said he could never forget, was to dwindle into his wife, domesticated, tamed, transformed into something other than she was: the courageous libertarian and dissident, the original and controversial writer, the outstandingly forward-looking woman of the age, of whom he does not speak in his diary, his letters, or his fiction.

The diary indicates many of the advantages he would gain if only he could persuade her or force her to marry him—he actually uses the word *force*. His attitude toward marriage as an ideal haven of quiet domesticity was common to his day and extremely conventional, as was his view of the husband's role. He believed that as Germaine's husband he would no longer be the secondary figure in the relationship; instead, he would be the master, the dominant partner. In addition, his reputation would be restored: his present equivocal position looked dishonorable because people could readily conceive that he was being financed by a wealthy woman, and Benjamin was always bothered about what people thought. He did not consider that such people would believe that he married her for financial reasons. He was genuinely worried about his name, his position, and his social standing, and was constantly harassed by his family on this theme, whereas Germaine remained thoroughly unconventional and scornful of mediocrity in all its forms, already a Romantic who considered herself, as an imaginative artist, to be an exceptional and superior being, one who rises above such petty considerations.

Benjamin could dream that, at a stroke, all his financial problems, including his perennial gambling debts, would be settled. Since the law regarded women as minors, he might have access to Necker's fortune—and Necker himself was no longer available to devise some sensible nuptial arrangement as he had done to limit the depredations of Eric de Staël. As her husband, protector, and guide, Benjamin imagined that he could change her and direct her, after having first grasped the helm of their life together: "I could have made her into a really excellent woman, if I had been able to seize hold of her," he assured himself in August 1804.[5]

Moreover, he could demand an end to all those discussions of hers that lingered on until three or four o'clock in the morning, so that at last he could enjoy a decent night's sleep. She had the energy to survive such intellectual and emotional marathons, whereas he had not. Besides, she suffered from insomnia, and talk could be a substitute for opium, a substance she used and abused. Her exhausting lifestyle is corroborated, humorously, by a member of her circle, Charles-Victor de Bonstetten, a near contemporary of her mother's: "I have just come back from Coppet and I am now quite stupefied, torn from my sweet repose and worn out by an orgy of intelligence. More wit is expended at Coppet in a day than in many a country in a year. I am so weary of it that I am lying half dead."[6] Benjamin often felt the same.

Above all, he decided, there would be no more of the "imprudent" conduct that was endangering his peace, including the extremely risky clandestine expeditions to Paris to meet her friends. Certainly, there would be an end to her moving around the French provinces and traveling abroad where and when she chose; on the contrary, she would be obliged to accompany him to Germany if he decided to go there to study. "The direction of her life must be seized authoritatively," he confided to his diary in January 1805, in her absence. "Since she does not want us to separate, she must be guided, but forced to do what I want. . . . Let us rule her then, since she must be ruled."[7] After Germaine left for Italy, a journey she had been contemplating for some time, Benjamin grew ever more daring. Although he was doubtful about whether she would be pleased by what he had to say to her in one of the (lost) letters he composed whose masterful contents are mentioned in his diary he concluded, "Since I am taking charge of her life, I cannot forgo directing it to suit myself. I have tried to make her realize this in the gentlest possible way."[8] It is doubtful that he actually sent this letter; if he did, it seems unlikely that this line of thought would have impressed Germaine.

Benjamin did not really expect to be any happier when they were married—he knew only too well the difference in their respective characters and temperaments—but he believed that his social and financial position would be regularized. He saw that it was difficult to reconcile her happiness with his own. Quite simply, marriage to her was the best solution to his problems, "and things will go on afterward as they may."[9] It was a gambler's answer: you throw the dice and accept whatever chance decrees.

As for Germaine, what would she gain by marriage to Benjamin?

For months she procrastinated and prevaricated: she did not want to lose him as her "best friend" or *ami* (an equivocal word that could be interpreted in several ways), her "brother," her devoted and entertaining companion, her aide-de-camp in negotiations with Napoleon's officials. She certainly was not interested in submitting to him as her husband, master, and guide, for she regarded with some contempt any rosy views like his on wifely domesticity and subordination, as she reveals in *Corinne*. As his wife she would no longer be free to engage in the *coquetteries de femmes*, the tender *amitiés amoureuses*, often with handsome or dashing young men, that were so important to her self-image. She felt that these did not impinge on her longstanding, tried-and-tested liaison with Benjamin. According to the law, moreover, she would have to put Necker's fortune at risk by placing it in the hands of a husband who was no less adept than Eric de Staël in accumulating huge debts and who had no intention of refraining from gambling—a diversion that would ultimately force him to sell his much loved home, Les Herbages, five years later. His cousin Rosalie, outraged by his gambling, treated him as another Beverley, a well-known character in a play, a gambler who ends in total collapse and ruin. Germaine regarded Necker's fortune as a sacred trust that she held on behalf of her children, a fortune that she had rapidly learned to control with the aid of her father's loyal agents.

There was another drawback to marriage with Benjamin: she would become plain Mme Constant, in a society where "de" had value. Unlike members of his family, he chose not to use this sign of aristocracy, having disdained it since the days when his father registered him as baron Benjamin de Constant at Edinburgh University. She would cease to be known as Madame de Staël, the name she had made famous throughout Europe with her writings; she would no longer be remembered as *"madame l'ambassadrice,"* with ready access to European royalty. Even Benjamin could appreciate that the change of name would cause embarrassment for her and for the children, as he noted in his diary on December 6, 1804, doubtless after hearing arguments of hers. He thought that perhaps a secret marriage on her return from Italy might be more reasonable. She proposed that they postpone their own public union until after the children were married—an outcome that was quite a way off in the future. In short, Germaine felt that she would gain nothing and lose a great deal. She would be no happier, and she knew that he would be dissatisfied and unfaithful. Why should she move from a situation in which she held the reins to one in which she was under the legal control of another?

The crux of the matter was this: she wanted to preserve the status quo and keep him on her terms, while he was prepared to stay at her side only on his own terms. When he finally realized that she was unlikely to marry him, he began seriously to look elsewhere and present her with a fait accompli. Amélie Fabri had faded from view as an eligible bride, but now his family urged the merits of Antoinette de Loys, a sixteen-year-old girl with a sizable dowry whom he estimated as someone he could rule. But Antoinette, too, ceased to be a candidate when the sought-after, twice-married Charlotte von Hardenberg, formerly Charlotte von Marenholz and now Mme du Tertre, arrived "at last" in Paris on December 27, like a goddess descending from the skies in an opera to unravel the plot, with the offer of a dowry of a hundred thousand francs, a sum that would turn out to be somewhat exaggerated. Charlotte came of a distinguished German family. Divorced from her first husband, she had married a French émigré, Alexandre du Tertre—a foolish move, in Constant's view—and she was thoroughly unhappy. True, Benjamin had a low opinion of her intelligence, and he had thought her "boring and full of romantic notions," but he had been "madly in love" with her "for a few days" in Brunswick, and he was longing to meet again the woman he had jilted for Germaine.[10] In Charlotte he would find someone who seemed utterly devoted to him, and whose patience and long-suffering would prove to be little short of exemplary.

Benjamin breathed a sigh of relief when, a few days before Charlotte's arrival, Germaine departed on December 19 or 20, 1804, for Italy, where she was to stay until June 1805. He had his regrets about staying behind: he said that he would have liked to visit a country so celebrated for its beauty. Clearly, however, the idea of regaining his freedom for a few months and the prospect of seeing Charlotte again were preferable. Germaine, unaware of the true reason, was disappointed when he chose not to accompany her. As though he were partly contrite, he surprised and pleased her by joining her en route and staying with her for a few days in Lyons. "I love her with all my heart and soul," he noted in his diary at the beginning of December. "She loves me more than ever and clings to me as though to her last affection, her last bond on this earth."[11] Germaine left with regret at finding herself for the first time without the company of her "best friend," but she was hardly alone. Her children were with her, as was Schlegel, and she was joined in Milan by Jean-Charles-Léonard Simonde, usually known as Sismondi, a promising Geneva-born economist and historian some years younger than herself, whom she had met a few years previously and who would remain her loyal though critical friend and support.

Before she left for Italy, Germaine had given Benjamin a token of trust in their association: together they had invested in a house on the rue des Mathurins in Paris, with her agent acting under the name of his aunt, Mme de Nassau. What financial contribution Benjamin made is unclear, but thenceforward he possessed "for life" a rent-free pied-à-terre in the capital. This was in addition to his delightful room at Coppet, which, according to Bonstetten, who once occupied it, looked out over the trees, the charming mill, and to the east over Lausanne, the Alps and the Lake of Geneva. Before departing from Coppet for Italy Germaine had written a brief testament, addressed to Benjamin, dated November 1, 1804: "Dear friend, Rejoice if Providence decides that I go before you into the tomb; after the loss of my father, it would have been impossible for me to bear yours." As for her, in death she would be rejoining her father and awaiting Benjamin. She asked him to stay close to her children, having urged them in a note "to love in you the one their mother has deeply loved!" She then passed to more mundane affairs. "You know that, following arrangements we have made together, a house in the rue des Mathurins bought by M. Fourcault [her agent] under the name of Mme de Nassau, belongs to us both, with this condition, that the income is yours, and the capital, after you, is my daughter's. Should it suit you to sell it, you would restore the money in a manner approved by my children's guardians." Then she added sorrowfully but hopefully, "Farewell, dear Benjamin, at least I hope that you will be near me when I die. Alas! I did not close my father's eyes: will you close mine?" Time would provide a deeply ironic answer.[12]

It must have seemed to her on second thought that this document, which might have to be shown to indifferent parties, was far too personal and insufficiently clear. In a second version, also dated November 1, 1804, the phrase "the one their mother has deeply loved" is replaced by the more formal and less compromising "the one who has been so faithful a friend to their mother." She also made clear that the arrangement for Albertine was separate from the rest of Germaine's legacy. Should he sell his half, with the consent of "the guardians of my daughter," the capital should be invested "in a solid manner," but the income from it belongs to him for life.[13] Most notably, this more formal version omits the touching farewell to Benjamin. The whole matter gives some inkling of the complexity of their joint financial commitments, and goes some way to explain Benjamin's later desire to be free of his financial dependence.

Winter and spring came and went, with Germaine and Benjamin now leading separate lives. Nonetheless, letters passed frequently between them, all of which have been lost or destroyed, the two versions of the testament she had addressed to him being rare survivors of their voluminous correspondence. When his letters were delayed Germaine imagined all sorts of disasters, just like Corinne when she did not hear from Oswald, and frenziedly importuned him. Her constant worry thoroughly irritated Benjamin, but when her letters failed to arrive he too worried about what was happening to her. As he noted privately in January 1805: "Whatever I say and consequently whatever I often write in this diary whenever some circumstance causes me worries about Minette, I feel that the tie that unites us lies in the deepest place in my heart, and that it is there that I live and shall live always."[14]

In accordance with his varying moods, Germaine appears in the diary in at least four incarnations. Called simply Germaine, she is compared with his prospective bride Amélie; indeed, all his women are eventually compared and contrasted with the chatelaine of Coppet. If he is feeling particularly affectionate toward Germaine she is given her family pet name, Minette. Otherwise she is Biondetta, from the fantastic fable *Le Diable amoureux* by Jacques Cazotte, published in 1772. In the story, a Spaniard raises a devil who takes female form as the enchantress Biondetta: in this guise Germaine figures as a sort of magical being, often but not always his tormentor. Then, in the diary's later pages, she is mentioned more formally as Mme de Staël. These names are a form of shorthand for the changing state of his feelings toward her.

Once he admitted, "I love Biondetta. Whatever I write in the bitterness of my heart it does not prevent me from appreciating her qualities and feeling sorry for her. . . . If I leave her, her image will follow me."[15] On another occasion he asked himself, "Could I live without you, without this being who watches over me more than I do myself?" His reply to this query was, "No, I could never bear the misfortune of losing Minette."[16] A few years later, when railing against her, he owned to his cousin Rosalie that he simultaneously felt such a deep wave of affection for Germaine that he could scarcely resist "the need to take her in my arms to console her."[17] Such admissions have to be borne in mind when one puzzles over why he faltered for so long and vacillated so much.

And vacillate he did, miserably, interminably, for years. His diary records every changing mood, which, like a pool stirred by the passing breeze, depends on whether he receives what he takes to be a sweet or a sour letter from Germaine. So many conflicting thoughts and feelings clash in his mind and heart, forming an endless series of variations on an array of irreconcilable themes: emotional ties, affection, memories, Albertine, love, no love, marriage, no marriage, weariness, gratitude, anger, fury, resentment, ambition, worries about social status and public opinion, desire for freedom, longing for tranquility, dislike and fear of causing pain, dread of possible reprisals from Germaine or her friends in high places. Indeed, Benjamin came to see how often the same responses recurred, and he devised a kind of shortcut to avoid constantly repeating himself. In his abbreviated diary from May 8, 1805, he selected seventeen recurring topics and assigned them each a number: "1 means physical [sexual] satisfaction. 2 desire to break my everlasting tie [with Germaine]. 3 return to this tie through memories or some passing enchantment. 4 work. . . . 8 marriage plans. . . . 11 hesitations about my plans with Mme du Tertre [Charlotte]. 12 love for Mme du Tertre. 13 uncertainty about everything . . ."[18] Later, he would simply refer to the issue by number, sometimes repeating the numbers for urgent emphasis and as if in an uncontrollable rage; for instance, "2 2 2" signified the pressing need of a break with Germaine.

In theory, Benjamin's intention was to devote himself to his work during the period of liberty provided by her absence in Italy, but he made frequent visits to Paris from Les Herbages. Some of these were occasioned by his efforts on Germaine's behalf to relax the decree of exile against her and to recover the famous two millions that Necker had lent to the treasury. This activity led him to call on Fouché, and on others he had known under the Directoire and in the Tribunate who were now serving Napoleon. It was actually Benjamin who forged the strategy that would govern Germaine's life in the following years, and hence his own: he advised her to acquire a property as close to Paris as possible, with the prospect of somehow being able to return to the capital. Hopes for this plan appear to have been founded on the Declaration of the Rights of Man of 1789 and the Constitution of Year III (1795), which both held that property was a natural and inalienable right. These hopes were to remain unfulfilled, especially after Napoleon heard about the maneuver and insisted to Fouché that the distance of forty *lieues* be maintained. The fact that Benjamin had devised this strategy would not prevent him from complaining later that he had followed Germaine from inn to inn.

Along with these "business" meetings largely on her account, he spent many pleasurable evenings in Parisian society. The season was in full swing. He was a frequent visitor to the salon of Sophie de Condorcet, widow of the liberal *philosophe*, and he attended her musical soirées. There, he could speak relatively freely with his friend Claude Fauriel. It was there, too, that he encountered his former mistress, Anna Lindsay, beautiful and charming as ever, and evidently still in love with him: he wondered whether he was at all in love with her. He met her also in the salon of the novelist Sophie Gay, mother of the more famous Delphine. And he attended the salon of Germaine's close friend Juliette Récamier, who remained one of the leading lights in Parisian society. Notably, he renewed his friendship with Julie Talma, who was seriously ill: he kept watch by her bedside and was deeply affected by her painful decline and her death early in May 1805, an experience of loss that moved this onetime disciple of the atheist Helvétius toward meditation on mortality and spiritual matters.

And then there was Charlotte, whom he had been so anxious to meet after their lengthy separation. He thought his connection with her was "bizarre." It soon became evident to him, however, that she was keen to renew their association and that she had loved him more than he had loved her. He hesitated briefly. Admittedly, an evening at Charlotte's could prove "long, sad, sometimes boring," and the people who attended her soirées were mere gossips and thoroughly "mediocre." It was not like an evening at Germaine's, but he had had enough wit for the moment. "This woman loves me passionately and I would be able to get her to do whatever I'd want," he concluded.[19]

Meanwhile, Germaine was enjoying the sights and sounds of Italy—the churches and monuments, the music and paintings, the lively popular culture, the beauty of the landscape—as she made her slow way from Milan to Bologna and then to Rome. She was engaged in a warm friendship with the celebrated poet Vincenzo Monti. Monti, who was fifty years old and married, encouraged her to revise some of the views on Italian writers that she had expressed in *De la littérature* and to oppose commonly held prejudices about his country. They were both "enthusiasts," soul mates in their love of the arts. As she was to write to him, "What is so lovely about enthusiasm, about this feeling that is more lively than friendship, purer than love, is an affection so deep and so intricate, an affection that unites all the qualities of tenderness and admiration. Oh! I am too revealing about how much I love you: does one captivate people in this manner?"[20] This was a declaration of the warmest friendship rather than a declaration of love as commonly understood today.

The borderline between such "enthusiasm" and love, however, can easily be crossed. Above all, Germaine wanted to please; she wanted to be loved. Any person she loved she had to admire. She needed to hear the language of love, as Benjamin observed, a language that he could no longer bring himself to address to her. She was always in quest of a soul mate, and throughout her life found a number of figures who appeared to fulfill her dream, occasionally women but usually younger men whose talent and potential she recognized and sought to encourage.

Among these was a delicate, sensitive young Portuguese nobleman she met in Rome. Pedro de Souza had lost his father, an ambassador to the Holy See, just over a year before. Germaine and her new friend could commiserate with each other over the loss of a beloved parent. She recognized his qualities, and her estimation of them would prove to be correct, for he would later become prime minister of Portugal. Young Pedro, who knew the eternal city well, accompanied her on visits to the antiquities of Rome, to the great churches, museums, and galleries. The treasured memory of that blissful companionship is enshrined in *Corinne ou l'Italie*, where, in a role reversal, the eponymous heroine introduces Oswald to the inspiring splendors of the fine arts and the elevation of Italian culture and civilization. Germaine would invite Pedro to visit her at Coppet, as she did all the esteemed friends she favored on her travels, and he would also be found among the numerous visitors at her various places of exile in the French provinces. Her stay in Naples and her return journey home via Florence would also figure in *Corinne*. By the end of June 1805 Germaine was back at Coppet, and she was joined by Benjamin in July.

The idea of seizing the day and marrying Charlotte had already taken shape in his mind by the beginning of May, at the time of his deep sorrow at Julie Talma's death.

After Germaine's return from Italy there were two young men who would follow Pedro de Souza in her affections. The first of these was the gifted twenty-three-year-old son of an important government official, the préfet du Léman, who was strongly opposed to his son's association with Mme de Staël. Some sixteen years her junior, dazzled by her and moved by her interest in him, young Prosper de Barante fell under her spell. Their liaison, which lasted from the summer of 1805 until 1811, appears to have largely consisted at first of tenderly sensuous embraces. Later, she even proposed marriage. Whether they were lovers remains a matter of conjecture. What did Benjamin know about the nature of this connection at the time, busy as he was with his own affairs, with Charlotte? He did notice how the young man progressed in Germaine's favors. When, according to social custom, Prosper de Barante had called on him in Paris at the end of December 1804, Benjamin saw "a fairly distinguished young man, rather pretentious, with some of the shortcomings of the present generation . . . but retaining many liberal ideas."[21] Prosper's father had determined that his son should follow in his own footsteps and adopt a career in the service of the state, whereas Germaine, perceiving his talent, urged him to trust his instincts and pursue a career in literature. Victory went to his father: Prosper's first post would take him away from Germaine's constant influence. All the same, he would be present at the Grands Jours de Coppet, the gatherings of distinguished writers and thinkers that took place there beginning in 1805; he would also visit her during her exile in the French provinces. He would, moreover, give proof of her judgment through his notable works as a historian and his contribution to liberal politics under later regimes.

The second young man entered the scene before Prosper de Barante left it, and after a serious crisis erupted between Germaine and Benjamin. He was a dashing twenty-seven-year-old Austrian officer of Irish descent whom she had met briefly in Venice in 1805, and again on her first visit to Austria in 1808. Count Maurice O'Donnell was an extremely touchy fellow, imagining slights, readily taking offense over trifles and withdrawing into sulks that were very upsetting to Germaine, so that she was obliged to justify herself and protest her innocence. Any tender words he proferred, such as "dear child," would keep her enraptured for months. Never noted for her tact, she made a signal error in sending him, unasked, a gift of money for his equipment when he was recalled to the colors, thus seriously offending him. More explanations were needed to placate him. It seems unlikely that Benjamin knew of his existence or his importance to her.

On leaving Vienna she wrote a note to O'Donnell from Budwitz on May 23, 1808: "Dearest noble friend, *appui* [support] that cannot fail me, I confide in you with all the powers of my heart and soul: I shall see you in four months less a day, is that not so? . . . Ah! I have heard your horses approaching and I have pictured your charming face, so sad and touching, just as I saw it all day, the little red cravat, the yellow waistcoat. . . . I saw it all again in my imagination. . . . My friend, my friend, why must we be separated? We must not part: you will take me with you, everything is so easy, Poland, the ends of the earth, but not to see you, that is what is impossible!" And, of course, she meant every word—at the time of writing. Celebrated for her intelligence, she seems not to have perceived the absurdity of a distinguished middle-aged woman who is ready to jettison everything, not least her children, her friends, her *gloire*, to follow her hero to the wars like some camp follower. Later, when she is feeling ill at the second staging post, her servants place her gingerly on the grass, prompting her to write, "I thought of the protective kindness of my friend. Could all the bustling care around me equal that expression 'dear child' with which in your enchanting voice you so often addressed me! . . . You who are my life . . . Ah! I beg you never to forget that I can no longer live without you."[22] But, of course, she could.

Only a week earlier, on May 15, she had written to Benjamin from Vienna one of the rare missives to survive. It reveals the decline in their intimacy:

> I am writing to you on the eve of my departure. I am still hoping for letters from you tomorrow. When one of them arrives that is rather kind in tone it sustains me for two or three days, and then I tell myself that your mood has passed and that at the moment when my soul is resting confidently upon you perhaps I am wrong to put my trust in this. Well, God will dispose! I am returning to you with the same affection for you, one that no homage has touched even lightly, one that does not compare you with anyone else on earth; my heart, my life, everything is yours if you want it and as you want it. Think about it; I am convinced that nobody will replace Albertine and myself with you, and that you flee happiness and *gloire* on this earth by disturbing our relationship so cruelly, by not using the kind of delicacy that so restores the spirit and makes it content with itself.

There follows some gossip about the visit to Vienna of Mlle George, Napoleon's favorite actress and mistress, about her own friendship with the egregious cosmopolitan Prince de Ligne, about the lack of wit in Viennese conversation. Then she writes, "This year I want to work night and day. Perhaps that will do my soul some good; but in my opinion I shall only know true good to the soul if you treat me with tenderness: that is all I desire."[23]

In this letter to Benjamin she complains about his change of tone and lack of tenderness, but she also strikes a note of disillusion and doubt about his attachment to her. Her words look truthful in one respect: she claims that she does not compare him with anyone else, that her esteem is unchanging, that she retains the sense of a special relationship with him. In that regard her affection for Benjamin can indeed be said to be "the same." She has been touched, however, by the gallantry and *galanterie* of dashing Maurice O'Donnell, her present imagined *appui* (compared with Benjamin, who has failed her in this role), the friend of her heart, the confidant of her soul. Just one week later she will say to Maurice, "You who are my life . . . I can no longer live without you," after having assured Benjamin that "my heart, my life, everything is yours if you want it." What to believe? She must know that the relationship with Maurice, who is about to depart with the Austrian armies, just as she is about to leave for Coppet, is unlikely to be permanent. These phrases of deep feeling, outward signs of the sensibility valued and favored in the eighteenth century and propagated especially by Jean-Jacques Rousseau, the author to whom she had devoted her early study, rise easily when she is speaking or writing, and prove soothing to her in spite of the harsh realities of experience. Germaine once admitted to Albertine Necker de Saussure that "when she held her pen in her hand she was carried away." Benjamin offers a more jaundiced view of veracity in *Adolphe:* "There is no total unity in man, and hardly ever is anyone quite sincere or quite insincere."[24] This subtle epigram is remarkably convenient for himself as well as for his antihero.

Just as Benjamin did not know the full extent of her amorous episodes, Germaine did not know that by the time of her 1808 letter he was set on marrying Charlotte, who had become his mistress. "Charlotte has yielded," he noted triumphantly in a diary entry from October 1806. "Consequently 1." This remark was soon followed by "1 for the second time, no possible doubt on this occasion." There are frequent allusions to 1 (sexual satisfaction) and to 12 (love for Charlotte).

"Love took hold of me again in all its violence. I did not believe my old heart to be capable of such feeling," he wrote in November. He experienced again "the delirium of love," "the delirium of the senses."[25] What a contrast there was between Germaine with her tantrums and Charlotte, who was all sweetness and light, tranquility, humility, and modesty! Charlotte was an "adorable angel," the source of his sexual fulfillment and happiness. Life with Germaine could never be the same again.

There was, admittedly, the little matter of Charlotte's marriage to Alexandre du Tertre, who was making difficulties. She would have to return to Germany for the purpose of gaining her divorce from her second husband. And then, of course, as a twice-divorced woman, she would risk being rejected by society, a risk that made Benjamin hesitate more than once. Germaine discovered Benjamin's relationship (as she surmised) with another woman when he refused to show her the letter he was writing and burned it. But it seems unlikely that he then confessed to her the true nature of his involvement; he would have had to reveal his promises to Charlotte and his marriage plans. There were stormy scenes enough: what if Germaine had known everything? He prevaricated for months. He did not like dissimulation, but he went on dissimulating, telling himself that he behaved in this manner out of affection for Germaine. But there were other reasons as well, not least his uncertainty about whether he was acting wisely, and his sense that he could be cementing his union with Charlotte simply to rid himself of his bond with Germaine.

On June 5, 1808, only a few weeks after the exchange of letters between Germaine and Benjamin in May, he and Charlotte were secretly married at his father's house at Brevans. Though conducted by a Protestant pastor, the marriage was not strictly legal, but it provided the fait accompli he needed to make his escape from Germaine. The marriage was kept secret partly because Charlotte's divorce was not yet signed and sealed, and partly because Benjamin could not bring himself to tell Germaine, who would remain in the dark for another eighteen months.

Before this denouement, the secret marriage to Charlotte, a crisis had arisen between Germaine and Benjamin. This was in 1807, before her visit to Vienna, her intense flirtation with Maurice O'Donnell, and her meeting with Friedrich von Gentz, one of Napoleon's most active opponents, an encounter that came to the ear of the emperor, as everything did, and caused him to take even more seriously her place in the political opposition to his rule. Germaine hoped that her novel, *Corinne ou l'Italie*, published on May 1, 1807, and acclaimed by the public if not by the critics, would merit Napoleon's esteem. Far from it: he was extremely displeased that although he was crowned king of Italy during the time she traveled and resided there, his name and his resounding deeds were not mentioned. He was also annoyed when he read—or was informed about—passages that appeared to be derogatory; for instance, when Corinne is on her way to be crowned for her art in the Capitol in Rome, it is said that "her victorious chariot cost nobody any tears," words taken as an oblique allusion to the large number of those killed in his conquest of Italy.[26]

Benjamin disapproved of political allusions of this kind, and he prided himself on the fact that none could be found in his play *Wallstein*. After having consulted those he knew who were familiar with his republican views and the state of his relations with the imperial regime, he told Claude Hochet in December 1807, "Indeed, I have taken great care to avoid anything like an allusion. With my kind of talent I do not go looking for them, because in my opinion they detract from the true and lasting merit of a literary work."[27] This judgment offers an oblique criticism of the author of *Corinne* and her intentions as a politically committed writer.

In the spring and summer of 1807 Coppet was at its most brilliant: a gathering of princes, diplomats, writers, and other notabilities from France, Switzerland, and the rest of Europe figured among the guests. Germaine required Benjamin's presence at her court; if he delayed, she sent Schlegel to fetch him or, as on one occasion, dispatched her majordomo Eugène with her carriage. Benjamin, humiliated and bitterly resentful, felt obliged to comply: he returned to Coppet to endure scenes of reproach and invective, interspersed with moments of tender reconciliation.

With the assistance of some of her guests, her children, and a servant or two, Germaine indulged her passion for the theater and arranged a series of remarkable performances, fully staged with painted curtain backdrops and splendid costumes, at Coppet and also in Geneva, which were attended by all her friends and the local gentry. She usually chose tragedies by Racine or Voltaire, or sometimes even composed the plays herself. It was in her favorite role as Racine's tormented Phèdre, bewailing her fate in her doomed passion for her stepson Hippolyte, that Germaine excelled: she could figure admirably as the fated prey of the implacable goddess Venus, a victim who ends her agonies by taking poison. Another performance of hers that impressed her audience deeply was in Racine's *Andromaque*, with Juliette Récamier as Hector's grieving widow, herself as Hermione, and Benjamin as Pyrrhus. When the impassioned princess Hermione, betrayed by Pyrrhus, her betrothed, rails against him in her fury, Rosalie de Constant thought that Germaine and Benjamin came perilously close to their own personal predicament: how could the two of them dare to put what was happening to them so blatantly before the public? Indeed, it almost looks as if the passion of Phèdre or Hermione seized hold of the self-dramatizing Germaine in her fiery arguments with Benjamin.

Meanwhile, he had decided to put forth his case and convince the influential members of his family, especially his aunt, Mme de Nassau, for he reckoned that in order to placate society, which strongly disapproved of divorce, he would need them to acknowledge and accept his marriage to the twice-divorced Charlotte. He chose as his "sole" confidante and adviser his sharp-witted, disabled cousin Rosalie, who was fond of gossip, unmarried, and presumably inexperienced in matters of the heart. She was a rather sober and correct person who had never taken to "*la trop célèbre,*" despite Germaine's sometimes tactless attempts to win her friendship. Benjamin trusted that Rosalie would convey a sympathetic account of his difficulties to his aunt. He revealed to his cousin what he felt she needed to know for his purpose, though it could not be the whole truth of his long, intricate, confused, confusing, and complex involvement with Germaine. In choosing Rosalie as his confidante he did not take into account the effect on her: "His situation, the sort of share in it that he has given me through his confidence, torments me more than I say or allow to be seen," she told her brother Charles.[28]

It was only considerably later that he would admit to Claude Hochet the part played by faults of his own: "Now that the whole struggle is over, I am ready to recognize that it is the faults of my character, as much as other circumstances, that prevented our relationship from always being smooth, and I should suffer much more to see her misjudged because of me than if I were being misjudged because of her." He would make a similar admission to Rosalie: "Perhaps there are faults on my side, and if there are wrongs on hers, let them rest buried in silence. It is not at her expense that I would wish to justify myself."[29] His admission to his cousin about his shortcomings was rather less gracious than that to his friend. These confessions, however, lay in the future.

On August 31, following his aunt's advice, Benjamin took the drastic step of delivering an ultimatum to Germaine: they must either marry at once or agree to an amicable separation. He told Rosalie the unfortunate result: Germaine was outraged. She called her children— along with Schlegel—and in their presence she accused Benjamin of compromising their position in life and their inheritance. At this, he furiously declared that he would never marry her. With dreadful cries she sank to the floor, whereupon he did his best to console her. According to his diary, the very next morning at seven o'clock, he saddled a horse and rode headlong to Rosalie, who lived with her aunt, Mme de Charrière-Bavois, outside Lausanne. They took him into their care and tried to calm him.

Soon, according to Rosalie's account to her brother Charles, Germaine arrived, after looking for Benjamin everywhere. Rosalie found her lying on the staircase, her hair outspread, her bosom uncovered, crying, "Where is he? I must find him." She was carried into the drawing room. Benjamin, hearing Germaine's voice, came to the door. She ran toward him, sank into his arms, and then collapsed, uttering wild reproaches. To Rosalie's astonishment, Benjamin meekly followed Germaine back to Coppet. He promised to stay with her for six or eight weeks until she was due to leave for Vienna.

Rosalie could not believe her eyes and ears. He talked about "a power stronger than his own and as though moved by this dreadful last proof of love." She declared indignantly that she would never see "that woman" again or mention her name. Much as she admired *Corinne*, she insisted, "I have even taken a vow never to read what she writes. A woman who puts herself in the position I saw, who yields to such uncontrollable passions, degrades all the intelligence she may have."[30] The whole incident is seen through Rosalie's censure. It was only later, on reflection, that she understood to what extent Benjamin had been parsimonious with the truth and had made her his dupe. On the back of a letter she left a note, written in the third person, that expressed her disillusion: "He had the art of deceiving all his partisans, without being untrue to them. He deceived R[osalie] more than all the others, and she judged him to be weak and indecisive so as not to admit to herself that she was a dupe."[31] She now realized that there was far more to his relationship with Germaine than he had chosen to admit to her.

Charlotte, meanwhile, was expected to wait patiently, being reassured by his promise that he would never abandon her. Yet he would return time and again to Coppet, or wherever Germaine found herself in her provincial exile, even when Charlotte was ill, drawn as if by a magic power, he said, and possibly also by Germaine's interesting guests and the lively activities that were always going on in her circle. Like so many others whose talents she fostered, he acknowledged that he profited from her invaluable criticism, which was said to be always thorough, impartial, and positive: it proved to be of great benefit to him. No creature defended her young more fiercely than Germaine did the works written by her friends: she regarded his play *Wallstein* as a masterpiece, sharply reproving one of her associates who ventured to judge otherwise, and she did everything she could to promote it.

That there had been, for some time, a change in Benjamin's attitude was obvious to Germaine, especially after the burning of his letter to prevent her reading it, and this was confirmed after his hasty early morning departure from her home. Despite her secret longstanding involvement with Prosper de Barante, and also her flirtation with Maurice O'Donnell, she went on assuring Juliette Récamier that Benjamin was the one she loved: "my heart is always his"; "I feel I love him more every day"; "I would rather he blew out my brains than that he should abandon me"; "without exaggeration I can say that I should die if he left me."[32] Always there was the threat of death that so intimidated Benjamin, but as Sismondi once pertinently observed, she did not carry it out. She needed Benjamin, not just for his presence, his wit, his contribution to entertaining and meaningful conversation, but also for his advice on all kinds of subjects. So why did she drive him away with her violent reproaches? What had he said or done—or omitted to say or do—that caused her such anger?

In essence, they inhabited distinct realms. She was all emotion and openness—not that she was above guile of a political sort to make a case—and whatever was in her heart rose to her lips. Very often the outpouring led to dramatic excess. Germaine doubtless had reason to feel that she had "made" Benjamin, having brought him to France, introduced him to her influential friends, lauded him, encouraged him to take his first steps on the political ladder, taught him all she knew, entrusted him with her person and her innermost secrets, and aided him intellectually and materially. If he failed to show proper appreciation for all she had done for him, he was nothing but an ingrate. Benjamin knew all of that perfectly well—it formed part of his many difficulties in trying to withdraw from her web of enchantment—but he also felt that over the years he had done an enormous amount to repay his debt, by attending to her every whim, carrying out her errands in Paris, sharing her exile, sacrificing (as he believed) his career and his peace of mind, and much else. In short, he was tired of being grateful. He was not hard-hearted, but, like her, he had his vanity. He was not an open, emotional character: if something was on his mind he seethed inwardly, bitterly, and resentfully, and he mulled over it incessantly. Ultimately, he wanted an escape from the dominion of her pain; he wanted to be a free agent.

She could not help being aware of the problems between them, but she did not want to acknowledge the truth. "Benjamin tells you that I am annoyed with him," she commented to Juliette Récamier. "My God! I have only one sorrow but it is a cruel one: it is the fear of not being loved. If I believed I was loved all the miseries of my life would disappear. But neither he, nor you, nor anyone else will tell me the truth about that, and I myself feel that I cannot provoke the truth because it would hurt me so much if it was not what I want to hear."[33] The fear of not being loved explains much of her conduct.

Following Benjamin's secret marriage to Charlotte at Brevans in June 1808, he was determined to keep the knowledge from Germaine. The second Mme Constant had a great deal to endure. When he was at Les Herbages he came to Paris to visit his wife secretly, as if she were his mistress. While he was at Coppet, Charlotte stayed at the inn at Sécheron. After many months of this kind of separation, realizing that Benjamin was unlikely ever to bring himself to reveal their marriage to Germaine, Charlotte decided to take the initiative. On May 9, 1809, using her distinguished maiden name, Countess von Hardenberg, she invited Germaine to call on her at the inn, told her the truth, and faced down her rival, who was in shock. Charlotte told Benjamin how Germaine had cried to her, "In the eyes of the Lord I am more his wife than you are."[34] Possibly to avoid Germaine's public discomfort, it was agreed that the marriage was to be kept secret. Soon, however, curiosity was aroused, and unflattering rumors about the couple flourished as tongues began to wag.

Notwithstanding Charlotte's revelation, Germaine returned to Coppet with Benjamin. He visited his wife at Brevans where she was staying with his father. When Germaine traveled to Lyons to see the great actor Talma perform, Benjamin followed her. Charlotte was in despair. Benjamin told Rosalie, "I realize perfectly how badly I am treating a really angelic creature who . . . notwithstanding her gentleness, has been ill more than once from despair. But in the depths of my heart I have some mysterious fatal attraction to another person, which means that so long as I believe her to be of good faith in her suffering or in her affection, I could easily take a violent decision to be free of a situation that weighs heavily upon me. . . . If I could discover any sign of duplicity, bad faith, malevolence, the spell would be broken. Tell me in heaven's name what you know."[35] It was as if, although married to Charlotte, he still needed proof of Germaine's infidelity or malice to feel truly liberated from her. That autumn, Germaine was still telling Juliette Récamier that she could not live without seeing Benjamin and talking with him. On December 9, he informed Rosalie about Charlotte's manifold virtues, her simplicity, equanimity, and delicacy, adding, "But sources of suffering remain from a terrible, stormy, most deep liaison that lasted fifteen years. . . . There are times when shattering, searing expressions of suffering, along with almost magical images, written in a style that resounds within a spirit accustomed to yield to them, return suddenly to tear my heart to shreds and confuse my mind."[36] So he was still very conscious of Germaine's power over him when, later that same month, he and Charlotte were united in a civil marriage in Paris that permanently ratified the private ceremony of June 1808.

The two rich fictional works that grew out of the altercations between Germaine and Benjamin in 1806–1807, *Corinne* and *Adolphe*, are both stories of an ill-fated liaison and a betrayal: Oswald betrays Corinne, Adolphe betrays not only Ellénore but also himself. Both tales end in death. Indeed, Adolphe is already dead when the manuscript in which he relates his story is discovered.

In *Corinne* the tragic outcome is signposted early. Corinne and Oswald, though originally destined for each other, are separated not only by his father's disapproval of her display of talent as a young girl but also by their opposing aspirations. The early part of the book, the scenes of the Italian journey that Germaine regarded as absolutely essential to the work, indicated her cultural and political theme of Italian regeneration, liberation, and the dream of future unity, and also provided evidence of Corinne's breadth of intellect and heart. Half-English and half-Italian, she is nothing less than a female genius, a very difficult quality for a novelist to convey as successfully as Germaine does. The depiction of such an exceptional creature—who as a woman makes use of her gifts and encourages others to emulate them—formed part of the book's originality for the readers of the day, especially women, on whom it had a liberating effect. The mysterious Corinne, who turns out to be the elder daughter of an English nobleman, has fled from a narrow-minded, mediocre, closed society that stifles her and does not appreciate her all-embracing intellectual curiosity. She has taken refuge in her mother's native land, Italy, where she is welcomed, adored, and esteemed, especially as a poet who improvises in public, a talent not too far removed from the art of conversation in which Germaine is known to excel, since it depends on the ability to speak with ease and spontaneity.

Enter Oswald, Lord Nelvil, a young Scottish officer who, interestingly, is treated as a representative Englishman, embodying the values of northern Europe as distinct from those of the south. He is accustomed to the dominance of the social proprieties that so frustrated the young Corinne; he is governed by duty and the call of an active life in the service of his country; he does not seek an exceptional wife who is renowned and who seems different from what he regards as the worthy norm. However, when he sees Corinne acclaimed in Rome he is dazzled: they fall passionately in love, she being drawn by his sensibility and his physical courage, and he by the radiance of her *gloire* and the way she awakens his imagination and offers him entry into the inspiring world of the arts. Her faithful friend, Prince Castel-Forte, warns, "Do not approach her, if you are condemned to leave her: you would search in vain, as long as you live, for the creative spirit who shared and enlarged your feelings and your thoughts, you would never find her like again."[37] Oswald is struck by these words, which prove to be prophetic.

Eventually obliged to return home to rejoin his regiment, Oswald is soon absorbed into his former way of life. He finds himself especially attracted to Lucile, Corinne's half-sister, a lovely young girl who is timid and innocent, and whose heart is "unknown to itself."[38] She is also the betrothed chosen for him by his late father. Corinne, who has followed him to England without his knowledge, realizes what is happening and generously finds a way to return his ring, thus absolving him from his promise to her. Oswald believes, or wants to believe, that she has forgotten him, and he marries Lucile. Happiness does not ensue. Meanwhile, the hapless Corinne returns to Italy, loses all interest in her own gifts, and falls into a decline. "For the sake of her own happiness, Corinne was wrong to become attached to a man who would thwart her natural existence, and repress rather than stimulate her talents," intervenes the author.[39]

After some years Oswald and Lucile, who has grown jealous of Corinne's place in his heart, visit Italy with their young daughter, Juliette. Corinne, embittered by suffering, resolutely refuses to see Oswald. Yet she says she forgives him and, at the same time, exacts what can be seen as a subtle revenge: she contrives to teach Juliette everything she knows. "She says she wants me to be like Corinne," remarks Juliette innocently.[40] The girl makes astonishing progress in Italian and music and is taught an air to be repeated every year on a particular day, to remind Oswald of a certain significant moment in his relationship with Corinne. Winning Lucile's confidence, Corinne instructs her on how to please Oswald by enlivening her conversation and showing more interest in life: "You must be you and me at the same time. . . . My only remaining wish for myself is that Oswald finds in you and his daughter some traces of my influence, and that at least he may never know a feeling of delight without remembering Corinne."[41] How could one person simultaneously be so seemingly generous and yet also so vengeful? Could the author, normally so perceptive, have been unaware of such a baleful interpretation? After Corinne's death, the wretched and remorseful Oswald, who says he loves his wife, is obliged to remember Corinne at every moment. The novel ends with the unforgiving words of the author: "Did he forgive himself for his own past conduct? Did the approval of society console him? Was he satisfied with a common fate, after what he had lost? I do not know and, in this regard, I do not wish either to blame him or absolve him."[42] The rancor that Germaine would feel for Benjamin and his choice of a wife who might be her superior in rank but was otherwise far from being her equal is already suggested in the final pages of *Corinne* with the heroine's death after intolerable suffering, an end so often promised by the author herself.

Always ready to defend Germaine and infuriated by some of the disapproving critics of the novel, Benjamin wrote three remarkable articles on *Corinne* for *Le Publiciste* on May 12, 14, and 16, 1807, shortly after the book's publication. They are largely appreciative, especially the last, but occasionally his personal feelings obtrude. In the first article he discusses the character of Corinne, whom he sees as theatrical, calling attention to "this union of qualities and faults, strength and weakness, energy of mind and sensibility of heart." He is brilliantly ironic about the moralizing critics of the novel who take issue with the merit of "enthusiasm": "Where are they then, these men so carried away by enthusiasm that it is urgent to save them from it?" he inquires sardonically.[43]

Yet while he is probing the moral effect of *Corinne*, he pens an extraordinary, eloquent passage that runs counter to the whole intent of the novel: "No work offers with greater clarity this important lesson: that the more one possesses brilliant faculties, the more one should know how to keep them under control; that when one offers to the tempestuous winds such billowing sails one should not hold a shaky helm with trembling hand; that the more numerous, dazzling and various are the gifts of nature, the more one should tread in the midst of men with mistrust and discretion; that between the rebellious spirit and an indifferent, judgmental society the struggle is unequal; and that for penetrating spirits, proud and sensitive characters, ardent imaginations, wide-ranging minds, three things are essential, on pain of seeing misfortune descend upon them: to know how to live alone, how to suffer, and how to despise."[44] The metaphor he uses, of a ship that defiantly does not trim its sails to the tempestuous winds, repeats that of an entry in his diary on June 18, 1804, with the same underlying and intense disapproval of Germaine's attitude and conduct and of her challenging political stance vis-à-vis Napoleon in comparison with his own discretion and avowed contempt. By returning to this idea in his article of May 1807, he offers a sharp public reproof to the author of *Corinne*, whom he purports to defend. Moreover, he would repeat that reproof, word for word, in his essay on Germaine published years after her death. Clearly, he meant what he said.

Worse was to come. One of the major themes of the novel is the role of the highly gifted woman artist in a disapproving, unappreciative, mediocre society, specifically that of northern England or, by extension, France as Germaine has known it. As an exceptionally talented woman she once saw herself as an Indian pariah in her book on literature. It is plain that Benjamin has little sympathy with this female role, as evidenced in his discussion of the morality of *Corinne*, where at one point he writes in the first-person singular, "Much has been written in all ages on the need to confine women in their households and to keep them in a sheltered, humble, and circumscribed sphere, and in general I, too, believe in this need."[45] And this is the public declaration of the longstanding companion of a celebrated female writer. Besides, he adds, the author of *Corinne* does not assert anything different. In confirmation of this statement he has the gall to quote Corinne's conventional stepmother, the bane of the heroine's youth. This passage accords with his views on the primacy of a quiet domestic life of the sort that he formerly considered with Amélie Fabri and Antoinette de Loys and that, at the time of writing, he hoped to share with the compliant Charlotte. Whatever admiration he expresses for the novel in his articles, it appears that its true drift toward raising the consciousness of women does not appeal to him in the least.

Then, in the second article, Benjamin comes to the character of Oswald, and he finds an echo of himself in the novel. (He was not alone: Prosper de Barante also saw himself portrayed as Oswald, but unlike Benjamin he was mightily annoyed.) As if seeing himself in the mirror, Benjamin chooses to define the vulnerable Lord Nelvil as "a mixture of timidity and pride, sensibility and indecisiveness, taste for the arts and love for a regular life, attachment to common views and inclination toward enthusiasm." Once Corinne and Oswald have met, "they cannot be happy together; they will no longer be able to be happy apart." This comment applies aptly to the current state of his liaison with Germaine. "Oswald travels through Italy with Corinne and sees all its marvels. Her eloquent language, her musical voice, her poetic enthusiasm enhance everything with supernatural splendor. But in the midst of this delirium that overturns his heart and his senses, Oswald remembers his native land, his duties, the career set out for him." He is charmed without being subjugated, never satisfied with himself, full of regrets. "This poetry, these fine arts, these pictures, this music seem to him to be life's adornments, but he asks where life itself, active life, useful and nobly fulfilled, is to be found and he seeks it in vain."[46] Benjamin allows his own dissatisfaction, hesitation, frustrated ambition, and regret to pierce through his résumé of Oswald's responses. Moreover, along with the matter of a career, he considers Oswald's encounter with the virginal Lucile to be a powerful element in his absorption into his destined way of life.

Adolphe, qualified by Benjamin as an anecdote or a novel, gives an account of a liaison from which all reference to female genius, an idea that is central to *Corinne,* has been expunged. No wonder, then, that Germaine claimed to find no allusion to herself in its pages. Adolphe is a timid young man who wants to have a liaison because he thinks it is the thing to do, like the youthful Benjamin, who, at Erlangen, took a mistress he did not love. Quite deliberately he sets his sights on Ellénore, a Polish lady ten years his senior with no intellectual pretensions. Ellénore, after falling on hard times, had spent many years as the mistress of a nobleman, had children by him, served his interests with exemplary devotion, and contrived, precariously and with difficulty, to win respect in local society. Clearly, in much of its detail, this account is reminiscent of the life story and outlook of Anna Lindsay. At first Ellénore rejects Adolphe's attentions, but she is moved by his assiduity and soon is overcome by a passion such as she has never experienced before. He becomes her lover, and although he was merely feigning love at the start, in time he genuinely grows to feel it. For a brief while he is in ecstasy. Though Adolphe never envisaged a permanent union with her, he is drawn into a web of lies and half-truths when Ellénore willfully leaves the sanctuary of her protector and abandons her children to be with him. In so doing, she sacrifices all the respect she has gained through years of discretion. His love for her quickly fades.

It is from this point, as Adolphe, mired in Ellénore's pain, struggles in vain to be free of her, that the tale bears some resemblance to the stormy scenes between Benjamin and Germaine—scenes filled with words that mean something other than they say, words that once spoken cannot be retracted. Yet when Ellénore ceases to be an "aim" and becomes a "tie" and then a "burden," when she feels threatened and grows ever more demanding, she is following a course that Benjamin believed to be standard in all such liaisons, as he once maintained to Julie Talma. Adolphe regrets his failure to pursue a career suited to his station and dreams of marriage to some pure young girl—the Lucile figure, as it were.

The subtle strategies that Adolphe employs in his vain effort to break free, his attempts at self-justification that turn against him, provide one source of the tale's enduring power. By staying with her out of compassion he is doing her a disservice, because it is not his pity but his love that she needs. When, finally, Ellénore discovers that he has not told her the truth, that he does not love her, she falls ill and dies. Adolphe, however, does not enjoy his freedom: "How this liberty that I had missed so much weighed upon me! . . . I was indeed free, but I was no longer loved: in everyone's eyes I was a stranger."[47] He does not adopt a career or assume the position in society that is said to be rightfully his; he suffers from regret and remorse and dies alone. The liaison on which he embarked so casually and so thoughtlessly is seen as a destructive force for both Adolphe and Ellénore. The novel reflects the author's feelings of entrapment at the moment of writing.

Unlike Corinne and Adolphe, their creators did not conveniently die: the conclusion of their long liaison was to be far more messy. If his civil marriage in Paris marked in a sense the end of their intimacy, which had grown so fractured, it was far from being the end of their connection. For a good while they continued to meet at intervals and write to each other. Eventually they went their separate ways, until public events brought them together on the same side. Benjamin might feel torn, but he had the freedom he had so wanted. Germaine might be resentful, but she was not one to break with friends. Her musical voice, the web of her enchantment, her image would pursue him.

CHAPTER EIGHT

❧ *The Flight to Freedom* ☙

AS FREEDOM OF EXPRESSION WAS STIFLED with growing consistency under Napoleon's authoritarian rule, Germaine and Benjamin would, separately, make their escape abroad—but in very different circumstances. Benjamin took flight into what he called voluntary exile in an attempt to recover his personal freedom. Germaine, on the other hand, was forced into exile by persecution and by threat to her very existence.

At a time when there was genuine despotism and oppression, when some were languishing in prison for years without trial while others were summarily banished at the ruler's arbitrary command, Benjamin spoke of the "tyranny" and "despotism" of Germaine. In the wider context of oppression under Napoleon's regime, the word "despotism" seems excessive. Even Benjamin was aware of the word's strength. For instance, the original title of his later powerful attack on Bonaparte's dictatorship was *De l'esprit de conquête et du despotisme*, but he decided to substitute the word *usurpation* for *despotism*. As he told Charles de Villers, he thought *despotism* was possibly shocking and risky. Yet he did not consider it too shocking to use about Germaine.

He bared his soul to his friend Claude Hochet on the theme of

Germaine's behavior after she sent Schlegel to bring him back to Coppet from his father's house at Brevans. "Life is unbearable with this despotism," he wrote, "and the lingering feelings of affection that I preserve as a precious relic of [an association of] 12 years, collapse under this heavy and troubling weight of a tyranny that yields neither to reason nor pity."[1] Benjamin had not the temperament to be like "that madman" Schlegel, who had actually signed a declaration that he was Germaine's slave for life, and who regarded her as a "supernatural being" whose happiness should be everyone's first consideration.

Having somehow become aware of this accusation of despotism, Germaine denied that she was despotic: "Ah! My dear friend," she confessed to Juliette Récamier in one of her dazzling flashes of lucidity, "how painful is the incompleteness of feelings! I am a person with whom and without whom one cannot live, not that I am despotic or bitter, but I appear to everyone to be something strange that is worth both more and less than the ordinary course of life."[2] Her "despotism" was simply the force of character of an extremely strong-willed woman who was always throbbing with energy, always active, always demanding in her expectations and her quest for reassurance that she was loved as she wished to be. This mostly futile quest led to her bizarre strategy of juggling two or more love objects, soul mates, or suitors at the same time. She could be coolheaded in deducing general ideas from her observations and experiences, but she was already at times frenetically "Romantic" in the manner of the generation to come. On the contrary, Benjamin was usually cautious, a lifelong gambler who calculated the risks. He might have his frenzied moments, but he was not energetic; indeed, he often blamed himself for being lazy— rather unjustly, because usually he was busy writing, and he carried with him everywhere a trunk full of his unpublished manuscripts. Sometimes he needed prodding—but he did not always want to be prodded.

His sufferings were caused not only by his deteriorating eyesight, which sustained damage in his youth from voracious reading, and by a painful eye operation in the days before chloroform, but also by his chronic indecisiveness as much as by Germaine's conduct. In his misery he turned for advice to a quietist sect known as the *Âmes Intérieures*, or Inner Spirits. Its leader was his cousin, Charles de Langallerie, who opined that Germaine was the cross that Benjamin had to bear and counseled submission to God and the complete abnegation of the will. Benjamin did his best to put this difficult advice into practice, hoping for a similar conversion on Germaine's part that might rid him of her. She, too, became interested in mysticism at this time, but she remained uncommitted. So did he. He said he felt calmer, though, and took to peppering his diary with the initials "L v d D s f" — *"La volonté de Dieu soit faite,"* or "God's will be done."

Since he compared any woman in whom he expressed an interest with Germaine, he was drawn to contrast her with Charlotte, the long-suffering, compliant, softly feminine "angel." This comparison would lead him to his first full description of Germaine's appearance: it figures in his novel *Cécile*, an incomplete attempt to make amends to his second wife for the cavalier way he had treated her. Germaine, it will be recalled, had found Benjamin's appearance most unattractive when they first met, though perhaps she overdid her distaste for Ribbing's benefit. Did Benjamin feel the same about her? "In stature," wrote Benjamin of Mme de Malbée / Germaine, "short rather than tall, and too stocky to be slim, irregular and over prominent features, a not very pleasing complexion, the most beautiful eyes, fine arms, rather overlarge but strikingly white hands, a splendid bosom, excessively swift movements and poses that were too masculine, a very soft voice that broke in moments of feeling in an extremely touching way — all this formed a whole that struck one unfavorably at first glance, but became irresistibly seductive when Mme de Malbée spoke and became animated."[3] The stockiness, the beautiful eyes, the enchanting voice, the way her speech could make people forget any deficiencies in her appearance are all confirmed by many other witnesses. Curiously, although Benjamin had always stressed his admiration for her outstanding qualities of heart and mind, in this portrait he now reveals a certain distaste for the "man-woman" who featured in his diary when he was in a rage with her as well as for the virile aspects long attributed to women who were intellectually gifted.

After Benjamin's definitive marriage to Charlotte in Paris in December 1809, the couple did not depart at once, as might have been expected. On the contrary, early in 1810 Benjamin returned alone to Coppet, where he remained for several months while he and Germaine hammered out an arrangement of their complex financial affairs. The matter of the somewhat equivocal shared ownership of the house on the rue des Mathurins, for instance, was settled. In an agreement written in his own hand and signed also by Germaine, Benjamin acknowledged that he owed her eighty thousand francs. This large sum did not have to be repaid immediately—which was just as well, for he was about to flounder under the huge gambling debts that would force him to sell Les Herbages, his furniture, and many of his books—but it was to be left to her in his will. As Germaine would discover afterward when she consulted a lawyer, this document was not valid because, being a woman, she was a minor in the eyes of the law.

"Now that the struggle is over," Benjamin told Hochet in the spring of 1810, "I should like to erase from my memory and that of everybody else any bitterness in a liaison that so many ties of heart and mind could not save from the abyss where all liaisons are engulfed. It will not be my fault if at the least an affectionate and long-standing friendship does not survive."[4] He could adopt a lordly, moralizing, philosophical stance now that the end was at last in sight and his life was "out of her empire." For Germaine, however, serious troubles were looming on the horizon, in which Benjamin would play at first a lesser role as her support or adviser, and then no role at all.

That summer, having left his wife elsewhere, Benjamin spent a month in the Loire valley at the beautiful château of Chaumont that Germaine had rented from its current owner, an American citizen. She was living there in internal exile, as banishment from Paris was called, entertaining a large company of distinguished visitors as well as correcting the proofs of the book on which she had been working for six years, ever since she had the first idea for it in the form of letters from Germany in 1803. She had been reading widely for it, thinking about it, discussing it, and seeking advice from writers and scholars with knowledge of German culture. No doubt Benjamin, given his long stay in Germany in his youth and his familiarity with the German language, was consulted, though Schlegel, employed for the purpose, played a larger part in the book's composition. Benjamin told her that he thought *De l'Allemagne* was a fine work. Parts of it were unequalled, in his opinion. He praised it to Prosper de Barante: "It is a superb monument of the nineteenth century, perhaps the last."[5] This is a curious remark, considering that the century was in its infancy. Significantly, however, he did not allude to the outstanding importance of *De l'Allemagne* as a landmark in European literature in his writings on Germaine during her lifetime, though he would refer to it, briefly, immediately after her death. Benjamin had literary ambitions of his own; he wrote works in verse like the forthcoming *Le Siège de Soissons,* and he was a perceptive literary critic. With his interest in the "ferment" in German religion, philosophy and culture, the subject was, in theory at least, one that he himself might have chosen to treat, but he did not.

De l'Allemagne was written with high enthusiasm, the virtue on which Germaine expatiated in her moving final pages. Delightedly, she had found treasure in Germany, and, as always, she was eager to share it with her readers. It was not that her admiration was unalloyed: for example, she disapproved of a tendency in German society to submit supinely to authority. Yet by offering so much that was new and inspiring on which to reflect, the book would long prove a mine of information and enlightenment, to be plundered by her successors.

The very concept of *De l'Allemagne*, however, the work on which she pinned such high hopes, could not be gratifying to the imperial regime, which had no truck with freedom of thought. What was all this praise of Germany, a country that France had conquered? The author's failure to mention the emperor and his victories was offensive in itself. The French empire was the summit of civilization: its *gloire* and grandeur were paramount. Besides, the great writers of the age of Louis XIV, like Molière and Racine, could not be surpassed, so why look abroad for inspiration? To do so was simply unpatriotic. While Germaine had long recognized the supreme merits of seventeenth-century French literature, she felt that the modern age required a modern art, just as Benjamin would argue that it required a modern form of government. The whole work was libertarian in spirit; it was also full of political allusions that needled the powers that be. For instance, it was evident to readers accustomed to looking for such allusions that Napoleon was to be included among the tyrants Germaine described who abuse power, like Attila the Hun, and leave behind nothing but dust.

The fate of *De l'Allemagne* was about to be sealed. Censorship laws were reinforced in February 1810. In June, the minister of police, Fouché, duc d'Otrante, was replaced. He had treated Germaine relatively leniently despite being constantly admonished by Napoleon to take firm measures against that "bird of ill omen," Mme de Staël, and execute at once the decree of forty *lieues*. His successor, General Savary, duc de Rovigo, was firmly determined to obey Napoleon's wishes to the letter and implement the law.

The censors passed the first two volumes of *De l'Allemagne*, but troubles began while Germaine was correcting the third volume. By then she had moved from the château of Chaumont to a mansion at Fossé. From Paris on September 6, 1810, Benjamin wrote to her there, wishing to reassure her and also to entertain her. He said he could find out nothing of importance about the censors; also, he approved of the way her factotum, Eugène, was dealing with the matter, but he urged her to return the corrected proofs to the publisher as soon as possible. He thought that some articles he had read in *Le Publiciste* written by François Guizot (the future liberal leader) offered similar views to hers and that many people appeared to be in need of them, "so weary, stupefied, stifled are they by the opposite." And he went on amicably if somewhat ambiguously: "Your letters are what has most influence on my interior life, and you keep me in a perpetual sequence of sensations and emotions of all kinds. On receiving one I never know how I shall be after having read it." And he concluded, "*Adieu, chère amie,* I love you tenderly. I am eager to see your fine work appear and to be associated in thought with all the success you will have with the good part of humanity. *Rari nantes*" —words from a line in Virgil's *Aeneid* that allude to Aeneas and his few companions who escape from shipwreck, and that point here to a surviving elite of rare spirits capable of appreciating her.[6] Who would imagine that he was addressing a woman he had described only a couple of months earlier as a tyrant and a despot?

Germaine rallied all her friends to intervene with the authorities on her behalf. She even imagined that a letter to the emperor requesting an audience with him would resolve the matter. Then the blow fell: Rovigo, in the crudity of his zeal, ordered her to leave Fossé within forty-eight hours; the manuscript and all the proofs of *De l'Allemagne* were to be confiscated at once. On October 6, Napoleon himself personally gave the order for all copies of the work to be pulped, although he would later find it politic to deny his involvement. After all those years of effort she was being condemned to silence. What could be worse for a writer? Ever resourceful, with the aid of her son Auguste, she managed to conceal all the pages that mattered; she took them with her to Coppet and finally to England, where the book was published in 1813, while Schlegel carried a set of proofs to Vienna.

Being reluctant to leave France she lingered on the return journey to Coppet. She invited Benjamin to come to meet her at Briare, in the Loiret. He arrived with his wife on October 10, presumably much embarrassed to find himself between two jealous women, each ready to be offended by anything he might say or do. As Germaine chose to see it for the benefit of Juliette Récamier, "My two days at Briare have been really odd. There I had proof, proof positive, that Benjamin still loved me, and that he was unhappy with his lady wife and she with him." He did not respond sympathetically, however, to expressions of pain—they were, in effect, the one way to put him on his guard. She claimed that during their recent separation, "he has passionately felt need of me."[7] Although not entirely dissatisfied with the two-day encounter, she wanted Juliette to reassure her that she was right in her impression of the poor state of the Constant marriage, an impression that was, perhaps, somewhat premature.

There was one consolation for Germaine in the midst of all her troubles, weighed down as she was by the cruel attempt to silence her. In November 1810 she met a young officer of hussars, John Rocca, who promptly fell in love with her. He was very handsome, with dark curly hair and large dark eyes. Naturally, tongues wagged over the difference in their ages: at twenty-three he was nearer in age to her elder son Auguste than to Germaine, who was then forty-four. A well-born Genevan, the dashing Rocca had returned from fighting in Spain after being gravely wounded near Ronda; indeed, his health never fully recovered. He was endowed with the prestige of the uniform and the military glamor that had always attracted her, whether in Narbonne, Ribbing, or O'Donnell. What did it matter if he was neither a brilliant intellect nor a great conversationalist like Benjamin? He was utterly devoted to her. She spoke to Claude Hochet of his "most extraordinary devotion."[8]

When Benjamin visited Coppet—as he said, twice in three months— the susceptible young swordsman took umbrage at what he considered Constant's excessive attentiveness to Germaine and his tone of easy familiarity when conversing with her. Impetuously, Rocca challenged him to a duel. Whereas years before, in a similar situation, Benjamin had bequeathed all his worldly goods to Germaine, he now bequeathed them in due form to his wife. There was no mention of the debt of eighty thousand francs to be repaid to Germaine on his demise. He penned a note of eulogy to Charlotte, asking his angel's pardon; declaring his true, deep, unalterable love for her; and expressing his gratitude. His note for Germaine was far less warm: "I forgive Mme de Staël for the outcome for which she served as pretext and I do not hold her responsible for the rage of a young madman. Likewise I beg her to forgive me if, at certain times, I have caused her any distress. I do not question whether I was in the wrong or the right; to have pained her is enough to make me feel remorse about it."[9] The phrase "whether I was in the wrong or the right" sounds grudging; after all, this might have been his last communication with her. Somehow the contestants were appeased, however, and the duel did not take place. Later on, Rocca would challenge him once more, but again no blood was spilled.

Benjamin spent his last evening at Coppet—without Charlotte— on April 18, 1811. At the beginning of May, in the presence of a pastor, Germaine de Staël and John Rocca solemnly promised to marry when circumstances were propitious—a binding engagement in sight of God that was to be kept secret. Certainly, Benjamin was not told about it. On May 8, on the steps of the Hôtel de la Couronne in Lausanne,

Germaine and Benjamin took leave of each other. Two years afterward, he remembered what she said to him then: that "she believed we would never meet again in this life."[10]

A week later, on May 15, he set off with Charlotte for Germany, where he would spend almost three years in voluntary exile, for no one was forcing him to leave France. At last he was free: free to devote himself to fulfilling the talent he felt he had neglected; free to engage full-time in the scholarly life of a man of letters; free to devote himself to his work on religion that would establish his literary reputation once and for all; free of his troublesome association with a notorious, strong-willed woman who was always the center of controversy and politically compromised; indeed, altogether free of politics, which he had "renounced" three years earlier; free to move at his own pace; free to enjoy his ideal of a quiet domestic life with his placid wife, Charlotte; and free of all the emotional dramas and traumas he had experienced for so long with that fiery whirlwind Germaine.

Benjamin might have renounced politics, but he could not suppress his thoughts and responses to the situations he encountered in the course of what was otherwise a fairly uneventful journey. As he reported to his cousin Rosalie, in Strasbourg he met on quite amicable terms the marquis de Barthélemy's secretary, with whom he had quarreled violently during the Directoire in 1797: "Ever since the present regime has killed off all [political] opinions, we meet again like the dead on the other bank [of the Styx] and we exist like the dead in profound peace."[11] He was ready to communicate to his intimates his view that the imperial regime had totally suppressed free speech, one of the cornerstones of his political convictions. With even more savage irony he lashed out at the repressive measures he found in Heidelberg: "The governments are more repressive than ever. Anyone poor is suspect, and at the slightest opportunity every suspect is arrested. There are twenty prisons in Heidelberg, all of them full. Because some prisoners have tried to escape they are now chained to the wall at their waist, their neck, their arms and legs. . . . They can in no way lie down and they sleep only leaning on their chains. It is convenient for the jailers. Yet it cannot be said that any distinctions are made between the guilty and the innocent; for as the courts try only those who confess, and as the innocent cannot confess to anything, these last are detained indefinitely. It is no longer war of the have-nots against the haves, but of the haves against the have-nots, and the Revolution having given them [the reactionary oppressors] the experience of fear, they use great firmness in their measures. What a nice moment for the human race!"[12] This bitterness at the treatment meted out to the innocent and the defenseless poor demonstrates that Benjamin—like Germaine, who was judged tireless in her active compassion for the underdog—was concerned with their fate.

Once in Germany, he found that innkeepers insisted on calling him "Baron de Constant." He arrived at the ancestral home of the Hardenbergs to discover that Charlotte's relatives were all ministers, leading officials, and favorites at the court of Westphalia. He was the only person present who did not sport an embroidered coat, a sash, and the ribbon of an order. The castle, though somber in appearance, had the advantage of being very near the university town of Göttingen, which was endowed with one of the finest libraries in Europe. There he intended to consult various professors, philosophers, and authorities on religion and to complete his magnum opus on the subject. He proposed to rent an apartment and see Charlotte two or three times a week, but she insisted on coming to stay with him in Göttingen.

At first, everything seemed to fulfill his high expectations, and he was full of enthusiasm. His work was going well and, as he reported to friends and relatives, he was perfectly happy with his angelic wife, whose virtues he listed. After a while, though, his tone changed. The work was not always going so well. There was nobody to talk to except one Frenchman he knew from the journey to Metz with Germaine in 1803, Charles de Villers, an authority on Kant, who was not a cheerful man. There was no social life, he complained, no conversation, no lightness of touch, no wit of the sort found in Paris or at Coppet. German professors worked solidly all day in the library, and in the evening they returned to their wives and stayed at home. They might be perfect examples of that ideal of domestic life that he had pursued for so long—but how tedious that life was in actuality! He escaped to the gaming tables for a little entertainment and excitement, and suffered heavy losses at roulette.

Worse, in his view, than the total absorption of the German professors in the pursuits of academe, was their indifference to the fate of their fellow human beings. When the news of the destruction of Moscow reached Göttingen in the autumn of 1812, he sensed its importance. "But here," he wrote to Claude Hochet, "people are so far buried in their books and in learning that, what with Villers being away, I have not been able to find a soul with whom I could talk about it. A town of 500,000 inhabitants can be blown up without a Göttingen professor lifting his eyes from his book."[13] Characteristically, Benjamin was being drawn inexorably toward the opposite of the quiet life to which he had fled so expectantly. Then the war came closer, and the quiet life turned out to be not so quiet: troops were constantly on the march tramping everywhere and even the boom of cannon could be heard.

And what of Charlotte? Once regarded as not very bright and rather lazy, she now ventured to engage with him in a dispute over politics: "Bitter quarrel with Charlotte over politics," ran the diary entry, followed by the cutting observation, "She has not two ideas to put together." Other quarrels followed and were duly noted. For instance, "Charlotte's character changed," he now thought. "What a trap marriage is! Shall I ever get out of it?" Or again: "Stupid situation! Stupid chain. Formerly I was swept away by a torrent, now I labor under a burden." The fact was that satisfaction in the bedroom had declined, and that was, after all, Charlotte's main attraction. As he confided to his diary, "Quarrel with Charlotte. If she is not my wife in the essential relationship, she will not stay long in others." And later, "Bad night because Charlotte did not want to come to bed. Among other things I got married in order to sleep with my wife a good deal and to go to bed early. I never sleep with her, or hardly ever, and we stay up until 4 o'clock in the morning." Then came a cry from the heart when Charlotte left for a visit to Kassel: "Begun my life of solitude . . . what freedom! If only I had known how to win back all that without taking on another chain."[14] Here he was again, as before with Germaine, thinking about a burden he wished to lay down and a chain he wanted to break. He was ready for something else.

Meanwhile, after Benjamin's departure for Germany, the situation grew worse for Germaine at Coppet. Napoleon had kept her under close surveillance for many years; he even had spies in her household who reported her doings and sayings. He had his eye on her wherever he was in Europe and however preoccupied with war and matters of state he might otherwise be. But her difficulties increased when a zealous petty bureaucrat named Capelle replaced Prosper de Barante's moderate father as préfet du Léman. Capelle excelled at finding ways to make Germaine's life a misery. She was confined to Coppet, permitted to travel only the short distance to Geneva. Many of her friends feared to visit her because of the stigma and because they rightly feared banishment. Two remained loyal and suffered for it: Juliette Récamier insisted on coming to see Germaine and was exiled, and Mathieu de Montmorency also hastened to Coppet and suffered the same fate.

Germaine was deeply distressed by this persecution, which also gravely affected the lives of her dearest friends. Reminded of Mary, Queen of Scots, who was imprisoned for many years before being executed, Germaine lived in dread of suffering a similar fate. Indeed, it is now known that her future imprisonment was on the agenda. Yet she could do nothing because she was pregnant. She was on the threshold of forty-six when Louis-Alphonse, her son by Rocca, was born in secrecy and seclusion on April 7, 1812. It was only after the infant was placed in the care of a discreet pastor that she could contemplate making her escape.

Napoleon's underlings had not counted on her ingenuity. On the afternoon of May 23, 1812, accompanied by Albertine and carrying only her fan, she entered her carriage and set off as if going for a drive in the immediate environs. Auguste and Rocca rode alongside. The party met with Schlegel, then made for the border. Fearfully, she was embarking on the greatest and most perilous adventure of her life, one that was to take her through Austria, Poland, Russia, and Sweden to England and freedom. It was a journey that would cement her fame and help her further to define her views and bring them to the attention of the world's leaders. No other woman of the era undertook such a task.

Benjamin, in Germany, had heard about the persecution of Germaine and felt very sorry for her. He was not exactly surprised by what was happening to her at Coppet, but he told Hochet that he was sad at not being able to share in her suffering. He foresaw that matters would go from bad to worse. When he learned of her escape, he was "stunned"—and deeply worried.

Rumors about the circumstances of Germaine's private life, and about her association with a man young enough to be her son, reached Paris and aroused disapproval. Benjamin told Claude Hochet that he knew nothing about Germaine's movements: he attributed the whole adventure of her escape and her journey to eastern Europe to her imprudence and to the influence of impulsive Rocca rather than that of Schlegel, whom he judged far too incompetent in practical matters to have conceived the enterprise and put it into effect. In fact, Schlegel had been active in the arrangements of the escape, but Benjamin had never cared much for him—a rival of sorts—and his lofty abstractions. Moreover, he observed to Hochet, whom he sought to reassure, that Germaine, "notwithstanding her fatal taste for the theatrical," was far too sensible to take on a young man like Rocca, who, "such as I know her, cannot satisfy her in any way."[15] Less a friend of hers than of her sons, Rocca was nothing but an escort, Benjamin conjectured, remarking that he was pained by her mistaken choice of a traveling companion.

Benjamin then delivered a most touching eulogy of his erstwhile companion: "She will always be, and now more than ever, sacred to me: and I can see merely an act of imprudence whose consequences she has not foreseen, in accepting the only company that was left to her at a time when her friends either abandoned her or were violently torn from her side. Consider what she was, such grace, such a wonderful mind, such ease with others, such kindness of heart, such incomparable eloquence, such a spirited and childlike temperament that made her by turns a naive and vulnerable creature and the most potent genius. There were storms in that strong and impetuous spirit; there are none in the ruts where the water is full of mud. Yet in spite of her mistakes, in spite of all the sufferings I have endured, in spite of the even more bitter ones I feel at the harm that she has done to herself, she is a shining memory, and I am very glad to have known her." He concluded in English with an adaptation of Hamlet's loving words about the uniqueness of his dead father: "Take her all in all, you'll never see the like of her again."[16] ("He was a man, take him for all in all, / I shall not look upon his like again.") This moving testimonial of Benjamin's reads rather like an obituary.

Two days after Germaine, very much alive, left Vienna, where she and her party had waited for passports, Napoleon's armies invaded Russia. After traveling through Bohemia, Moravia, and Poland, she crossed the Russian frontier at Brody on July 14, 1812. To avoid the Grande Armée it was necessary to take a circuitous route, via Kiev and Moscow, and she was one of the last foreign travelers to see the oriental splendor of the city before the Russians put it to the torch. Only recently she had undergone a late pregnancy, and yet here she was, waiting for horses, staying at execrable inns, and being offered strange food. She was always treated with extreme courtesy although the country was at war with France. On August 14 she arrived in Saint Petersburg, where she was showered with invitations and lavishly entertained by the nobility, and she engaged in talks with English diplomats, among others. The royal family welcomed her; young Tsar Alexander I received her twice in audience, discussing with her as an equal his liberal intentions, especially concerning serfdom, and relating to her what Napoleon had said to him on the raft at Tilsit. Her chief concern now was to find some way of putting an end to the emperor's tyranny.

While Germaine was enriching her imagination, seeing strange sights and customs, drawing ideas from her impressions and experiences that would figure in her gripping account *Dix années d'exil*, conversing with prominent figures among the Allies, and actively working against Napoleon, Benjamin in Göttingen was increasingly in a state of high anxiety. "I can think only of her on her travels," he confided to his diary. The fact that so far he had received no letters increased his worry. What a relief when he heard from her on July 27. "God protect her on her travels," he prayed. As he was quarreling with

Charlotte and complaining about his marriage, he noted, "How I regret Mme de Staël!" And again, "How I regret Mme de Staël more than ever!"—even, he added, with all her faults. Then, after receiving a letter from her on December 24, he wrote, "So, all is finished between us. It was what I wanted. Let us make our way alone. But do not let us be incommoded by ties that are far less charming." So much for Charlotte! A few weeks later came an even stronger note of regret: "Mme de Staël is really lost to me. I shall never recover from this."[17] Such entries in the diary are disconcerting. Was he not married to another? Had he expected Germaine to resign herself to her fate and fade away when he left with Charlotte for Germany?

It was also during these months that Napoleon suffered his first major defeat. Already, in the autumn of 1812, a conspiracy led by General Malet, although ultimately unsuccessful, had revealed that there was serious discontent and opposition in France. Then, in the winter of 1812, the long retreat of the Grande Armée from Moscow, with its terrible casualties left to die in the snowy wastes, gave the signal that the conqueror might not be invincible after all. None of this development was lost on the attentive Benjamin, nor was the news of Germaine's activity in Russia when he read about it in the press.

A royal welcome awaited Germaine when she arrived in Sweden, on September 24, 1812, where she would stay more than eight months, until June 9, 1813. At last, she felt truly free and independent. Her old friend, General Jean-Baptiste Bernadotte, had been unanimously elected Crown Prince of Sweden in 1810. He was intelligent, handsome, ambitious, and a long-standing rival to Bonaparte. Having decided to work actively toward Napoleon's downfall, Germaine urged Bernadotte to declare his opposition openly with the aim of overthrowing the dictator and becoming the head of the French government. It seemed to her that Bernadotte's republican and libertarian principles under the Consulate in 1802, when she had been very closely associated with him, made him a most suitable candidate to lead France, although it would mean replacing one general who was a military genius with another who, however high his reputation, was not. In any case she thought his rule would be preferable to the restoration of the Bourbons, which was the only other option. She became his unofficial agent and propagandist. Bernadotte found posts for her sons—Auguste in the Swedish diplomatic service and Albert as a lieutenant in the hussars—while Schlegel was appointed his secretary-cum-publicist.

With full force it struck Benjamin that he had not played his cards well and that Schlegel had managed his career more successfully. He, Benjamin, could have accompanied Germaine in her encounters with the movers and shakers of Europe; he could have been Bernadotte's aide. He would later note in his diary, "I am as preoccupied with Mme de Staël as I was 10, 8, or 4 years ago."[18] He told Prosper de Barante, "From time to time, at fairly long intervals, I dream of her and for several hours after being awake these dreams cause an unusual stir in my life, as when our soldiers pass by some great fire, at Smolensk or crossing the river Berezina."[19] These disturbing images he drew from the retreat from Moscow: the flames of the French bombardment of Smolensk, a city that the French ultimately could not hold, and the skillful escape of the remnant of the Grande Armée by means of the hastily built pontoon bridges over the Berezina. As he saw it, he had foolishly stayed with Germaine while his political career suffered through her reckless provocation of Napoleon, and he had left her when the connection would have served his ambition. If only he had persevered, his hopes for advancement would now be realized: "I did something really stupid when I broke a tie that could have been useful to me, a tie I kept when it was harmful to me."[20] By now he was in the grip of ambition, just as he had been in 1795: "I don't know what mad stirring of ambition has seized hold of me again," he wrote on October 2, 1813, and a week later, "If I want to try active life again, this is the moment."[21] That "moment" was the buildup to the battle of Leipzig, which took place October 17 to 19, 1813, and in which Napoleon's forces suffered a significant defeat. Bernadotte emerged as the man of the hour, the controversial victor and hero.

By the spring of 1813 Germaine had not heard from Benjamin for two months, nor had he heard from her. Correspondence across war-torn Europe was not an easy matter. They had not seen each other for nearly two years. Eventually, in Stockholm, she managed to find a trustworthy traveler to carry to him a veiled note of her plans, informing him of her intention to go to "Doxat et Divett" (the London branch of her Swiss bankers), meaning England. She also urged him to act: "What I do not comprehend is how your taste for letters [meaning politics] has not declared itself sooner and how it has not done so by now. I am not speaking in any way about myself, but about you. How is it that the Doxats do not tempt you; in fine, what are you doing with your rare genius? What you lack is decisiveness. . . . I do not ask for anything in my name, but cannot you do something for yourself?"[22] She reminded him of her own decisiveness and how, years before, she had not waited to be asked before hastening to Rosalie's home at Lausanne to fetch him back to Coppet with her.

When writing to Benjamin from Stockholm she knew how to appeal to his sensibility as well as goad his ambition. He was a great one for recalling anniversaries, mulling over memories, and indulging in nostalgia, especially about Albertine—"Albertine, alas!" is a common refrain in his diary. Benjamin, in response, inquired whether Germaine had forgotten him. She reassured him that she certainly had not and expressed her regrets: "Do you remember your promise that we would never be separated? I can assure you that you have let a fine career slip through your fingers, without mentioning everything else."[23]

Just as he complained to Hochet that he had nobody to talk to in

Göttingen, she told Benjamin about her sense of mental isolation—in spite of the company of charming Albertine, who also wrote to him at intervals, and a good part of the Swedish nobility, to say nothing of Rocca. Evidently, she meant that she was unable to pursue the unique ongoing conversation with Benjamin. "I always have some of your letters with me, I never open my secrétaire without holding them, I look at the address. Everything I have suffered through these lines makes me shudder, and yet I should like to receive some again. My father, you, and Mathieu [de Montmorency] remain in a part of my heart that is forever closed—there I am always suffering and, in spite of all, there I am dead and there I live—and if I were to drown [she was dreading the sea journey to England] my voice would be calling on these three names, only one of which has been fatal to me. . . . Is it possible that despair like mine was unable to keep you?"[24] Always the same litany: Benjamin has left her life in ruins, but, she adds, no more of that. How is it that she could not retain his love when she loved him so deeply? Why was he not like her present gentle companion, Rocca, so devotedly loyal? Why could not fidelity accompany supreme intelligence? Why were feelings incomplete?

When Germaine arrived in London at last on June 18, 1813, she continued to urge Benjamin to act. She had two aims in mind, one public and one private: to promote the cause of Bernadotte and freedom, and to find a distinguished English husband for Albertine, who had reached the marriageable age of sixteen. As it turned out, neither prospective British suitors nor the idea of making her life in England appealed to her daughter. Germaine had not been in England for some ten years; then, she had lived in Surrey, with Narbonne and her aristocratic friends, and was seen as just one well-known exile among the numerous French refugees who fled revolutionary excesses. Now, however, she came as a prime mover in the struggle to defend freedom and defeat Napoleon.

She was lionized. Eager to talk with her, politicians—both Tories and Whigs, all revealing a deep sense of liberty, as she told Benjamin—together with leading figures in society called on her at her hotel. Aristocrats, who were on the point of leaving London for the summer as was their custom, invited her to their great country estates, including Bowood, Althrop, and Hatfield House. She met almost everyone of interest and importance, from Lord Erskine, the distinguished lord chancellor, with whom she discussed the penal code, to Sir James Mackintosh, the celebrated polymath, who recalled the astonishing young Benjamin Constant from his days at Edinburgh University. Among the poets she encountered were Coleridge, Southey, and, not least, Byron.

As much as Byron admired her and her works, the notorious creator of Childe Harold could not resist teasing her mercilessly. He told her that "all the moral world thought that her representing all the virtuous characters in *Corinne* as being dull, commonplace and tedious, was a most insidious blow aimed at virtue, and calculated to throw it in the shade. She was so excited and impatient to attempt a refutation that it was only by my volubility I could keep her silent. She interrupted me every moment by gesticulating, exclaiming—"*Quelle idée!*" "*Mon Dieu!*" "*Ecoutez donc!*" "*Vous m'impatientez!*" . . . Had you seen her! I now wonder how I had the courage to go on. . . . She told me that *I*, above *all people*, was the last person who ought to talk of morals, as nobody had done more to deteriorate them." She was outraged "and all the more so, as I appeared calm and in earnest, though I assure you it required an effort, as I was ready to laugh outright at the idea that *I*, who was at that period considered the most *mauvais sujet* of the day, should give Mme de Staël a lecture on morals." With characteristic lordly nonchalance Byron could not bring himself to believe that so great a man as Napoleon, whom he deeply admired, knew about all the acts of persecution of which she complained or thought her of sufficient importance to be dangerous. How mistaken Byron was! All the same, while fully aware of her self-complacency and her lack of tact, he observed that "she was, notwithstanding her little defects, a fine creature, with great talents, and many qualities, and had a simplicity quite extraordinary," thus reinforcing Benjamin's view of the childlike element in her nature.[25]

And then *De l'Allemagne* was published to wide acclaim. She was living the high life in Regency society with its round of parties, routs, dinners, plays, and concerts, but that did not prevent her from reciting to Benjamin the familiar tale of his disastrous effect on her existence. Nor did the dreadful news of the death of her younger son, Albert. Always wilfull, he had quarreled with his partner during a game of cards at a spa in Germany where he was stationed, and he was killed in the ensuing duel. Byron expected her to indulge in a theatrical outpouring of emotion, but in her genuine grief she remained reticent.

Meanwhile, in spite of Germaine's prompting on the topic of Bernadotte, Benjamin appeared to be in no hurry to act: he had his reservations about the crown prince. Germaine emphasized how Bernadotte "holds you in such high regard, he has such a promising future so in conformity with our feelings." She pressed Benjamin: "Will you really do nothing for yourself, for that superior self you have taken away from me? . . . Certainly, to see you again would be to be reborn, but where and how? . . . All is lost for me, through you, by you! God forgive you! . . . I should not like to die without seeing you again, without speaking with you again as in the past."[26] However, by the time she wrote to him in this vein, on November 30, 1813, in a mixture of praise, prodding and reproach, condemnation and reconciliation, he had already joined the crown prince. Naturally, Germaine was pleased when she heard the news: "I was very moved to learn that you are with the Prince. . . . All the same, the chief difficulty remains to be dealt with, for it would be folly to hope to overturn the man [Napoleon] against the will of the nation. . . . Do whatever suits you and do not waste your rare gifts any longer, that is all I desire."²⁷ She was so gratified that she offered to help to have his book on religion published in London.

A number of factors had moved Benjamin, after many months of reflection and hesitation, to abandon caution at last and take political action. These included his dissatisfaction with Charlotte, with Göttingen, and with both the domestic and the academic style of life; as well as his realization that large cracks were appearing in the solid-seeming walls of Bonaparte's conquests, demonstrated by the resounding defeat at Leipzig—"What an overthrow! Nemesis! . . . The collapse is confirmed."—and that a change of regime was possible in France.²⁸ Finally, and not least, was the positive example of Germaine's activities in Russia, Sweden, and England, and her repeated urging that he not waste his God-given talent but instead embark on the political career for which he was destined. He left Göttingen for Hanover, where he met with Bernadotte and dined frequently with him. By November 10 he had decided to join the crown prince: "My decision is taken. I am making a declaration. One must contribute to the great work: it is a duty."²⁹ Despite further hesitation, by November 13 he was in tête-à-tête with Bernadotte, discussing what he could write to promote the cause. Yet after doing what Germaine had urged him to do, he still worried about her attitude toward him. When Schlegel arrived with news of her, Benjamin confided regretfully to his diary that "it seems that she has really forgotten me."³⁰

He produced very rapidly his sizable "pamphlet" (in effect a book), *De l'esprit de conquête et de l'usurpation dans leurs rapports avec la civilisation européenne,* an indictment of Napoleon's dictatorship and its corrupting consequences, so telling in its Orwellian detail that it holds good today for all arbitrary governments. Based on the manuscript of an earlier treatise on politics, it is also an eloquent paean to the liberty of the individual that has not lost its power. As proof of his libertarian credentials the title page listed the author as "Benjamin de Constant-Rebecque, member of the Tribunate, purged in 1802, correspondent of the Royal Society of Göttingen." In *De l'esprit de conquête*, which shows traces of Germaine's unpublished book *Des circonstances actuelles*, he demonstrated how the rise of commerce in the burgeoning nineteenth century changed everything, making wars of conquest an anachronism: what people really wanted was privacy and peace to improve their lives. The work caused a great stir and ran to several editions, establishing Benjamin Constant as a major political thinker. He was extremely gratified when Bernadotte decorated him with the Polar Star: he was "devoted to Bernadotte for life," he said.[31]

But just as Benjamin was at last proclaiming his opposition to Napoleon after a public silence of ten years, Germaine, who had certainly not kept silent throughout that period, was beginning to wish for Napoleon's survival, after having worked publicly for his downfall. Their opposite routes were due nonetheless to the same circumstances: the decline and imminent defeat of the dictator and, especially, the consequences of that fall. For Germaine the dominant fact was the presence of foreign armies on French soil.

In London, news of the Allied invasion of France was convincing Germaine that the leaders of the Coalition were not going to make any distinction between Napoleon and France, as she did: both would be united in defeat. She was in disarray. Already, the previous year, at a reception at Prince Naryshkin's estate overlooking the Gulf of Finland, she had declined to drink a toast to the defeat of France and would raise her glass only to the downfall of Napoleon. She found it very difficult to accept that they would be seen as indistinguishable. Now she began to criticize Benjamin for failing to consider this factor: "Do you not see the danger for France? Do you not feel the wind of counterrevolution that . . . will soon overturn everything in France?

. . . Is this the time to speak ill of the French, when the flames of Moscow are threatening Paris?"[32] All the confusion and mixed emotions, a jumble of the personal and the public, poured from her. In the end, however, realism would prevail. Louis XVIII himself had been living in exile in England in a mansion near Aylesbury; she had seen the corpulent figure being carried in his wheelchair at Bath, and she had not warmed to him. But prominent royalists had made tentative proposals to her; for example, the duc de Berry (son of the comte d'Artois, future Charles X) had been to see her. She told Benjamin, "I am not in bad odor with the Bourbons. If they come back one will have to submit." It seemed to her that anything was better than the anarchy and chaos experienced in the 1790s, but, she added, "they have not changed one iota, especially the members of their entourage." How she wished she could talk about it all with Benjamin! "I should so like to discuss all this with you, but what would I not like to talk to you about? . . . At least our minds will always be attuned to each other," she mused.[33]

She then returned to her theme: "It is no longer the time to incite people against the French, they are hated too much already. As for the man himself [Napoleon], what free spirit could want him to be over-thrown by the Cossacks?" She urged Benjamin to think about what he was doing, and about how a pamphlet, as distinct from a large, considered work, required close attention to the immediate circumstances: "One must not speak ill of the French when the Russians are at Langres. May God banish me from France rather than that I should be made to return there with the help of foreigners!" Whatever her criticism, though, she assured him that she would be of service to him and, in spite of everything, "I shall be your friend, you must never doubt it."[34] She wondered whether the senate could not invite Bernadotte to negotiate peace: he could be another William of Orange, the instigator of a peaceable revolution like that of 1688 in England. She encouraged Benjamin to discuss this with the crown prince. And, she inquired like everyone else, why did Bernadotte not press on alone with his army toward Paris?

The underlying complexity of her attitude toward Napoleon became apparent: admiration for the military genius vied with disdain for the oppressor and destroyer of individual liberties. Benjamin wanted her to continue exposing her ideas, and she wanted him to do the same. She wrote in March 1814, "You tell me that I am 'disinterested in my ideas,' yes, certainly I am; but as for you, your connections have made you into a chamberlain. Do you really think that Bonaparte could not appear in a gathering of princes? Forty battles are also a title of nobility. I hate the man, but I blame events that force me at this time to wish him success. Do you want France to be trodden underfoot?" She foresaw how, with the return of the Bourbons, twenty-five years of history—that is, everything from 1789—would be made into one long crime: the early principles of the Revolution to which she had always adhered would be totally condemned. She declared, "I shall do nothing against France," the country where in 1789 women had knelt on the ground as Necker passed by. "You are not French, Benjamin. All your childhood memories are not attached to this land—that is where the difference arises between you and me." To charge him with not being French must have struck him as harsh, for it was the very accusation that had dogged him and would often frustrate his political ambitions. Besides, this was an accusation that she herself, with her Swiss ancestry and Swedish husband, had not eluded, despite being born in Paris. "I feel in myself that I am right," she told Benjamin, "for my feeling is involuntary and contrary to my personal interests."[35] Her views were not consistent, but they were human: they arose from what Constant, in the essay about her that he published twelve years after her death, named her indestructible love for France.

She also assured Benjamin that Rocca—who had been kept as far as possible out of sight from high society—had changed and would behave impeccably toward him when they met again. She informed Benjamin about the nature of the relationship: "Our mutual affection is established for life, he has supported me in my misfortune with such generous and tender care that I shall never forget it." And she underlined Rocca's new malleability: "*Do not think of him as an obstacle.*" Yet in spite of this apparently happy union she could not forgo her lamentations and reproaches: "Ah! The past, the past! It is you who destroyed our lives through the instability of your character—we would be united here and leaning upon each other for support if you had not unleashed everything against me. Farewell! Be loyal to France and freedom, there is nothing without friendship."[36]

While Germaine agonized in England in the spring of 1814 Benjamin was serving as publicist for the procrastinating Bernadotte. In March 1814 he joined the crown prince at his headquarters in Liège in the Low Countries to await the advance of the Swedish army on Paris. Then, rapidly, for Benjamin as for Germaine, the illusions faded. Bernadotte did not reach beyond Nancy, the capital of Lorraine. On March 31, Paris fell to the Allies, who brought the Bourbons in their train. "So Paris has really been taken. . . . What a fall! . . . Divine justice. L v d D s f."[37] Benjamin left for Brussels with Bernadotte, who then returned to Sweden, ultimately to be satisfied with inheriting the Swedish throne. Germaine told Benjamin that there was nothing to do but to rally to the Bourbons and that she was returning to Paris, wearing the white cockade of the monarchy with perfect sincerity "while thinking much more about independence than freedom, for in truth the French are not in the least worthy of it."[38] She could be as scathing about the failings of her fellow countrymen as he was. She declared that she was finished with politics, while maintaining that what was important now was to end the Allied occupation of France. She assured Benjamin that when she returned to Paris she would be delighted to welcome him and Charlotte. Unbeknownst to her, Charlotte, left behind in Germany, was finding consolation with Adolphus Frederick, Duke of Cambridge, one of the sons of George III.

Benjamin's short-lived attempt to revive his political career after a gap of many years had not so far proved a dazzling success. After Louis XVIII was established on the French throne, and a few days before the abdication of Napoleon at Fontainebleau, Benjamin decided, "Liberty is not lost. Let us try to make a place for us in a peaceable system. It is worth the trouble of trying."[39] All the same, he wrongly surmised at first that he had no contacts or patrons in France; he even thought of writing to Talleyrand, who had masterminded the restoration of the monarchy. Then Germaine's son Auguste happened to arrive in Brussels and in the course of conversation he showed Benjamin a letter from his mother. This letter produced an unexpected effect, a veritable explosion of disgust in Benjamin's diary.

As Benjamin, who was preparing to make his own moves, saw it, Germaine was engaged in some contemptible intrigue. What was it precisely? He does not say. It seems unlikely that Auguste would have shown him anything that might prove detrimental to his mother's reputation. Entrusted with negotiating on her behalf, the young man was no fool: in Chambéry in December 1807, he, only seventeen, had held his own while pleading her cause with Napoleon himself, who admitted afterward that he had treated the youth with severity. In her recent letters to Benjamin, moreover, Germaine had made no secret of the approaches she had received from the Bourbons and their representatives or of her negotiations with them and her reluctant acceptance of the inevitable, the restoration of the monarchy. He was familiar with all her stratagems and strategies; after all, he had helped to shape some of them and had been engaged for many years as her spokesman in her dealings with those in high office. Perhaps he was just tired of it all. He claimed that her conduct, whatever it was, "sickened me and severed in my mind the last ties between us; and she is bringing up her daughter on the same lines. Poor Albertine!"[40] Nostalgia for the past, concern, regrets, all vanished in an instant. This did not bode well for his forthcoming reunion with Germaine.

Together with Auguste, Benjamin left Brussels for Paris. His spirits revived somewhat. "Let us serve the good cause and serve ourselves," he candidly advised himself in his diary, an ambitious politician eager to establish himself as well as his liberal principles.[41] Germaine's attitude was rather different. Only two days before, she had invoked France: "May she be reborn under her kings and under liberty!" At least, unlike the usurper, Louis XVIII was likely to be favorable to literature, she thought. "Well, let us be content since tyranny is overthrown," she observed to Hochet, as she tried to make the best of an outcome she had not desired.[42]

Benjamin arrived in Paris from Brussels on April 15; Germaine followed from London on May 12. The two ardent republicans were going to live as subjects under the restored Bourbon monarchy. And they were going to meet again, face to face, after an eventful separation of three years.

CHAPTER NINE

⁓ *Reunion in Paris—and After* ⁓

GERMAINE WAS LOOKING FORWARD most keenly to meeting Benjamin again in Paris, as she repeatedly told him in her letters from London. After alluding to her poor health and, in a socially acceptable, round-about way, to pains due to menopause, she assured him, "I really should like to see you again, in case I am to die soon. . . . So write to me about what you will be doing. . . . Adieu, remember me." And to encourage and sustain him, as she often did, she enthused about his qualities: "Your intelligence and your talents will always arouse my admiration, and to talk with you, if you still care for my conversation, will always be the chief of all my pleasures."[1] She longed to discuss everything with him, just as they used to do with so much enjoyment, and especially the meaning of all the momentous changes that were taking place in the world. Would there be established in France a truly constitutional monarchy? Would there be a parliament of two chambers like the one in England that they admired?

Benjamin, on the contrary, felt no such feelings of warm anticipation. When they met in Paris her disillusion was great: "During the two months I have spent in Paris," she told her intimate friend Juliette Récamier, "I have not received from him the slightest indication of friendship and I did not imagine it was possible to be so insensitive."[2] She bewailed the way that fifteen wasted years had vanished into a chasm. On the same day she conveyed her deep disappointment to Benjamin himself: "When you saw that I would be coming back to reside near you the tone of your letters changed and those you wrote from Paris to me in London wounded me deeply. When I arrived I found you in harmony with your letters, not a glance, not a hint in your voice that betrayed a memory," she complained.[3]

Albertine had warned him that her mother's health was poor, that she had grown very thin and pale. Had Germaine truly recovered from the birth of Louis-Alphonse, which took place during a period of intense persecution and when she was already in her mid-forties? The cumulative strain, struggle, and agitation during the years of exile, the uncertainties and difficulties she experienced when she was traveling across war-torn Europe, her constant worries about the future of Albertine and Auguste and about Rocca's declining health, and the dreadful, futile death of her younger son Albert in a duel—all these had taken their toll, as had her abuse of opium to combat insomnia and the symptoms associated with menopause.

This decline in her health was no passing phase. Germaine's appearance had changed noticeably: she was "no longer the historian but the victim of *Dix années d'exil*," recalled the liberal literary scholar and future minister Abel-François Villemain, who was deeply saddened when he saw her some months after her return to Paris. "Beneath the finery, at once striking and careless, that she usually wore, beneath that scarlet turban partly covering her thick black hair and which blended with the expressive splendor of her gaze, Mme de Staël no longer seemed the same person. Her face was downcast and as if sick with sadness. That fiery spirit, which usually enlivened her expression with countless swiftly passing nuances, was no longer in evidence." In its place Villemain, who fully recognized in her present state the physical cost of her long resistance against absolute power, observed in her "a look of changing, insightful disquiet, a sort of foreboding in sorrow."[4]

At the very least Benjamin might be expected to show some understanding or express some concern when he perceived the changed appearance and condition of his former lover and companion. He did not. He was entirely wrapped up in his own concerns, especially his attempt to make a place for himself in the political life of the Restoration. The time he spent working with Bernadotte had renewed his confidence and his taste for political action.

In the weeks before Germaine's arrival in Paris, and certainly after it, Benjamin paid a great many visits to the eminent and influential; he met with those apparently indestructible pillars of all regimes, Talleyrand and Fouché, as well as General Sébastiani and others he had known during the Directoire and the Consulate. Some he had encountered in the course of his efforts to alleviate Germaine's exile and recover Necker's millions. He was trying to establish himself and his reputation as a leading political journalist, a committed opponent of Napoleon, a supporter of the Bourbons in their proclaimed liberal guise. The impression he gave was that, instead of keeping silent in public, he had been a dissident voice and an emblem of resistance to the tyrant in the years between his dismissal from the Tribunate in 1802 and the publication of his impressive attack on the usurper, *De l'esprit de conquête*, in 1813, now in its third edition. He published various important articles, including his observations on constitutions and his views on the responsibility of ministers, much admired by Germaine. In these articles he defended free speech and freedom of the press at a time when, notwithstanding Louis XVIII's promulgation of the liberal *Charte*, or Charter, there were very strong currents of reaction.

Benjamin was truly shocked when he saw Germaine at last. "Did not work much because of my visit to Mme de Staël. She has changed, she is thin and pale. I did not allow myself to show any feeling. What would be the use? Albertine is charming, extremely witty, adorable. She is the one I regret. I should like to spend my life with her."[5] His apparent indifference to Germaine, confided to his diary, did not prevent him from dining with her almost every afternoon at the customary hour of four or four-thirty. Her salon was again celebrated for its brilliance and frequented by luminaries from all over Europe, crowned heads, statesmen, diplomats, generals, and distinguished writers and scholars, offering Benjamin an excellent chance to make contact with the eminent and powerful who flooded into the capital. "Dined with Mme de Staël. She has changed in every way. She is withdrawn, almost cold, thinking only of herself, scarcely listening to others, attached to nothing, even to her daughter, except out of duty, to myself not at all."[6] Instead, he concentrated all his affection on Albertine: she "is completely myself in her manner of thinking, I am pleased with what has been done with my handiwork," he commented complacently, although he had played no part in her upbringing.[7] A few days later he noted, "Read my poem to Mme de Staël. It is easy to see that she no longer loves me, because she scarcely praised me."[8] Clearly her praise, which he had relied on in the past to give him support and encouragement, did still matter to him. A great weight was lifted from his shoulders, he claimed, after seeing Germaine, for whom he said he no longer felt any affection. Indeed, he preferred his wife, who was still in Germany and whom he had not seen for a long while or even thought about much during his involvement with Bernadotte.

The reunion of Germaine and Benjamin in Paris in the spring of 1814, then, was far from being a romantic affair. It was not even a moment of amicable reconciliation, as perhaps Germaine had hoped or imagined. Despite his journalism and his socializing, Benjamin felt somewhat at a loss when Germaine departed for Coppet with Albertine and Rocca in July. Life seemed empty: he missed Charlotte, who was managing perfectly well without him. It seemed that nobody loved him, and there was nobody in Paris whom he loved: in short, he was bored and he felt at a low ebb. In his apathy he failed to correspond with Germaine: Albertine wrote to complain that he had not written to them at Coppet when he must know how her mother relied on his letters for the latest news and gossip from Paris.

Then, suddenly, the vacuum was filled. Benjamin succumbed to a most turbulent midlife crisis: he fell madly in love. "Am I losing my mind?" he inquired on August 31, 1814. Indeed, in some sense he did lose his head, such was his frenzy. His passion took command, bringing an abiding interest into his loveless existence. Timid expressions of lifelong devotion to his beloved, bitter outpourings of despair, wild threats of suicide—these were, as ever with Benjamin, the forms of his love strategy, but in this instance, they were all to no avail. He could see that it was rather absurd for an experienced man of forty-seven to be behaving like a lovesick adolescent. All the same, he was in the grip of "passion in a novel as at 18," words that echo his condemnation of Germaine's shortcomings a decade earlier, and especially her longing for the romance of passionate love and its expression: "It is . . . the demand for love as at 18," he had complained about her then.[9] It seems unlikely that, governed by his new passion, he would have remembered the phrase he had used to characterize what he had perceived as Germaine's emotional immaturity.

Who was the object of this *grande passion?* It was none other than Juliette Récamier, Germaine's most deeply cherished female friend. He had known her for at least fourteen years without ever transgressing a tone of social playfulness. Indeed, on occasion he had remarked to Prosper de Barante that she was ageless and good-hearted, but frivolous. Once, he had traveled amicably with her in close proximity in a carriage to meet Germaine. He had, moreover, acted in *Andromaque* alongside Juliette at Coppet without joining her queue of admirers. It seems not to have occurred to him that Germaine would interpret his conduct, when she learned of it on her return to Paris at the end of September, as a further "betrayal" of their companionship and association, not far short of that of his secret marriage. Could he seriously have expected her to give her blessing to the union of her ex-lover and her best friend? Of course, he did not attempt to see matters from her point of view; he was the only one who counted. Germaine told him, referring to the effect of his obsession with Juliette, "I know that since you are not bored I no longer mean anything to you. . . . I appear to you as a form of remorse that one feels only when one is unhappy. I have the sad ability to see into the depths of the human heart."[10] He now regarded Germaine simply as an obstacle, and a detested obstacle at that; he was convinced that she would do all she could to frustrate his passion and harm him in every way. For him, she had been transformed into the serpent in the garden. He wanted his family to know nothing about his feelings for Juliette, so he informed Rosalie that Germaine was spreading rumors about his nonexistent amours with various ladies, and that his happiness with the angelic Charlotte was complete. He reproved his friend Hochet for criticizing him and doubting his ability to be a statesman or a minister in Germaine's presence, for fear that she would undermine his reputation.

Ever since the Directoire, Juliette Récamier, a vision in fashionable diaphanous white as she reclined on her chaise longue in the iconic paintings by Baron Gérard and Jacques-Louis David, had been famous for being famous. Admired throughout Europe for her grace, charm, elegance, finesse, and beauty, she was one of the great celebrities of the day. Germaine would tempt her friends to Coppet by saying that Juliette would be coming to stay. They had met for the first time around 1800 when Juliette's husband, the banker Jacques Récamier, bought a Parisian mansion that Necker had put up for sale, and from that moment their friendship had blossomed. It has been called *"une amitié amoureuse*," a friendship that is barely distinguishable from love—and so it was, at least on Germaine's part. She once compared her feelings for Juliette, endowed with "mysterious qualities" as well as charm, with the depth of her feeling for Benjamin. For Germaine, this was no mundane or social friendship—she enjoyed a countless number of such friendships with distinguished women—but one that was intense, ideal, sublime, visceral, and unique. To discover that Benjamin had joined the extremely long list of Juliette's suitors, from Lucien Bonaparte and Adrien de Montmorency to Prince Augustus of Prussia, Prosper de Barante, and her own son Auguste, must have been painful. Germaine warned Juliette, just as Mathieu de Montmorency had once warned *her*, against becoming involved with such a volatile character as Benjamin.

Locked in a *mariage blanc,* or unconsummated union (with, so it was murmured, a man who was really her father), a marriage of convenience to protect property during the Revolution, Juliette was deemed not only ravishingly beautiful but pure and unattainable. She posed a challenge few men could resist. Benjamin felt impelled to try his luck. When he alluded to his timidity Juliette encouraged him: "Dare!" she said famously. Intelligent, of equable temperament, she was also a practised coquette, and Germaine later reproached her, saying that she would have been too perfect if she had put friendship before coquetry. Juliette was partly mistrustful and partly intrigued by Benjamin's ardor, unable to resist making another conquest. Later, he noted in his diary: "Perhaps also, as Mme de Staël said, . . . fundamentally she [Juliette] wants from men only the sort of physical sensations that their desire evokes in her, *faute de mieux,* and that my timidity often prevented me from arousing in her. I gained little profit from several encounters with her."[11] He addressed her as an enchanting woman, an angel descended from heaven, a five-year-old child, but in his diary he would apply to her the usual complaints he leveled against most of the women he knew: he said that she dominated him and that he was her slave. When he did not get his way he followed his customary pattern of behavior, from wild passion and suffering to mutterings of loathing, and, toward the end, studied indifference.

His intentions were not platonic: "This cursed woman is impregnable," he declared.[12] Gambler that he was, he thought that he should have risked everything on a single throw, that he should have seized a moment when she was emotionally vulnerable (as he had done, successfully, when wooing Charlotte) or taken her by force after threatening to commit suicide. He acknowledged that he had failed to "profit" from several tête-à-têtes through his timidity: "I have been a great fool."[13] He remained in thrall to her for more than a year, and his obsession led him into some curious and unexpected areas. For instance, although he had long scorned privilege, he asked Rosalie for a print of the family coat of arms because, under the Bourbon Restoration, everyone was resurrecting old titles or adopting new ones, and because "my seal 'Benjamin Constant' makes me look like a draper."[14] Perhaps he fancied that as Benjamin *de* Constant, the appellation his father had favored, he might appear to be a person of more consequence in Juliette's eyes.

Meanwhile, how was he to pass the time while waiting around for Juliette to look kindly on him? Apart from his writing there was always gambling, of course. A tremendous stroke of luck at the roulette table in November enabled him to buy a fine house on the rue Neuve-de-Berry with a fairly large garden and a superb view: unfortunately, his later heavy losses prevented him from being able to afford its upkeep. In addition, there were, as in the past, visits to prostitutes. But what he really needed was to find ways to win Juliette's attention and hold her interest.

To please Juliette, who was a friend of Napoleon's sister, Queen Caroline of Naples, he wrote a memorandum addressed to the Allies in favor of Caroline's husband, Joachim Murat, who wanted to stay on the Neapolitan throne. And in order to enjoy closer contact with the object of his pursuit, Benjamin encouraged Juliette to compose her memoirs: she would speak to him about her life while he put what she said into order. He was working on these memoirs in the winter of 1815. Among the papers that survive is a section on Germaine doubtless composed entirely by Benjamin: chapter 3 was patently a means for him to unburden his current bitterness about his former companion. These pages are satirical, sharper even than anything he wrote about Germaine as Mme de Malbée in *Cécile*.

The friendship of Germaine and Juliette occupies relatively little place in this cruel chapter. Germaine is depicted as swift in expressing new thoughts, which the idealized Juliette is swift to comprehend and judge; a strong, virile temperament contrasts with a delicate, refined, feminine one. The substance of chapter 3 does not lie here, however, but in the analysis of Germaine's character by a man who knows intimately her every flaw. After the allusions to her controversial appearance, her splendid gaze, her customary expression of benevolence, and her astonishing conversation comes the sword thrust: her conviction of her own superiority. He never admits that she has a good deal to be proud about, not least her writings that changed the face of literature and of culture in general. He writes, "Mme de Staël unites two things that make her perhaps the most astounding woman in the entire world, a combination that deceives others as well as herself. Her imagination, full of eloquence and poetry, endows her words with a nobility, a loftiness, a mark of generosity and devotion to others that charm and captivate, but she has such a sense of her superiority and of the huge distance that separates her from the rest of humanity that it is primarily in her favor that this nobility, this loftiness and this generosity are brought to bear. It is not egoism, it is a cult." What precisely does he mean? He suggests that egoism has its shameful aspect whereas "Mme de Staël's cult of herself inspires a certain religious awe."[15] Egoism, in short, is far too small a word to express Germaine's self-worship. In contrast with this view, her cousin Albertine Necker de Saussure, who was by no means blind to her faults, declared that Germaine believed in the equality of all human beings before God and never felt herself to be superior because of her genius.

On one brilliant page he attacks her sincerity by presenting her eloquently expressed yet contradictory views one after the other; it seems almost possible to hear her voice, so vivid is his mimicry. Mme de Staël is perfectly sincere, he says, when she declares that family and filial obligations should take second place to the right to happiness of magnanimous souls endowed with sensibility, after the manner of Rousseau's *La Nouvelle Héloïse*. He is alluding, of course, to the time when she demanded that Benjamin leave his father's home, where filial duty called him, to attend on her at Coppet. She is equally sincere, he maintains, when as a mother she advocates the complete opposite and insists on filial piety and duty against the claims of love. Here he is alluding to her son Auguste's wooing of Juliette, of which Germaine strongly disapproved. The peculiar irony of the situation is that Benjamin himself held that a truth is not complete unless it embraces its contrary. He once maintained, moreover, that there are a thousand different ways of looking at a question. On almost every page of his diary there are feelings and thoughts that directly contradict each other. Indeed, it is this very contradictory integrity that makes his diary such a remarkable document.

Perhaps the most cruel page of all concerns her love for her father, which verged on idolatry. Nobody knew about this love more intimately than Benjamin, who a decade earlier had ridden night and day to Germany to protect her by being the first to tell her of Necker's death. Then, however, he had marriage in mind. He notes how her lavish praise for her father in her writings has been ridiculed—mistakenly, he claims, "because nothing true is ridiculous" (a dubious assertion). It is Benjamin, though, who has raised the subject of ridicule in the mind of his potential reader. What would Germaine have thought if she had read how "Necker was too weak for the circumstances in which he was placed or placed himself"? In all likelihood she would have cared more about the words "or placed himself" and the damaging assessment of her father's standing in history than about all the allusions to her self-worship. Benjamin knew well enough that by the time Necker became finance minister it was too late to save France, and he would say as much in his later writings. This satirical portrait is particularly shocking coming from a professed friend whom Necker loved as a son. Necker, he declared, thought of himself and his daughter as belonging to a privileged species, almost above humanity: "The vanity of Mme de Staël, often satisfied but sometimes wounded in society, because society judges harshly any person engaged in self-promotion, never suffered at her father's hands."[16] A final dig alludes to Germaine's remorse at leaving Necker alone at Coppet, rather than staying with him and caring for him in his old age, simply so she could enjoy the satisfactions of vanity. He disregards the fact that Necker encouraged her to travel abroad, and that she did so not only to escape her underlying melancholy but also to discover new worlds of ideas and culture to share with her readers. These terrible pages, which one hopes she never saw, combine wounding accuracy of aim with the worst possible interpretation of her character and motives. They date from a period when Benjamin felt nothing for Germaine but hatred, occupied as he was in trying to remove Juliette from her influence.

It was also in the hope of impressing Juliette that he sought to establish himself as a spokesman for the Bourbon regime, especially regarding its professed liberal aspirations. Unfortunately, his efforts, which sometimes made him sound more royalist than the king himself, did not win approval from traditional supporters of the monarchy. His former republican allies were not pleased either. Germaine lectured him on the extreme and risky course he was taking and gave him the benefit of what he called "another political sermon."[17] Nonetheless, when on March 6, 1815, the astonishing news reached the public in Paris that Napoleon had escaped from Elba and had landed at Golfe-Juan on March 1, intent on hastening to the capital, Benjamin threw caution to the winds. With all the force of his eloquence he violently attacked Napoleon in two notorious articles published on March 11 in the *Journal de Paris* and March 19 in the *Journal des Débats*. In the second article he declared, "It is Attila, it is Genghis Khan, more fearsome and hateful because the resources of civilization are at his disposal" for pillage and massacre. "I say today without fear of being misunderstood: I wanted freedom under diverse forms; I saw it was possible under the monarchy; I saw the King rally to the nation: I shall not go, like a wretched renegade, dragging myself from one power to another, disguising infamy with sophistry and stammering words that have been profaned in order to ransom a shameful life."[18] These resounding phrases would come to haunt him. The very next day, Louis XVIII, to whom he had so loudly pledged his faith, departed in ignominious haste for Ghent with all his court.

Benjamin had tried to rally some resistance to Napoleon, and, though carried away by his rhetoric, he knew that he was risking his life. He had gambled and lost: all he could do now, he thought, was to die nobly, for he fully expected the emperor to have him put to death. Germaine feared for him. During a talk with her one morning her solicitude touched him: "She moved me, and I felt that, in spite of my anger, I did not really hate her."[19] She urged him to flee from the capital without delay: "I beg you for the sake of our old affection to leave immediately."[20] Fearing that all hopes for liberty were at an end, she herself departed hurriedly for Coppet. En route, at six o'clock the next morning, she found time to write a note to Juliette: "My dear friend, do me one more favor, see that Benjamin leaves. I am greatly worried about him after what he has written."[21] Benjamin hastily departed to join Prosper de Barante in the Vendée. Napoleon entered the capital on March 20. A week later Benjamin returned to Paris, discovering to his great surprise that all was quiet.

Not the least surprising aspect of Napoleon's astonishing and variegated career was his pragmatic decision to establish a liberal regime in 1815, a decision that baffled a great many people. Could Napoleon really be sincere in his liberal-minded talk? Would his new regime last? Who was to be believed? Above all, what if Napoleon had returned for good? Even Germaine received kind words from elevated quarters. Her friend of many years, Joseph Bonaparte, informed her that the emperor had not forgotten her magnanimity in contriving to let him know, when he was a prisoner on Elba, about a plot to assassinate him. Joseph assured her that if she were to return to Paris now, she would be permitted to speak and write freely. To placate her Napoleon claimed that it was not himself but his underlings who had ordered the destruction of *De l'Allemagne*—a blatant lie. She was not convinced by these blandishments or the new liberal order, telling her cousin Albertine: "He managed very well to do without a constitution and without me for twelve years, and even now he cares as little for the one as for the other."[22]

Although Germaine would convey the impression in her influential *Considérations sur les principaux événements de la Révolution française* that she stood firm, she in fact wavered for a while. There was something epic to appeal to her imagination in Napoleon's daring escape from Elba, his reconquest of the country in just under three weeks, the swift restoration of all the trappings of his rule, and his decision to adapt the constitution to the time, the circumstances, and his own current requirements. "Mme de Staël would really like to mend fences," thought Benjamin.[23] She admitted to him that although she had gone along with the monarchy she was not committed to the royalist party and, therefore, "if the Emperor grants freedom he will be the legitimate power in my view." Besides, he seemed to be invincible: "Above all, since the landing at Antibes [Golfe-Juan] I do not know who could resist him. I should be less capable of doing so now than in the past, so the nation would be even more unlikely to oppose him."[24] There was, moreover, the outstanding question of the repayment of Necker's loan, promised by Louis XVIII. Her son Auguste was employed in negotiations in Paris, but he had little hope of success, for the state coffers were far from full. Nonetheless, Benjamin was optimistic, according to Auguste. Germaine told Juliette that if Napoleon were to settle the debt her gratitude would prevent her from doing or saying anything to oppose him.

Yet, as much as Germaine desired the repayment, she soon discovered that it would come at much too high a price. As Auguste reported to her, Lucien Bonaparte had made clear to him that Napoleon "would not take the first step. He wants your mother to receive her payment from his generosity, not from justice, he wants her to cross the Rubicon."[25] She would have to come to Paris to undertake negotiations in person and rally to the emperor's new cause. Germaine refused, though she could not help wondering if she was putting her pride before the interests of her children. She decided to keep away from Paris and stay discreetly at Coppet, criticizing those of her friends and associates, like Lafayette, Sismondi, and Benjamin himself, who chose to rally to the liberal Empire.

It was, temporarily, a parting of political ways for Germaine and Benjamin. Yet, throughout the months of his passion for Juliette and his professed loathing for Germaine, and throughout the period of his new political involvement, the two former companions—despite further personal differences—continued to comment on political affairs at a distance. And Auguste stayed at Benjamin's during the abortive negotiations for repayment, in which his host continued to take an active personal interest.

Benjamin Constant was far too useful a writer to be punished for his virulent attacks on Napoleon. A brilliant polemicist and publicist with impeccable liberal credentials like his was just what the new regime required. He paid visits to Fouché and Sébastiani, who made offers and promises to him, giving him serious hopes of advancement. Often he dined with Savary, duc de Rovigo, who had behaved so harshly to Germaine over *De l'Allemagne*. He visited Joseph Bonaparte, though after talking with him he could not help wondering whether there were real prospects for liberty: "So what! Let's accept," he decided. He was hardly more convinced by the liberal assurances of the new regime than was Germaine: "Intentions are liberal. Practice will be despotic. Never mind. Shall I get what I want?"[26] What he wanted was a position that would establish him permanently in France and in French political life, one that would also impress Juliette and win her respect and admiration.

When Germaine learned that Benjamin had been appointed one of the commissioners to prepare the additions to the constitution, she urged him to consider guarantees rather than the declaration of rights. She did not hesitate, moreover, to remind him of his rash words, so quickly contradicted by his actions, in his notorious pro-Bourbon and anti-Napoleon article of March 19, when he proclaimed, "I shall not go, like a wretched renegade, dragging myself from one power to another, disguising infamy with sophistry and stammering words that have been profaned in order to ransom a shameful life." Germaine hit home by quoting from this bold declaration, which he would doubtless have preferred to be forgotten: "I do not want to say anything about politics, I cannot 'stammer words that have been profaned,'" she remarked acidly.[27]

On April 14 Benjamin had a long conversation with the emperor himself, the first of many: "He is an astounding man. Tomorrow I shall bring him a draft for a constitution. Shall I make it at last? Should I want to do so? The future is dark. L v d D s f." On the following day Napoleon again received him in audience, but his draft met with little favor: "It is not exactly liberty that they want," noted Benjamin. On April 18, he spent two hours with Napoleon: Benjamin's revised draft received greater approval. He knew that many were criticizing him severely, "but I am doing good, and also I want to get out of the position I am in."[28] However, one member of Germaine's circle of sharp-witted women friends was more amused at Benjamin's volte-face than judgmental about the way he candidly revealed his utter astonishment at Napoleon, whom he called a "phenomenon," a "prodigy," profoundly impressed as he was by the range and flexibility of the great man's mind.[29] On April 19 he had another long audience with the emperor, who accepted many of his ideas. As a reward Constant was nominated for the Council of State: "If my nomination goes through, I am on my way without forgoing any of my principles."[30] How entertaining political affairs were! Within a few days, he was wearing the gold embroidered uniform of a councillor of state. "So here I am, a member of the new court," he commented approvingly.[31]

On the whole he was pleased with himself, despite receiving anonymous letters every day that conveyed disapproval both of him and of the Additional Act to the constitution, familiarly known as *la benjamine*, though he was not the only person who worked on it. Germaine was divided between approval and criticism: "I was extremely satisfied with the constitution yet I have some objections to it." She showered him with queries about important details. As regards the councillors of state, are they responsible or inviolable? What will be the role of the peers? "A Chamber of military men would be no guarantee of liberty," she cautioned. Were the administrators in the provinces subject to election? "However, what is praiseworthy must be praised, and I understand that you are very pleased to have collaborated on it. But this satisfaction you tell me you feel does not seem to derive solely from your conscience," she observed perspicaciously, letting him know that she could readily assess the part played by ambition.[32]

There were further audiences with Napoleon, but Benjamin still wondered, "How can one venture to say that liberty exists?"[33] He caught a glimpse of the lion's claws whenever the emperor angrily resisted any constraint on his power. All the same, things were going well for Benjamin: at the beginning of June he published a work with which he had been engaged for some years, his great liberal manifesto *Principes de politique*. His political principles were conveniently applicable to all regimes.

Then, suddenly, came debacle, collapse, Waterloo, the end of the Hundred Days of the liberal empire, Napoleon's second abdication, and the second restoration of Louis XVIII, all in quick succession. And with these events came the end of Benjamin's brief period in high office.

During the Hundred Days the most sordid quarrel broke out between Germaine and Benjamin: it was over money. This dispute raged during their political discussions, during the impasse of his continuing passion for Juliette, and during his political rise. Just as Benjamin lost his head over Juliette, Germaine lost hers over Albertine's prospective marriage and dowry. Accustomed to entertaining on a lavish scale and dispensing largesse very freely to those in need, Germaine now found it difficult to gain access to her foreign investments because of political upheavals. In addition, her frequent comings and goings during her exile and her travels through Europe with her party, whom she maintained and subsidized, had depleted her funds, as had the months she spent in England, a country where living was known to be expensive and in her view three times as costly as anywhere else. All this, along with her dismay at her failure to recover Necker's millions, caused her to panic and made her believe that she was on the brink of destitution. Matters were pressing because she had discovered the most suitable— though impecunious—husband for Albertine, one who also found favor with her daughter. Not only was Victor, duc de Broglie, the scion of a great family, but also he enjoyed the advantage of sharing her own liberal views. Without the requisite and promised dowry, however, this eminently desirable marriage might not take place.

To whom should she apply but to Benjamin? In the past, along with her father, she had supplied him with considerable funds, and at present he was in high office and receiving a sizable salary. He had, moreover, promised some years before to repay the debt of eighty thousand francs he owed her—she was asking simply for half of this sum. Besides, she knew that he was utterly devoted to Albertine. Did he not privately consider the girl to be "completely myself in her manner of thinking"? Did he not express satisfaction with "my handiwork"? Did he not treat her with fatherly affection and pride? Who else was more likely to help? Indeed, Germaine does not appear to have approached anyone else among her large acquaintance.

Benjamin, however, had always had a fixation about money. It was largely on this score that he and his father quarreled bitterly. When the two children of his father's second marriage—described by Benjamin as "the bastards"—were born, he feared for his inheritance. While he was engaged in research in Göttingen he took time from his books to occupy himself with his wife's complex financial affairs; Rosalie complained to him that his letters were full of little else. Despite his reckless gambling, or because of it, the improvement of his financial standing, his assets, and everything connected with "*ma fortune*" bothered him as much as his desire for a political role.

Letters passed between Germaine at Coppet and Benjamin in Paris, with Auguste sometimes acting as the messenger. In the records from this distasteful interlude in their relationship, their voices can clearly be heard, raised in anger and at times quivering with hatred. There is venom as well as pain in her reactions to the extremely cruel remarks in his letters. Although his missives are lost, she often alludes to them or quotes from them word for word in her replies to him. There is venom, too, in the furious comments in his diary. Insults flew, and some home truths were exchanged.

Germaine's request for repayment of forty thousand francs came out of the blue while Benjamin was engaged in negotiations with leading Bonapartists. In his diary he denied that he owed her anything of the sort. His mind was made up from the start, and he never deviated from outright refusal. On April 20, after he had enjoyed numerous discussions with Napoleon, been appointed to the Council of State, and become totally committed to the new regime, he noted in his diary, "She would like me to do nothing for *ma fortune* [my finances] and give her the little I have. Nice arrangement. Neither the one nor the other." Already, months before, in November 1814, in the midst of his frenzy over Juliette, he had thought of protecting his purse: "As for Mme de Staël, she is a snake whose vanity is savage. In reality she hates me and I return the favor. Let's put *ma fortune* in a place that is safe from her harpy's claws. Besides, I have little fear of her and, in this connection, I have pretty good means of defending myself."[34] By this threat, he implied the drastic course of revealing her letters—definitely not the act of a gentleman.

In the beginning she apologized to him for having to ask for the repayment of half his debt. She assured him that she would not be approaching him if Albertine's marriage did not hang in the balance. Auguste was bringing him the document or promissory note that Benjamin had drawn up and signed in Switzerland in 1811, but

Benjamin knew it was not worth the paper it was written on, and by now so did she: "You *promised* to return to me 40,000 francs out of the 80, on the marriage of my daughter." She knew that his financial situation had improved considerably, but he was not going to acknowledge it: "You write to me in your letter before last that your engagement to myself and Albertine depended on your hope of becoming a député. Now that you have become a councillor of state you are being more highly remunerated. You claim now that your position cannot last, but you say yourself that the emperor is invincible, so what are you afraid of?" These allusions to his present elevation and salary produced an outburst in the diary: "Letter from Mme de Staël. What a harpy! She won't have me as cheaply as she believes."[35]

What he then wrote to her can be gleaned from Germaine's reply; he evidently threatened to go public, and she retorted, "I can have no idea of how to reply to your letter, it exceeds everything I believed possible of the human heart." She vowed to consult the law. "Even if I were to lose I should have the bitter pleasure of assembling facts that will arouse deep pity for a person unfortunate enough to have been bound to you for fifteen years! You dare to make use of the generosity I showed you when I loved you, as a right! . . . You tell me that my children will have the greater part of your wealth after your demise— yours? Mine, since I lent you 80 thousand francs for life without interest." If she could not make him keep his promise, "at least the conduct of each of us will be known."[36] On May 19, after mentioning in his journal a session of the Council of State and a reception at the Elysée where Napoleon held court, Benjamin fumed, "Letter from Mme de Staël. So it is to be war between us. I welcome it. I shall wage it willingly."[37] In another letter to him, Germaine raged, "What man would not beg me on his knees to be allowed to share in Albertine's happiness?" She added that in the hour of his death the memory of his life would make him tremble. "Besides, all is over between you and me, between you and Albertine."[38] Henceforward, she declared, all communication would be through lawyers.

This parting shot turned out to be premature. She had not intended to write to him any further on the subject, but she could not allow his letters, brought by Auguste, to pass without a rejoinder. Benjamin was threatening to publish her correspondence with him, a most ungallant course of action for one who prided himself on his chivalry. He apparently felt secure in his new position with the regime, whereas she remained powerless. He had long resisted breaking with her for many reasons, including fear of reprisals. These he no longer seemed to dread, now that he was part of Napoleon's court circle. Germaine was thoroughly riled: "You threaten me 'with my letters.' This touch is worthy of you, to threaten a woman with intimate letters that can compromise her and her family so as not to pay her the money one owes her, this is a touch that eluded M. de Sade. If so . . . it will be proved before the whole of Europe that you owe me 80 thousand francs, of which 34 thousand were due to my father for Hérivaux . . . etc., etc., no interest for ten years." She continued, "This new method of enrichment will become known because before you nobody would have dared to imagine it. This lack of money that you now parade, when you spent the whole winter gambling, is a mockery." Her own assets, she said, were reduced by her exile, and by the twenty thousand francs pension she paid to Schlegel and to Fanny Randall, an English lady who had long served her devotedly. As for Benjamin, he had displayed neither honor nor kindliness, for "money alone governs your political and private life." She quoted from his letter to her: "You write to me that you wanted to break with me and that 'I held you back from doing so by my financial assistance to you'—I believe it, but it was strange to say it."[39] There is little doubt, though, that she did sometimes use her wealth to try to keep people attached to her. This last well-aimed barb of hers elicited from Benjamin a further outburst: "Furious letter from Mme de Staël. I am waiting for her and I'll crush her. Elysée." His important work, *Principes de politique*, was about to be published, and he was riding high: "Council of State . . . Elysée. Letter from Mme de Staël. What a fury!" he noted two days later, reduced again to his limited vocabulary of invective, harpies, and furies.[40]

Then he tried to stun her with an unflattering Latin quotation relating to her appearance. Naturally, she had been sensitive about his subject ever since her father had told her when she was a young girl that she would have to rely on her intelligence. Her outraged reply is dated June 12, a few days before Napoleon's defeat at Waterloo. "You tell me that I am an offensive woman and, to give an example of moderation, you quote the Latin words '*spretaeque injuria formae*' that you consider the most insulting of all for a woman." This phrase from Virgil's *Aeneid* concerns the goddess Juno, who is furious with the young Trojan prince Paris because of "his insulting scorn for her beauty"; he has given the prize for beauty not to her but to Venus—or Juliette Récamier in the present context. Germaine was devastated but not silenced: "If you had treated as you do me a servant who was as ugly as she was stupid but who loved you as I loved you, you would still be what you are: the most deeply acerbic and insensitive man alive today. You tell me that for six thousand years women have complained about men who did not love them, but also for six thousand years men have loved money and I do not think you have shown yourself indifferent to it in the last two months. . . . You say that in the past my pain left a deeper impression on you. Would you please tell me if it prevented you from marrying another, all unbeknown to me, in spite of having promised to marry me, and transferring to another the wealth that you had from my father and myself?" Here, she conveniently forgot that she had refused his proposal of marriage. She went on: "You inform me 'you will speak ill of me.' I am sorry to have to tell you that I have ten letters that urge me to let it be known that I no longer have any connection with you. . . . You had to say in front of my daughter and myself that you never loved a woman for more than three months, a disgusting remark typical of a roué that you should have spared Albertine in her innocence. . . . As for me, since I now see in our liaison nothing but a spell cast upon me by the vengeance of hell, I am obsessed with the idea that I apparently deserved it, that even my father himself could not obtain my pardon. . . . In short, I suffer as much as when I loved you."[41] What more could she say about the effect of words than that they still had power to inflict pain?

Then, as suddenly as it had arisen, the violent storm subsided. Louis XVIII sanctioned the settlement of the debt incurred in the reign of his martyred brother, Louis XVI, and Albertine's marriage to Victor de Broglie was able to proceed. On July 21, 1815, Germaine wrote from Coppet to tell Benjamin that she was now more favorably inclined toward him. The change in tone was due not only to the end of her fears for her daughter's marriage but also to her knowledge that he must be miserable at the fall of the imperial regime and the consequent loss of his elevated position. She could never fail to respond to anyone who was unhappy or in trouble, and Benjamin knew it: "Mme de Staël has given up her claims since my position has changed and her letters are friendly again because she knows I am unhappy," he told Rosalie.[42]

Germaine tried to do all she could to raise his spirits: if he failed to become a député, she encouraged, he should finish his book on religion and publish it. "Your talent will always sustain you," she added.[43] To encourage him further she reported flattering remarks she heard about him, such as when a visitor from England praised his understanding of the English constitution, and a Swiss legislator observed that since Montesquieu there had been no works as powerful as Constant's. She advised him to stay in Paris if he could, for time would surely moderate party hatreds. Besides, she assured him, "the shining aspects of your life, your love of liberty and your talent will again come to the fore."[44] She urged that they write to each other and forget the whole matter that had come between them.

As a proclaimed adherent of Louis XVIII under the First Restoration who became a prominent member of Napoleon's regime during the Hundred Days, Benjamin had made many enemies; his present position was difficult and precarious. Some military figures who changed sides, such as Marshal Ney and Colonel de La Bédoyère, were soon to pay with their lives. Vengeful monarchists who were in power under the Second Restoration saw Benjamin Constant as the turncoat that only a few months before he had said he would never be. He was frozen out of the salons he had once frequented; and he even wondered whether Germaine would continue to receive him. "As for me," she wrote from Coppet, "can you have the slightest doubt that if I were to return to Paris I should see you as before?" She assured him that she was not the sort of person to pay attention to social prejudices. "You have been senseless and cruel," she declared, but what mattered now was for him to make good use of his great gifts. "What a fine career will be yours if you can teach France liberty," she prophesied.[45]

The apologia Benjamin composed in justification of his recent political conduct, and which he thought admirable for its moderation and nobility, met with Germaine's approval. As a sure sign of trust he gave her permission to show it to others so long as it did not leave her hands. Fortunately, Louis XVIII approved it. When Benjamin was congratulated on its success in convincing Louis XVIII, he coolly observed, "I should think so, it almost convinced me."[46] The king himself arranged for Benjamin's name to be removed from the list of those to be exiled, and he wanted Benjamin to know, as the author of the apologia, that he had taken this action.

Benjamin had submitted his apologia through the royal favorite, Elie, later duc Decazes, whom the childless King treated as a son, and who was soon to be minister of police. He saw a good deal of Decazes, who doubtless would not have been averse to having Benjamin's pen on the royalist side again. Benjamin published an eloquent article to try to save Colonel de La Bédoyère from execution, employing the argument that "millions" like him had changed sides. He approached Decazes, too, in quest of clemency, to no avail. Did Benjamin, as later suggested, spend the condemned man's last hours with him, reminiscing about Germaine de Staël, about life at Coppet and how they had performed there together in Voltaire's *Zaïre?* It seems rather soon after the outpouring of venomous remarks about her in his diary, but perhaps the volatile Benjamin was mollified by mid-August, when the unfortunate La Bédoyère faced the firing squad.

Were Germaine and Benjamin reconciled? Certainly, she appeared ready to forgive and forget; she truly wished them to remain in contact. Yet things could never be the same. Too many harsh and bitter words had been exchanged that could not be entirely expunged from the memory. Moreover, their paths were about to diverge once again.

By September 1815 Benjamin, who was still writing and publishing articles, was forty-eight and feeling tired. He was weary of having to face the hostility of many members of society toward him, weary with humanity in general and with Juliette Récamier in particular, for his suit was obviously getting nowhere. His mood shifted from intense emotionalism and activity to its opposite: he felt again the need for *repos,* peace, and tranquillity. After some hesitation, as "a cure for love," he decided to depart for Brussels, sending for Charlotte to join him there. She arrived in December, less out of love, he realized, than a sense of wifely duty; evidently, she would have preferred to stay in Germany. Together, on January 16, 1816, they left for England.

Benjamin did not want to look as if he had come to London without any purpose in mind: "In England I want to be the representative of France under oppression."[47] This role was problematic, despite being identical to the one that Germaine had performed so eminently in 1813–1814 when, as an exile, she tried to help put an end to Napoleon's tyranny. At that time, apart from the British "Napoleonists" who blindly swallowed and regurgitated the myth of Bonaparte as the savior of the Revolution, opinion in the country, which was at war with France, was largely on her side. Benjamin, however, was in exile voluntarily. He might be out of favor in Paris, but he was not under surveillance or persecuted, as Germaine had been; he had not daringly escaped and traveled across Europe to promote freedom. Besides, circumstances had changed. Louis XVIII, who had found refuge in Hertfordshire, was generally regarded as an ally; it was by traveling "in the baggage train" of the British and Allied armies that he twice recovered his throne. Sympathy lay with Napoleon's victims rather than with those who suffered from the outrages being committed by royalist extremists during the White Terror.

Consequently, although leading members of English society, especially those prominent among the liberal Whigs, welcomed Benjamin Constant as an intriguing figure of high intelligence and a controversial political thinker and activist, he was not exactly a celebrity like Mme de Staël, that astonishing woman known throughout Europe for her writings, her eloquence, and her courageous defiance of Napoleon. She was a personality whom those eminent in society and in the world of politics, science, literature, and the arts wished to meet, even if only at times to mock her volubility, her décolleté, and her lack of tact. All the same, there was scarcely an evening when Benjamin was not attending some distinguished soirée or rout: Lord Holland (Henry Fox) and his wife invited him to their elite gatherings, as did Lord Grey and the Duke of Devonshire, among other prominent aristocrats. Benjamin was at Lady Jersey's reception on April 8 when Byron was ostracized; the poet left England forever shortly afterward, later to be most gratified when Germaine warmly welcomed him at Coppet. Moreover, Benjamin met many of Germaine's English friends and a number of his own associates from his student days in Edinburgh, including Lord Kinnaird and Sir James Mackintosh, who had become very friendly with Germaine during her London stay. Like Germaine, Benjamin found the cost of living ruinously expensive; like her, he went to the theater and saw Kean in his most famous role as Richard III; like her, he visited Parliament and was impressed by the debates; and like her, he was invited to stay at the country mansions of various grandees.

The only trouble was that any social invitations Benjamin received were addressed to him alone, even though his wife was living with him throughout the months he spent in London. Although she was born in England and was of high birth, Charlotte was regarded as persona non grata because she was twice divorced. Society, with the dissolute Prince Regent at its head, was not distinguished for its high moral tone: it has been said that many men's mistresses lived in finer style than their wife. On the subject of divorce, however, opinion was strict. Similar hypocrisy prevailed in France: friends had warned Germaine about the risk of ostracism when she was thinking of divorcing her husband. Charlotte's health suffered from the English "climate" in more senses than one, but Benjamin, despite his bad conscience, was not deterred from accepting invitations.

The publication of his novella, *Adolphe*, on May 8, 1816, was a *succès de scandale*. He had given many private readings from it in the salons in Paris and London, and a wider public was equally fascinated by the simple notion that the composite figure of Ellénore stood for the famous Mme de Staël, no matter how many prefaces he issued to the contrary. Among his various intentions Benjamin said he desired to present the general through the particular "situation," to demonstrate the fatal nature of all such liaisons and the ineluctable tragic consequences for both leading characters. The fact that he did not entirely succeed in diverting attention from Germaine did not detract from the impact of his story. Albertine, with whom he corresponded from time to time, let him know that she felt irritated and did not care much for the "hero." Not surprisingly, she found characteristics of the author in Adolphe; she disliked especially the Byronic tendency to reveal the worst side of one's character. Germaine, of course, was acquainted with the novella, for Benjamin had read parts of it to her since he began working on it in 1806. Doubtless if Albertine was irritated by it so was she. Germaine gave her true unfavorable opinion to her friend, the duchesse de Duras, future author of the subtle novella *Ourika:* "I do not care for Benjamin Constant's novel." She did not think that all men were like Adolphe, only those who were full of vanity—a reflection on Benjamin as well as on the autobiographical elements in his protagonist. "It is what must be avoided as the death of feeling," she added.[48]

Benjamin was afraid that Germaine would feel wounded by the publication of *Adolphe* and that there would be a new dispute between them, in spite of all his public attempts to separate fiction from fact. Apparently, she did not think the matter was worth another rift. He was relieved to learn that "my novel has not set us at odds."[49] The one person who *was* furious and who let him know it, he told Juliette, was his discarded mistress, Anna Lindsay.

From the autumn of 1815 correspondence between Germaine and Benjamin seems to have been fitful. In September 1815, a few months before he crossed the English Channel, she left for Italy, accompanied by Rocca, who was not well and might improve in a more favorable climate, and by the ever-attentive Schlegel and Albertine. They spent the winter in Pisa, where, on February 20, 1816, Albertine and Victor de Broglie were married according to both the Protestant and Catholic rites. Germaine left it to Albertine to inform Benjamin of the marriage, while she herself assured him that her daughter's attachment to him was unchanged and that she had done nothing to lessen it. Albertine wrote of her great happiness, regretting only the "sad combination of circumstances" that prevented him from being present at her wedding. "I would not have believed it six years ago," she told him.[50] The party then went on to Florence. Germaine heard about Benjamin's activities in London, presumably from her many English friends, although she had no letters from him. She had already complained to Juliette the previous autumn, just after leaving for Italy, that she had no contact with Benjamin. In February 1816, a few days before the wedding, she asked Juliette, "What has become of Benjamin?"[51]

Germaine spent the summer of 1816 at Coppet, where the great gatherings of European luminaries, writers, thinkers, and notabilities continued to flourish. Stendhal, who was never actually there but knew of them by repute, called them "the States General of European thought" and remarked on their political significance.[52] These famous assemblies took place without Benjamin, who had not set foot in Coppet since 1811.

It was in her family home that Germaine and Rocca were married, in strictest privacy, on October 10, 1816. Shortly afterward they left for Paris, where Benjamin had arrived some three months earlier. He was busy writing articles and pamphlets, including *De la doctrine politique qui peut réunir tous les partis,* an attempt to reach a compromise between opposing political parties. This compromise had been an objective of Germaine's and was one of the major themes of her unpublished work *Des circonstances actuelles,* on which he had collaborated at the beginning of their relationship. Did their paths cross in Paris? It is unclear. Benjamin's diary ends on September 26, 1816, so his detailed and informative agenda is lacking.

The time had come in both of their lives for mature regrets. One of Germaine's last known letters to Benjamin, written on May 30, 1816, tells him about Albertine's happiness with Victor de Broglie and about her own contentment, which would be complete if only Rocca's health were to improve. Notably, she regrets all the time she wasted in unhappiness—implying that a good deal of it was spent with Benjamin or bewailing their separation. All that counts now, she realizes, is the heart's affections.

As for Benjamin, he often liked to reminisce, recalling the most significant dates in his life: the birth of Albertine, for example, or the anniversary of the scene at Sécheron when Germaine was finally told of his secret marriage to Charlotte. A few days before he closed his diary, and with it an entire period of his existence, he remembered his first encounter with Germaine: "Twenty-two years ago at the same hour I saw Mme de Staël for the first time. I should have done better not to embark on this liaison and afterward not to break it off."[53] With this brief observation he summed up his current attitude to his long-standing, complex, tempestuous, but ultimately fruitful relationship with Germaine. After so many storms, so much pain mutually inflicted, so many veerings on his part, he had reached the conclusion that in severing the connection he had made the wrong decision. It is an extraordinary admission.

CHAPTER TEN

⁓ *The Death of Corinne* ⁓

THE WINTER SEASON IN PARIS was as brilliant as ever. Although Germaine's health was visibly failing, she went on entertaining her large circle of guests from all over Europe and accepting invitations to grand balls and soirées. On February 21, 1817, while attending a reception given by the minister Decazes, she collapsed on the staircase, paralyzed by a stroke. Carried to her house on the rue Royale, she could still speak, her mind was clear, but she was scarcely able to move and fell into a kind of torpor. She was gripped by premonitions of death more intense than those she had previously conveyed to Benjamin.

Up to the moment of her collapse she had been as active as usual, engaged in writing her *Considérations sur les principaux événements de la Révolution française,* one of the earliest books to seek to assess the significance of the French Revolution. Moreover, she had been busy with the movement to put an end to the slave trade through her connection with leading abolitionist William Wilberforce, whom she had met in London; she had also been intervening with the Duke of Wellington and others in an attempt to lighten the heavy burden of the Allied demand for French reparations. Her energy seemed inexhaustible. Germaine had never taken particular care of her health; her constitution was known to be robust, and consequently some, like Rosalie de Constant in Lausanne, were sure that she would recover.

For Germaine to find herself condemned to the stagnation she had always dreaded and sedulously avoided, was hard indeed: she regarded it as "divine punishment when the most active person is so to speak petrified, though not in my mind and heart."[1] Her sufferings were exacerbated by her fear of death.

In constant attendance hovered a pale shadow, her husband, the dying John Rocca. Schlegel and Fanny Randall were usually on call as well, along with Albertine and Victor de Broglie. Germaine continued to invite friends to dinner, although she herself could rarely sit at the table and Albertine had to act as hostess in her stead. Among the many friends who visited her there were the now extremely devout and ultraconservative but always loyal Mathieu de Montmorency, later to be minister of foreign affairs; stalwarts like Prosper de Barante and Sismondi; and the victorious Wellington. There was also Chateaubriand, whose eyes met those of Juliette Récamier at Germaine's bedside—and so began the celebrated affair that lasted until the death of the creator of *René* some thirty-one years later. While Chateaubriand had opposed Germaine in the past, he was by now "my dear Francis," an attentive and esteemed colleague but by no means a longstanding intimate friend like Mathieu de Montmorency.

But where was Benjamin, the one person who might have been expected to be present among the numerous friends and acquaintances who gathered to hearten Germaine? At the beginning of 1817 he was in Paris, much occupied with the attempt by a number of liberal writers to restore the fortunes of the venerable *Mercure de France*, founded in 1672 to give weekly news of Louis XIV's court, and later an organ of the *idéologues* and then of a conservative group around Chateaubriand. The aim was to establish it as a liberal journal. As soon as Benjamin heard of Germaine's collapse he rushed to her house on the rue Royale. He was not admitted.

A desperate note scribbled to Schlegel, undated and unsigned but evidently written by Benjamin, was discovered toward the end of the nineteenth century among Schlegel's papers. Benjamin was in a state of complete disarray and despair. He could scarcely comprehend what he was being told: that he, of all people, was not being allowed to visit her, to console and sustain her, when others could do so, and that the door was firmly closed against him because, it was claimed, his presence would upset her. "I am very worried about what I have heard. Is there really no way for me to see Mme de Staël? Others are seeing her. I cannot describe what I am feeling. Does she not want to see me? Believe me, the past haunts you dreadfully when you are afraid for those you have made to suffer. Do tell me what the situation is, I beg you, and, if it does not distress her too much, arrange for me to see her."[2] In spite of this poignant note, which reveals how much he longed to visit her and talk with her, the decision was final.

By April 17 he knew, at second hand, that his former companion was unlikely to recover. He was devastated, but he did not tell Rosalie that he had not been allowed to see the dying Germaine. Many years before, he had written in his diary, "No, I could never bear the misfortune of losing Minette."[3] During those five months of her protracted agony, he, aware of her mental and physical suffering, had plenty of time to recall his indifference to her changed appearance at their reunion in the spring of 1814.

When Julie Talma lay dying in 1805 he had stayed with her to the end, deeply shaken by her long agony and the physical changes that had overtaken her, and moved by profound reflections on mortality and religion. He was not married then; Julie Talma was divorced, her famous actor husband had remarried, her sons had died, and but for a few solicitous friends she was virtually alone. The present circumstances were very different and precluded so intimate and touching a deathbed scene. Germaine was surrounded by her husband, her children, her friends, and her loyal entourage. Did she recall the words of the first version of her testament of November 1, 1804, composed soon after her father's death, in which she expressed her sorrow at not having been present to close Necker's eyes and her hope that Benjamin would close hers? Did he remember them?

Who was it that decided Benjamin should not be admitted? Was it the view of those who had taken charge of the sickroom, Rocca and Schlegel, Auguste and Albertine, all thinking that they had the invalid's best interests at heart and that Benjamin's presence would be too disturbing for her? Or was it the decision of Germaine herself? She would have known that Benjamin, who could be so acutely sensitive to suffering, would want to be at her side and would be distraught and desperate at being refused entry; she was, moreover, in possession of her faculties of "mind and heart," and she had five months in which to countermand any decision by her entourage if she so wished. "I have loved where I love no longer, I have esteemed where I no longer esteem; life's current has carried everything away except that great shade on the summit of the mountain who points to the life to come," she wrote in the chapter on Necker's last days in *Considérations*.[4] Apparently, she did not want to rake over the ashes with Benjamin to no purpose; she did not seek a grand scene of his repentance and their reconciliation.

The situation is reminiscent of the very long death scene at the end of *Corinne* where the eponymous heroine, in the grip of unbearable suffering, refuses to see her former lover, Oswald, who has betrayed her, although she welcomes others, including his wife and daughter. Unlike Corinne, Germaine was not dying of bitter disillusion at the loss of her ideal soul mate and the sickness of unrequited love, but their fates have much in common. Oswald broke his vow to stay with Corinne always, as well as his promise to marry her, although she contrived generously to release him from it. He forgot their secret link with the divine that transformed their two souls into one. Similarly, Benjamin, the trusted bosom friend, broke his vow to Germaine that they would always be together, although she declined to marry him. Like Oswald, Benjamin married another and threw away a pearl of great price—that was the gist of many of Germaine's reproaches in her surviving letters to him. "What have you done with this unique affection?" asks Corinne.[5]

Corinne does not give any specific reason for her refusal to see Oswald; for instance, she does not suggest that his presence would distress her, although she is deeply distressed on learning of his return to Italy. It is his conduct that has caused the chasm between them. "Are you not another's husband?" she asks rhetorically in her reply to his letter. "What could I possibly have to say to you? Was I granted permission to die in your arms?"[6] The negative answers to these questions provide the cause for her refusal. If the decision to reject Benjamin in 1817 was Germaine's, it looks like a case of life imitating art. Oswald falls at the feet of the dying heroine at the last moment, but the scene of bedside reconciliation does not take place in *Corinne*, nor did it occur in actuality. After being moved to a quiet house on the rue Neuve-des-Mathurins with a garden she was able to enjoy, Germaine died in her sleep, with the faithful Fanny Randall holding her hand, on July 14, 1817. She had only recently turned fifty-one.

Now Benjamin was allowed to keep watch over her body in the company of Victor de Broglie. He had had several months to brood on her illness as well as his own sorrow and imminent loss, but this final moment was terrible. In his memoirs, published many years later, the duc de Broglie left a brief, rather bland and banal account: "We kept watch together at the foot of Mme de Staël's bed. I was touched to the quick and deeply moved. After having exhausted personal memories and regrets about the past, we devoted long hours to serious reflections.

All the problems that arise naturally within us in the presence of death we probed and resolved in a manner that satisfied us both."[7] Benjamin had memories and regrets in abundance, no doubt, but he always scorned conventional words of mourning and condolence: it seems unlikely that at such a moment he would have been "satisfied" with any discussion of the ultimate questions of life and death that had always preoccupied him. He was haunted by death, by all the friends he had lost; he sometimes felt closer to them than to the living. At such times he was tormented by thoughts that left him in a state of deep melancholy and depression.

Something of his pain and grief at the loss of his dazzling companion is conveyed in the tributes he paid to her in the following days. On July 18 he published a long, unsigned article, "On Mme de Staël," in the liberal *Journal général de France*. The authorship of the article, which bears many touches of his hand, was confirmed when he sent a signed copy to Albertine and Auguste. "What I should like to depict, what all her friends would still find it a painful pleasure to describe, if a profound grief did not rather lead all those who cherished her to reject every form of consolation, is this kindness, this nobility, the enduring loftiness of feeling, this warmth of friendship, this compassion, this respect for weakness, this ardor in pleading for the oppressed, in fine, this strength of affection that spread over the lives of all who met her a charm it is impossible to replace, and whose loss they cannot conceive how they can bear."[8] The phrasing and rhythm of "this kindness, this nobility, . . . this compassion" recall the cruel passage in chapter 3 of the memoirs of Mme Récamier, a chapter written by Benjamin, in which these very qualities were connected with Germaine's vanity and self-worship. In the article of July 18, however, the list sounds like an act of reparation. The note of genuine grief and irreparable loss is manifest in its pages.

The article also offers a résumé of her life and writings, presenting a more just assessment of her, of her father, and of their exceptional relationship. Benjamin briefly discusses her works, from her early study of Rousseau through her book on the passions, with its "faulty plan" but wealth of striking and original ideas, especially on society in the modern era, to *Delphine* and *Corinne*, and even including a rare though uninspiring mention of *De l'Allemagne*. He honors her courage, suggesting that her long exile may have shortened her life. Occasionally, he covers some episodes with a discreet veil, for instance when implying that he was reconciled with her in perfect amity after their return to France in 1814, the period of his mad passion for Juliette and his loathing for the viper of Coppet: "Friends long separated saw her again and reconquered her goodwill." He concluded with the ineffaceable impact she made: "All those who had any connection with her have retained an indelible impression. . . . No one could have spent an hour with her without giving this hour a separate place in his memory; her life was essential to those who had known her, even when they no longer saw her"—an evident allusion not only to their separation but also to his exclusion from the inner circle of family and friends who cared for her in her last illness.[9]

There followed, a week later, on July 26, an article published in the *Mercure de France*. It is better known than its predecessor because parts of it were incorporated into the chapter "On Mme de Staël and her Works," put together in 1829, the year before his death, in an anthology of his writings, *Mélanges de littérature et de politique*. This chapter also contained extracts from his review of *Corinne* in *Le Publiciste* in 1807 as well as passages from his review of her *Considérations sur les principaux événements de la Révolution française* in the *Mercure de France* in 1818. By 1829 he was not concerned with producing a totally new or revised assessment.

The remarkable preamble to the article of July 26, 1817, which he did not retain in 1829, offers the most potent expression of his grief at her loss. Here, the impersonal phrase "her friends," a discreet expression that is meant to include or stand for himself, yields suddenly under the pressure of emotion to the deeply felt personal "I" that he has tried in vain to conceal.

> At the time of Mme de Staël's death many of her friends have felt the need to pay a final tribute to [her] memory. . . . I want others to succeed in carrying out this duty: the more I try to fulfill this painful task the more I feel it is beyond my strength. When I recount in my mind the details of this life devoted in turn to winning fame and succoring misfortune, these details crowd in upon me so vividly that, forgetting the work I had undertaken, I allow my thoughts to wander over those impressions which are never to be repeated for her friends who are still living, and the hours drift by without my being able to write a line that satisfies me, a line that may be able to convey to others a part of the emotion that it seems to me everyone should be feeling. When I reread her works that I was intending to examine, I pause in spite of myself at each of those expressions which, while she was alive, struck her friends by their eloquence, but whose predictions they preferred to elude and which now appear as fearful prophecies that events have made real. Finally, when, making an effort, I manage to put together a few words that render imperfectly one of her innumerable qualities, I am overcome with pain and bitterness. It was to her that her friends should have said how much they loved her: they did not succeed in convincing her. It was feared that the emotion, which perhaps her spirit needed, would prove too much for her now that her body had grown so frail. . . . Death took her from us, we all remained as if foundering under the weight of words we had forbidden ourselves to utter. To utter them now would be, in my view, a kind of profanation.[10]

He tells his reader to expect neither order in his ideas nor the full expression of the feeling she inspired in members of her intimate circle. Her friends (that is, himself) can think only of her: they write for her in the hope that she would have been satisfied with their words and would have found in them "a further proof" of affection. It seems clear that, if he had been permitted to see Germaine, he not only would have reassured her of his love but also would have stirred up the profound thoughts on mortality and "the emotion which perhaps her spirit needed," in his view. He was obviously bitter at being excluded, convinced that he knew her better than anyone else, and completely shattered by her death.

In this poignant preamble to the article in the *Mercure de France* he speaks of being unable to discuss her works as he would like, yet he had already done so in the article of July 18. Perhaps the preamble was composed in the first moments of grief, before any other obituary tributes, as its depth of personal feeling suggests. In the article in the *Mercure* he alludes to her love of liberty and justice, proposes that her unfinished study of Necker's life represents the essence of her finest attainment, and reminisces about her gift for friendship, how readily she understood and responded to the most fleeting impressions in others, enhancing the value of their formless aperçus in their own eyes. It is an acknowledgment of his debt to her. Even when one was not with her, he reflects, one stayed under her spell: all one's thoughts turned to her, and one longed to discuss one's ideas and emotions with her. Indeed she, too, had shared a similar longing to discuss everything with him.

Benjamin was not present at the funeral. His one-time rival Schlegel took his place. The cortège traveled to Coppet, and on July 28 Germaine's coffin was carried into the mausoleum where her parents lay. Members of the commune of Coppet served as pallbearers, and among those present were relatives, friends, and leading citizens of

Geneva and its environs. Germaine had asked for alms to be given to the poor; in her will she made known her marriage to John Rocca—who died the following year—and acknowledged the birth of their son.

Sismondi, who saw Benjamin after Germaine's death, recalled how he was "so broken in spirit" that he scarcely appeared to be the same man.[11] Writing to Juliette in August 1817, Benjamin owned, "I am melancholy and above all indifferent [to everything]. . . . All in all, I am no longer alive."[12] Everything seemed empty, meaningless, and pointless. As he had informed Rosalie when he knew Germaine was at death's door, "I am so tired of wandering that I lie down where I am, with indifference and solely because I am there. . . . Everything is so fleeting, one is so close to leaving everything seen and to be seen that I am no longer able to value the acquisition of what must shortly be placed on the edge of the great abyss, and I am no longer curious to understand a world where I shall be staying so briefly."[13] This kind of despondency, which frequently descended on him, particularly at the loss of his friends, and seemed to draw color from all his activities, could not last. "Dear Benjamin," wrote Rosalie, on learning of his nihilism in the months immediately after Germaine's collapse, "Quite old as you say you are, your ambition is very young, yet you lie down and you say: 'Everything is all the same because I shall die and perhaps soon.' When you speak like that I guess your state of mind. But you know very well that you will go on living, that you will be taking action."[14] Rosalie recognized the slough of despond and apathy into which he often fell throughout his life; she understood her cousin sufficiently to realize that his somber mood would change and that he would not succumb to darkness.

In the period after Germaine's death Benjamin could not help but defend her and preserve her memory, since he continued to uphold the principles they had shared. He did not, however, turn into a keeper of the flame. Two women fulfilled that role. One was Benjamin's putative daughter, Albertine de Broglie, whose liberal salon he frequented: she fiercely and religiously protected her mother's reputation. The other was Juliette Récamier, who cherished her friend's memory in a veritable cult. Those who visited her in her famous apartment in the convent of l'Abbaye-aux-Bois could gaze on Baron Gérard's evocative painting of an idealized Mme de Staël as Corinne at Cape Misenum, where the inspired poet is seen improvising her verses before a spellbound audience that includes Oswald, lost in admiration. Benjamin would have seen it every time he entered Juliette's drawing room, where Chateaubriand presided.

☙ *Epilogue* ❧

BENJAMIN'S CAREER AS A DARING AND FORMIDABLE liberal politician did not really take off until after Germaine's death. All those long, intense discussions of theirs, often into the small hours when he wanted an early night, left their mark on him. It was she who had the bold flashes of imaginative insight and poetic enthusiasm and who in the beginning helped him to give shape to his perceptions. If, in her novels and her works of nonfiction she defended, propagated, and popularized the notion and value of what she called "liberal ideas," it was he who elaborated on these ideas, defined them, developed them, and eventually put them to practical use in the political arena. She was the high flyer, while he kept closer to the ground: their ideas, however, belonged to the same family. In that sense they would remain linked together, as they had been in life, in the history of literature, culture, ideas, and politics.

The values inherited from the Enlightenment that Germaine and Benjamin cherished—freedom to practice one's religion; freedom of thought, inquiry, and expression; freedom of the press; emphasis on individual human worth and dignity; and representative government and liberty with order—could be seen in their day as modern, destructive of the established authority of church and state, and dangerous. They had not yet become commonplace. Taken for granted by those who now enjoy such liberties, they had to be achieved at the cost of arduous struggles. Benjamin would continue to fight the battles in which Germaine had been engaged right up to her last illness.

How could he fail to do this when he thought largely along the same lines as she did? Their intellectual companionship was so intimate that it has often been regarded as the chief element and basis of their relationship. Many of those who knew them were convinced of it. Benjamin and Germaine consulted and advised each other, discussed everything from literature and politics to religion and philosophy, and examined and interpreted the meaning of contemporary events for the future. She relied on him for counsel on her practical or family concerns, often calling on him to intervene diplomatically with influential figures during her exile. He relied on her not just for his comforts and her subventions but also for her encouragement and her editorial expertise. "Oh! If only our friend [Germaine]. . . ," sighed Benjamin in a letter to Prosper de Barante from Göttingen in August 1812, when he was at a crucial point in his book on polytheism and longed for her advice about the choice of material to be cut from his manuscript. He did not have to finish his sentence, for he knew that Prosper would have experienced the detailed care she lavished on the literary endeavors of her friends.[1]

Yet, vital for Germaine and Benjamin as this harmony of minds proved to be, there was also a long-lasting, deep emotional tie that was a potent force in both their lives. Paradoxically, even her refusal to see him in her last months testifies to the lasting potency of their bond. Contentedly married, as she claimed, why should she care if she saw Benjamin unless she feared his power to move her? This visceral bond is among the reasons for his long delay in making a break, and, after the break, for his desperate worries about her safety and his regrets during her daring and dangerous journey across Europe in 1812. Above all, it is manifest in his intense grief at her death. In spite of everything, their storms, their rages, their threats, their betrayals, even their hatred, they not only understood each other but also loved one another—in their fashion.

It was on a foundation of unhappiness and dissatisfaction that they built their hopes for a better future. In her case these hopes were a kind of noble poetic prayer, for she conceived politics as a form of poetry, morality, and religion; in his, they were mainly resurgent when he was engaged in action. While they did not see eye to eye on such matters as "the destiny of woman," so dear to Germaine's heart, the one theme on which they were always agreed was liberty, a word that had not yet acquired today's multiple meanings or any hint of ambiguity. People who are without liberty usually know what it is that they lack. Germaine had unshakable faith in freedom as a natural right that, she trusted, would eventually be extended through enlightenment to reach everyone, everywhere, whatever their station and background. "Liberty! Let us repeat her name . . . without fear of wounding any power worthy of respect, for everything we love and honor is contained in it," she wrote lyrically in the conclusion to *Considérations sur les principaux événements de la Révolution française.*[7]

Benjamin's enduring faith in freedom was born out of his private yearning for independence. Despite his disillusion with humankind in general, which Germaine did not share, or to which she refused to yield, his passion for freedom was no less keen than hers. During the triumph of Napoleon's power and arbitrary rule he may have been outwardly more prudent but he privately opposed it and its deadening effect on the general mind, whereas she provoked the emperor in public and paid a heavy price. Benjamin later said, rightly, that Napoleon's harsh treatment of her was a blot on his reputation as a great man.

Many of Benjamin's political ideas were already formulated in his writings under the Directoire when his attachment to Germaine was especially close. "It will soon be twenty years," he declaimed in the foreword to *Principes de politique,* published in May 1815 at the height of his commitment to Napoleon's liberal empire, "that I have been concerned with political matters, and I have always proclaimed the same views, expressed the same aims. What I asked for then was individual freedom, the freedom of the press, no arbitrary rule, respect for the rights of all. That is what I call for to-day with no less fervor and hope."[3] Twenty years: he was counting from May 25, 1795, the moment when he arrived in Paris with Germaine with the aim of making a mark on the political scene. In this way he could always maintain that he had not betrayed his principles in working for the emperor in his liberal guise during the Hundred Days—a view that other libertarians then or later did not readily share or forgive.

No one was ever more resolute than Benjamin on the subject of individual liberty, and he remained consistent to the end. In the preface to his *Mélanges* of 1829, he famously expanded on this earlier passage, now venturing to date his credo from 1789: "For forty years I have defended the same principle, liberty in everything, in religion, in philosophy, in literature, in industry, in politics: and by liberty I mean the triumph of individuality both over authority that would seek to govern by despotism and over the masses who demand the right to enslave the minority to the majority. Despotism has no right. The majority has that of constraining the minority to respect order." But, he continued, everything that does not disturb order, everything that is private and intimately personal, like opinion, provided it does not harm others, "should not be subject by law to the social power."[4] His ringing defense of the freedom of the individual from government intervention (which Isaiah Berlin described as negative liberty) differed in tone from Germaine's paean to liberty at the conclusion of

Considérations, where she was seeking not to define it but to elevate it. It was with lyric enthusiasm and an appeal to the soul and to God that she called for the abolition of the slave trade and for the freedom of the press. These were two of the causes that Benjamin would continue to uphold faithfully.

Very soon after Germaine's death the opportunity arose for Benjamin to hasten to her defense, as he had so often done in the past. The posthumous publication of *Considérations sur les principaux événements de la Révolution française* in 1818 prompted an extremely heated public debate. Most of her works, from the studies of the passions and of literature to *Delphine* and *Corinne* and beyond, had aroused controversy and were intended to do so. *Considérations*, with its mixture of history, memoir, and reflections on politics, including a special emphasis on the merits of the English constitution as a model for France, inspired a volley of attacks and ripostes, including a tome by the leading conservative Catholic philosopher Louis de Bonald, a theocrat who insisted that such lofty subjects of governance did not fall within the sphere and capacities of a woman better suited to writing novels.

Benjamin opened his review with a further expression of pain and regret at her death: these had not lessened, he admitted. He wanted to pay a last tribute to her, calling *Considérations* "one of the finest monuments ever raised to liberty and human dignity."[5] Her view of the French Revolution as one of the greatest epochs of the social order contradicted all the pieties of the reactionaries, who were obsessed with the glories of the past and ignored all its shortcomings. Her well-known, forward-looking views, which he shared, were expressed in this work with renewed vigor. In short, from the moment of the publication of *Considérations* in 1818 under the Bourbon Restoration, the significance of the conflict that had raged since the Revolution was examined and made clear. The battle lines were drawn between those who looked only to the so-called superior values of the past and those who wanted to pursue what was modern as well as build on the reforms brought about by the Revolution of 1789—and the battle would continue for years to come.

In discussing Germaine's examination of "the social organization of modern peoples," Benjamin noted perspicaciously, "Liberty seems to many who seek and desire it to be far less precious than equality."[6] The theme of equality was to dominate and sometimes predominate in the future. He recognized that the relationship between the privileged and the nonprivileged was going to be of prime importance. Germaine and Benjamin based their liberal principles upon the inviolability of property, for they held that ownership encouraged a sense of responsibility, so it was not difficult to brand them in terms of class as "bourgeois"—already a term of opprobrium—and as figures who disregarded the suffering poor and disadvantaged.

Yet Germaine was far from indifferent to the peasants and serfs she saw on her travels; she was aware of the wretched condition of those unfortunate men and women who fell outside of what was then regarded as "society." As an individual she did all she could to alleviate the misery she encountered, but, like many of her contemporaries in quest of reform, her gaze was fixed on how the nation as a whole could be governed for the better, which she thought depended on its social organization and a proper constitution as the source of national well-being and improvement. It was only after her death and around 1825 that utopian socialists, who followed Henri de Saint-Simon in their concern with the economy and with industry, would exert an influence on thinkers, writers, and poets. By the 1820s Benjamin, however, was fully aware of the deleterious effects of the delayed industrial revolution in France.

He had long been conscious of the sufferings of the underprivileged, which was evident, for example, in his bitter comments to Rosalie in 1811 on the maltreatment of the innocent poor in Heidelberg. In his later eloquent speeches in the Chambre des Députés, he railed against the privileged few whose selfish acquisitiveness was driving the "proletarians" to revolt. "Hunger does not wear out. If through my laws I had reduced forty thousand workers of the capital and perhaps a hundred thousand in the kingdom to have neither work nor livelihood, I feel that a sumptuous banquet would weigh on me," he declared with characteristic irony in 1827.[7]

Was this Benjamin of 1827 the same man who had been careful to avoid giving offense to the emperor for so long? Who would have thought, during the years when he was regaling his friends and relatives with dismal, self-flagellating accounts of his world-weariness, contempt for mankind, apathy, indifference, and laziness, that he would turn into a tireless champion of the defenseless and unemployed and a fighter for justice, considered by Germaine the supreme law, or that he would figure as the hammer of the *ultras,* the extreme monarchists and reactionaries? As a député he found his opportunity, his métier, and his way. A gifted orator, he took up the defense of victims of injustice. Notable among these was an ordinary citizen, Wilfrid Regnault, who was condemned to death for a murder he did not commit. "I hold more than anyone that all Frenchmen are equal," Benjamin observed, but for this salutary opinion to be established the judges must not be drawn solely from the prejudiced and privileged class that views all underdogs with suspicion. How can "obscure and defenseless" men of the people find a way to approach the powerful and influential?[8] He wielded the rapier of his eloquence and wit, leading his opponent to stumble and then moving in to deliver the coup de grâce.

Germaine would surely have been gratified that he was making such good use of the gifts she had recognized when they first met. There is a meaningful passage that he crossed out from the manuscript of the preface to *Mélanges* of 1829, one that—underneath the familiar tone of world weariness—contains an echo of her wishes for him: "When one has reached the stage in life when ambition is at an end, when one asks nothing of men and hopes for nothing from them, when one can at least flatter oneself on having come more or less close to the aim one set for oneself at the beginning of one's career—that is, to have contributed to explain to a free nation the nature of liberty—one feels oneself to be liberated from acting with any special care and caution." It was Germaine who, after he lost his elevated position during the Hundred Days, had tried to console him with the idea that "yours would be a fine career if you could teach France liberty."[9] To explain the nature of liberty—that was indeed what he had done in the years since her death.

Not long after Germaine died, Benjamin suffered a serious fall from which he never recovered; from 1818 on, he could walk only with the aid of crutches. Despite this disability, added to his failing eyesight and declining health, which had never been robust, in his last years he became as loudly active in the struggle for freedom as she had been. Never short of physical courage, as he proved by his propensity for fighting duels whenever honor was at the stake—indeed, in 1822, he met one opponent while seated on a chair—he also revealed exemplary moral courage as a député. His numerous enemies tried to implicate him in the conspiracy led by the Bonapartist General Berton. Benjamin protested his innocence, but he was tried in absentia, fined, and sentenced to six months in prison, although the sentence was not carried out. This worrying affair did not prevent him from making every effort to save the conspirators from execution. He even proposed to the prime minister, Joseph de Villèle, that he would not stand as a candidate in the forthcoming elections if the life of one of the condemned men, Caffé, a doctor whom he believed to be innocent and to whom he felt an obligation, were spared. Benjamin saw himself as "perhaps the involuntary cause" of the doctor's misfortune.[10] As in the case of La

Bédoyère some years earlier, his intervention proved bootless: Caffé committed suicide, and General Berton and his co-conspirators were executed. Benjamin's action was, nonetheless, reminiscent of Germaine's many generous attempts to rescue her friends and acquaintances during the Revolution and the Directoire, which he had enumerated so admiringly in his obituary of July 1817 in the *Mercure de France.*

There were disappointments: he had set his heart on being elected to the Académie Française, but he failed three times. The third attempt was in November 1830, so despite what he said in the passage deleted from the preface to *Mélanges,* his ambitions were indeed keen to the last. In these years he appeared to live quietly with Charlotte; he confessed, though, that every evening he ate his vegetable soup and then made for the gambling house, where he continued to amass huge debts.

When the Revolution broke out in July 1830 Benjamin had already been in contact with the future king, the liberal-minded Louis-Philippe, duc d'Orléans, and he helped to draw up a declaration in his favor. Many, and particularly the young, regarded Benjamin Constant as a hero, the outstanding indefatigable defender of the underdog, the champion of freedom of thought, expression, and speech, the advocate of the rights of the individual and the inviolable liberty of the press during the hardening censorship, obscurantism, and reactionary folly that characterized not only the reign of Louis XVIII but also, to an even greater degree, that of his brother, Charles X. Benjamin was carried on a litter at the front of the procession that brought the duc d'Orléans from the Palais-Royal to the Hôtel de Ville. Louis-Philippe made him a gift of two hundred thousand francs to settle his debts. All the same, Benjamin insisted that he must retain the freedom to speak his mind. Although some, such as the chief of the Romantic poets, Victor Hugo, triumphant after the notorious "battle of *Hernani,*" had expected that the liberal leader would be made a minister, Benjamin was not invited to join the government. He was, however, appointed president of the legislative committee of the Council of State. This position could hardly have represented the peak of his ambitions.

Toward the end of his life, Benjamin put together selected passages from his writings about Germaine and her works to be published as an essay in *Mélanges* in 1829. She was on his mind, for he had already alluded to some of the essay's themes in the autumn of the previous year. Then, he had dictated to his secretary, Jean-Jacques Coulmann, his recollections of the dangerous period under the Convention and the Directoire when he came to Paris with her to try his fortune. His memory was sharp even though many of the events he described so vividly had happened more than thirty years before. Seated by the fireside in Coulmann's country retreat, he spoke freely of such leading personalities of the time as Sieyès; of Germaine and her confused state of mind, which he shared; of the signal ingratitude of men she helped to power, such as Talleyrand, or whose lives she saved; of the persecution she suffered that "certainly shortened her life"; of those who dared to make light of her exile; of his own (supposed) naiveté—all delivered with extraordinary precision and characteristic self-denigration, in a tone of ironic detachment through which filtered much lingering sympathy for her and her generosity of spirit.[11]

In March 1830, dreading paralysis in his already weakened, disabled state, Benjamin expressed his fears, recalling how Germaine had been paralyzed after a stroke and had suffered in her last months: "That is the way Mme de Staël died," he shuddered.[12] Like her and her mother, he too was haunted by the terror of being buried alive.

Benjamin died on December 8, 1830. He was sixty-four. The onetime adventurer, whose French nationality had so often been questioned, was honored with a state funeral. An escort of cavalry rode in front of the bier, with a number of ministers and députés following on foot, to the cemetery of Père Lachaise, where that icon of freedom, Lafayette, was to deliver the eulogy. Behind them a huge crowd that included many young people surged along the boulevards. "To the Panthéon!" cried some who wanted him to be laid to rest with Voltaire and Rousseau in the national mausoleum of the great.

The state funeral on December 12 was a sufficiently momentous occasion for one of the leading poets of the new Romantic school, the thirty-three-year-old Alfred de Vigny, to record it on that very day in his diary, though he did not say whether he had been present. A disgruntled partisan of the nobility, with humanitarian leanings, Vigny took the opportunity to recall how he met Benjamin Constant once, during the previous winter. He saw the author of *Wallstein* as a figure of superior intelligence, ultimately disinterested as a fighter, an uncommon blend of man of the world and man of letters, but his feelings toward the elder writer were ambivalent. Vigny thought the goal of Constant's ambition a very lofty one, to be sure, but noted that Constant had not attained it. He would not have been satisfied with being prime minister; perhaps he needed a republic where he could be president, suggested Vigny. In his view, Constant had "helped to overthrow" the Bourbon dynasty without founding anything on the ruins.[13]

A more sympathetic assessment was composed by Sismondi, Germaine's faithful friend, on December 13, 1830, the day following the state funeral. After recalling the brilliant conversational encounters between Germaine and Benjamin, he went on to defend Benjamin against unjust criticism: "I do feel that he remained far below what he could have been, but at the same time he seems to me to have risen far above all his contemporaries." Here, Sismondi listed prominent figures of the age in politics, religion and philosophy whom he thought Benjamin surpassed. "Even in literature he seems to me to be far superior to the whole Académie [française] that judged him unfavorably. It is only in comparison with himself that one feels where he is wanting," claimed Sismondi in his generous tribute.[14] Germaine, with her high expectations of her companion, might have said as much.

Whatever the splendors and miseries of their liaison, whatever their all-too-human private shortcomings, in the public sphere Germaine and Benjamin contributed not only to the creation of a new "modern" literature but also to the establishment of political liberalism in France in the nineteenth century and beyond. They devoted themselves to fighting for freedom of thought and expression against despotism and the closed mind and for the liberty of the individual against the subtle depredations of power—she with exaltation, he with quiet desperation. That the libertarian legacy has survived, albeit precariously, is due in no small measure to the struggles, the writings, and the combined labors of Germaine de Staël and Benjamin Constant.

NOTES

All translations are my own.

Prologue

1. Sismondi to Eulalie de Saint-Aulaire, December 13, 1830, *Epistolario*, vol. 3, p. 109.
2. Jacques Necker, *Nouveaux mélanges*, in Staël, *Correspondance générale*, vol. 4, part 2, p. 441n.

1. A Chance Encounter

1. Constant, *Cécile*, p. 183.
2. Benjamin Constant to Mme de Charrière, August 16 and 23, 1793, *Correspondance générale*, vol. 2, pp. 116, 120.
3. Mme de Charrière to Benjamin Constant, September 24, 1794, ibid., pp. 445–446.
4. Benjamin Constant to Mme de Charrière, September 30, 1794, ibid., p. 459.
5. Ibid.
6. Staël, *Correspondance générale*, vol. 3, part 1, pp. 132, 135; Benjamin Constant to Mme de Charrière, September 30, 1794, *Correspondance générale*, vol. 2, p. 460.
7. Benjamin Constant to Mme de Charrière, October 21 and April 5, 1794, ibid., pp. 276, 481–482.
8. Necker de Saussure, *Notice*, p. cclxxviii.
9. Mme de Staël to Adolph Ribbing, September 18, 1794, *Correspondance générale*, vol. 3, part 1, p. 117.
10. Mme de Staël to Adolph Ribbing, October 8, 1794, ibid., p. 149.

11. Mme de Staël to Adolph Ribbing, October 22, 1794, ibid., p. 158.

12. Charles-Victor de Bonstetten to Stapfer, in Kohler, *Madame de Staël et la Suisse*, p. 497.

13. Mme de Staël to Adolph Ribbing, October 24, 1794, *Correspondance générale*, vol. 3, part 1, pp. 163–164.

14. Mme de Staël to Adolph Ribbing, November 15, 1794, ibid., p. 180.

15. Mme de Staël to Adolph Ribbing, December 8, 1794, ibid., p. 196.

16. Mme de Staël to Adolph Ribbing, March 3, 1795, ibid., p. 264.

17. Constant, *Le Cahier rouge*, pp. 130–131.

18. Ibid., pp. 136–141.

19. Norvins, *Mémorial*, vol. 2, pp. 95–99.

20. Ibid., p. 97.

21. General de Montesquiou to Mme de Montolieu, April 3, 1795, in Staël, *Correspondance générale*, vol. 3, part 1, p. 289n4.

22. Mme de Staël to Adolph Ribbing, April 1, 1795, ibid., p. 288.

23. Erich Bollmann, *Récit du sauvetage de Narbonne*, in Staël, *Lettres à Narbonne*, ed. Solovieff, p. 48.

24. Nils von Jacobsson, *Journal*, in Staël, *Lettres inédites à Narbonne*, ed. Jasinski, appendix 3, pp. 416–419.

25. Ibid., p. 420.

26. Stendhal (Henri Beyle) to Pauline Beyle, August 20, 1805, *Correspondance*, vol. 1, pp. 213–214; Stendhal, *Journal*, August 8, 1805, in *Oeuvres intimes*, p. 709.

27. Staël, *De l'influence des passions*, p. 37.

28. Ibid., pp. 124–125.

29. Staël, *Considérations sur la Révolution française*, ed. Godechot, pp. 281–282.

30. Mme de Staël to Adolph Ribbing, January 23, 1796, *Correspondance générale*, vol. 3, part 2, p. 120.

31. Mme de Staël to Adolph Ribbing, March 10, 1796, ibid., pp. 154–155.

32. Staël, *Considérations sur la Révolution française*, ed. Godechot, p. 168.

33. Benjamin Constant to Mme de Charrière, September 26, 1794, *Correspondance générale*, vol. 2, p. 453.

2. Prodigies

1. Gibbon, *Memoirs of My Life*, p. 107.
2. Catherine Huber in Andlau, *Jeunesse*, p. 31.
3. Mme de Staël (Mlle Necker) to Mme Necker, *Correspondance générale*, vol. 1, p. 6.
4. Ibid., pp. 7, 11–13.
5. Mme Necker to Mlle Necker, ibid., p. 39.
6. Catherine Huber in Andlau, *Jeunesse*, pp. 37, 39.
7. Mme de Staël (Mlle Necker), *Portrait de M. Necker* (1785), ibid., p. 51.
8. Catherine Huber in Andlau, *Jeunesse*, p. 31.
9. Rosalie de Constant in Rudler, *Jeunesse*, p. 36.
10. Benjamin Constant to Rose-Suzanne de Constant, November 19, 1779, *Correspondance générale*, vol. 1, p. 59.
11. Ibid.
12. Rudler, *Jeunesse*, p. 121.
13. Constant, *Le Cahier rouge*, p. 126.
14. Rudler, *Jeunesse*, p. 169.
15. Wood, *Benjamin Constant*, p. 55.
16. Constant, *Le Cahier rouge*, p. 149; Rudler, *Jeunesse*, p. 391.
17. Rudler, *Jeunesse*, pp. 261, 270.
18. Ibid., pp. 248, 493.
19. Ibid., p. 413.
20. Ibid., p. 470.
21. Benjamin Constant to Mme de Charrière, May 17, 1793, *Correspondance générale*, vol. 2, p. 89.
22. Benjamin Constant to Mme de Nassau, May 24, 1794, ibid., pp. 362–363.
23. Staël, *Considérations sur la Révolution française*, ed. Godechot, p. 285.
24. Ibid.
25. Ibid.
26. Benjamin Constant to Mme de Charrière, October 14, 1794, *Correspondance générale*, vol. 2, p. 470.
27. Rudler, *Jeunesse*, pp. 485–486.

28. Constant, *Journaux intimes*, April 28, 1805, in *Oeuvres*, p. 512.

29. Constant, *Le Cahier rouge*, in *Oeuvres*, p. 139.

30. Staël, *Lettres à Ribbing*, p. 10.

31. Mme de Staël to Louis de Narbonne, *Lettres à Narbonne*, ed. Solovieff, p. 23.

32. Susan Phillips to Fanny Burney, May 14 and 22, 1793, in Burney, *Journals and Letters*, vol. 2, p. 123n.

33. Mme de Staël to Edward Gibbon, June 10, 1793, *Correspondance générale*, vol. 2, part 2, p. 454.

34. Louis de Narbonne to Susan Phillips, in Burney, *Journals and Letters*, vol. 2, p. 158n; Gutwirth, *Madame de Staël, Novelist*, p. 130.

35. Benjamin Constant to Mme de Charrière, June 7, 1794, *Correspondance générale*, vol. 2, p. 381.

36. Rudler, *Jeunesse*, p. 406.

37. Mme de Staël to Adolph Ribbing, December 16, 1794, *Correspondance générale*, vol. 3, part 1, p. 202.

38. Staël, *Delphine*, in *Oeuvres complètes*, vol. 7, pp. 112, 140.

39. Staël, *De l'influence des passions*, pp. 217–218; Staël, *Correspondance générale*, vol. 3, part 1, p. 202n6.

3. A Bold Throw

1. Mme de Staël to M. de Staël, February 5, 1796, *Correspondance générale*, vol. 3, part 2, p. 133.

2. Gervinus to Hardenberg, May 29, 1795, in Staël, *Correspondance générale*, vol. 3, part 2, p. 3n6.

3. Mme de Staël to Pierre-Louis Roederer, July 17, 1796, ibid., p. 219.

4. Mme de Staël to the editors of *Nouvelles politiques*, May 31–June 2, 1795, ibid., p. 7.

5. Mme de Staël, *Réflexions sur la paix adressées à M. Pitt et aux Français*, in *Oeuvres complètes*, vol. 2, p. 52.

6. Benjamin Constant to Mme de Nassau, July 7, 1795, *Correspondance générale*, vol. 3, p. 99.

7. Benjamin Constant in Jasinski, *L'Engagement*, pp. 128–129.

8. Benjamin Constant to Rosalie de Constant, December 1827, in Constant and Constant, *Correspondance, 1786–1830*, p. 300.

9. Constant, *Cécile*, pp. 184–185.

10. Benjamin Constant to Mme de Nassau, August 9, 1796 and April 14, 1797, *Correspondance générale*, vol. 3, pp. 214, 252.

11. Benjamin Constant to Mme de Nassau, May 29, 1797, ibid., p. 110.

12. Benjamin Constant to Mme de Nassau, August 7, 1795, ibid., pp. 103–104.

13. Mme de Staël to Juste de Constant, October 10, 1795, *Correspondance générale*, vol. 3, part 2, p. 77.

14. Benjamin Constant to Mme de Nassau, June 28, 1798, *Correspondance générale*, vol. 3, p. 343.

15. Staël, *Correspondance générale*, vol. 3, part 2, p. 43.

16. Constant, *Journaux intimes*, October 7, 1804, p. 387.

17. Jasinski, *L'Engagement*, pp. 169–170.

18. Mme de Staël to François de Pange, December 27, 1795, *Correspondance générale*, vol. 3, part 2, p. 100; Mme de Staël to Adolph Ribbing, December 27, 1795, ibid., p. 102.

19. Fanny Burney to Dr. Burney, February 16–19, 1793, *Journals and Letters*, p. 17; Stendhal, *Journal*, August 8, 1805, and August 19, 1806, in *Oeuvres intimes*, pp. 709, 768; Rosalie de Constant in Staël, *Correspondance générale*, vol. 3, part 2, p. 215.

20. Staël, *Correspondance générale*, p. 204.

21. Mme de Staël to Pierre-Louis Roederer, July 17, 1796, ibid., pp. 217–218.

22. Ibid., p. 219.

23. Staël, *De l'influence des passions*, p. 142; Jasinski, *L'Engagement*, p. 200.

24. Benjamin Constant, *Recueil d'Articles, 1795–1817*, p. 42.

25. Mme de Staël, *De l'influence des passions*, p. 198.

26. Ibid.

27. Jasinski, *L'Engagement*, p. 27.

28. Mathieu de Montmorency to Albertine Necker de Saussure, December 14, 1796, in Staël, *Correspondance générale*, vol. 3, part 2, p. 257n2.

29. Mme de Staël to Adrien de Mun, October 15, 1796, ibid., p. 257.

30. Jasinski, *L'Engagement*, p. 224.

31. Ibid., p. 225.

32. Mme de Staël to Rosalie de Constant, July 31 and August 2, 1796, *Correspondance générale*, vol. 3, part 2, pp. 222, 224.

33. Pauline de Beaumont to Charles de Constant, October 20 or 22, 1796, ibid., p. 235n1.

4. Enter the Hero

1. Staël, *Correspondance générale*, vol. 3, part 2, p. 92n9.

2. La Tour du Pin, *Mémoires*, p. 250.

3. Staël, *Correspondance générale*, vol. 4, part 1, p. 83.

4. La Tour du Pin, *Mémoires*, p. 254.

5. Mme de Staël to Samuel de Constant, September 20, 1797, *Correspondance générale*, vol. 4, part 1, p. 94.

6. Staël, *Correspondance générale*, ibid., p. 88.

7. Ibid., p. 127.

8. Levaillant, *Les Amours de Benjamin Constant*, p. 54.

9. Benjamin Constant, *Lettre sur Julie*, in *Mélanges*, pp. 849–850, 1598n.

10. Burke, *Reflections on the French Revolution*, p. 68.

11. Mme de Staël to Jean-Marie Pictet-Diodati, April 28, 1798, *Correspondance générale*, vol. 4, part 1, p. 135.

12. Mme de Staël to Juste de Constant, April 30, 1798, ibid., p. 136.

13. Benjamin Constant to Mme de Nassau, May 15, 1798, *Correspondance générale*, vol. 3, pp. 334–337.

14. Ibid.

15. Constant, *Lettre sur Julie*, in *Mélanges*, pp. 844–845; Constant, *Adolphe*, in *Oeuvres*, p. 68.

16. Benjamin Constant to Mme de Nassau, June 28, 1798, *Correspondance générale*, vol. 3, pp. 342–343; Benjamin Constant to Mme de Nassau, July 16, 1798, ibid., p. 345.

17. Samuel de Constant to Rosalie de Constant, c. April 10, 1799, in Staël, *Correspondance générale*, vol. 4, part 1, p. 198.

18. Staël, *Des circonstances actuelles*, pp. 206–207; Benjamin Constant to Ludwig Ferdinand Huber, November 27, 1798, *Correspondance générale*, vol. 3, p. 383.

19. Benjamin Constant to Emmanuel-Joseph Sieyès, May 18, 1799, and July 9, 1799, *Correspondance générale*, vol. 3, p. 421, 433.

20. Alexis de Tocqueville, *L'Ancien régime et la Révolution*, in Bredin, *Sieyès*, p. 460n.

21. Bredin, *Sieyès*, p. 460; Constant, *Correspondance générale*, vol. 3, p. 456n4.

22. Haussonville, *Madame de Staël et M. Necker*, quoted in Staël, *Correspondance générale*, vol. 4, part 1, p. 246.

23. Benjamin Constant to Emmanuel-Joseph Sieyès, November 10, 1799, *Correspondance générale*, vol. 3, p. 455.

24. Benjamin Constant to Emmanuel-Joseph Sieyès, November 15, 1799, ibid., p. 457.

5. A New Order

1. Mme de Staël to Claude Hochet, August 17, 1800, *Correspondance générale*, vol. 4, part 1, p. 309.

2. Staël, *Dix années d'exil*, p. 84.

3. Ibid., p. 85.

4. Staël, *Correspondance générale*, vol. 4, part 1, p. 250n3.

5. Mme de Staël to Pierre-Louis Roederer, January 9, 1800, ibid., pp. 250–252.

6. Staël, *Correspondance générale*, p. 253n1.

7. Glachant, *Benjamin Constant*, p. 1.

8. Mme de Staël, *Discours préliminaire*, in *De la littérature*, ed. Gengembre and Goldzink, p. 66; Staël, *De la littérature*, in *Oeuvres complètes*, vol. 4, p. 392.

9. Staël, *De la littérature*, ed. Gengembre and Goldzink, p. 61.

10. Quoted in the Introduction to Staël, *De la littérature*, ed. Van Tieghem, vol. 1, p. xliv.

11. Staël, *De la littérature*, ed. Gengembre and Goldzink, p. 64, footnote of Mme de Staël; Mme de Staël to Pierre Daunou, August 17, 1800, *Correspondance générale*, vol. 4, part 1, pp. 303–304.

12. Constant, *Recueil d'articles, 1795–1817*, pp. 48–51, 52–56.

13. Benjamin Constant to Rosalie de Constant, October 19, 1800, in Constant and Constant, *Correspondance, 1786–1830*, pp. 25–26.

14. Benjamin Constant to Rosalie de Constant, August 21 and October 19, 1800, ibid., pp. 22, 25.

15. Staël, *Dix années d'exil*, p. 122n1.

16. Ibid., p. 107n3.

17. Staël, *De la littérature*, ed. Van Tieghem, vol. 2, p. 428.

18. Mme de Staël to Jacques Necker, mid-June 1800, *Correspondance générale*, vol. 4, part 1, p. 288.

19. Mme de Staël to Jacques Necker, August 27, 1800, ibid., p. 313.

20. Mme de Staël to Joseph-Marie de Gerando, October 8, 1800, ibid., p. 329.

21. Mme de Staël to Jacques Necker, November 15, 1801, ibid., p. 428.

22. Benjamin Constant to Rosalie de Constant, November 14, 1800, *Correspondance, 1786–1830*, p. 26.

23. Ibid., p. 27.

24. Levaillant, *Les Amours de Benjamin Constant*, p. 63.

25. Ibid., p. 64.

26. Ibid., p. 65.

27. Ibid., p. 66.

28. Ibid., p. 68.

29. Ibid., pp. 69–70.

30. Rosalie de Constant in Staël, *Correspondance générale*, vol. 4, part 2, p. 567.

31. Mme de Staël to Camille Jordan, February 20, 1802, ibid., p. 465.

32. Benjamin Constant to Claude Fauriel, July 15, 1802, in Glachant, *Benjamin Constant*, p. 64.

33. Mme de Staël to Camille Jordan, August 20, 1802, *Correspondance générale*, vol. 4, part 2, p. 548.

34. Mme de Staël to Jean-Marie Pictet-Diodati, August 12, 1802, ibid., pp. 544–545.

35. Mme de Staël to Claude Hochet, September 6, 1802, ibid., p. 554.

36. Mme de Staël to Camille Jordan, September 6, 1802, ibid., p. 556.

37. Glachant, *Benjamin Constant*, p. 76.

38. Mme de Staël to Mme Pastoret, June 9, 1800, *Correspondance générale*, vol. 4, part 1, p. 284.

39. Mme de Staël to Jean-Baptiste Suard, November 4, 1802, ibid., vol. 4, part 2, p. 570; Staël, *Delphine*, ed. Didier, vol. 1, p. 421.

40. Staël, *Delphine*, ed. Didier, vol. 2, p. 187.

41. Ibid., vol. 1, p. 421.

42. Constant, *Recueil d'articles, 1795–1817*, pp. 60–61.

43. Ibid. See also Simone Balayé, "*Delphine* et la presse sous le Consulat," in *Madame de Staël: Ecrire, lutter, vivre*, pp. 231–243.

44. Staël, *Delphine*, ed. Didier, vol. 1, p. 58.

45. Mme de Staël to Claude Hochet, March 3, 1803, *Correspondance générale*, vol. 4, part 2, pp. 593–594; Mme de Staël to Joseph Bonaparte, March 27, 1803, ibid., p. 602.

46. Editor's note in Staël, *Correspondance générale*, ibid., pp. 611–612.

47. Staël, *Delphine*, ed. Didier, vol. 1, p. 396.

48. Staël, *Quelques réflexions sur le but moral de Delphine*, in ibid., vol. 2, p. 371.

6. Journey into the Unknown

1. Mme de Staël to Jacques Necker, October 27, 1803, *Correspondance générale*, vol. 5, part 1, p. 85.

2. Mme de Staël to Jacques Necker, October 7, 1803, ibid., pp. 48–49.

3. Benjamin Constant, *Journaux intimes*, February 19, 1803, p. 247.

4. Ibid., December 18, 1804, pp. 428–429.

5. Mme de Staël to Jacques Necker, February 10, 1804, *Correspondance générale*, vol. 5, part 1, p. 227.

6. Constant, *Journaux intimes*, March 2, 1803, p. 247.

7. Ibid., p. 248.

8. Ibid., July 28, 1804, p. 344.

9. Ibid., January 6, 1803, pp. 225–226.

10. Ibid., p. 226.

11. Ibid., p. 226.

12. Ibid., March 2, 1803, p. 248.

13. Ibid., August 19, September 7, and October 14, 1804, pp. 355, 368, 390.

14. Constant, *Journal intime et lettres à sa famille*, p. 250.

15. Constant, *Journaux intimes*, January 6, 1803, p. 226.

16. Staël, *Correspondance générale*, vol. 5, part 1, p. 132.

17. Constant, *Journaux intimes*, January 6, 1803, pp. 226–227.

18. Mme de Staël, *Journal sur l'Allemagne*, November 15, 1803, in *Les Carnets de voyage*, p. 31.

19. Mme de Staël to Jacques Necker, December 18, 1803, *Correspondance générale*, vol. 5, part 1, p. 152.

20. Mme de Staël to Jacques Necker, January 6, 1804, ibid., p. 185; Mme de Staël to Albertine Necker de Saussure, January 11 and 31, 1804, ibid., pp. 189, 213–214.

21. Constant, *Journaux intimes*, February 16, 1804, pp. 268, 1489n9.

22. Ibid., March 21, 1804, p. 280; Benjamin Constant to Rosalie de Constant, February 27, 1804, in Constant and Constant, *Correspondance, 1786–1830*, pp. 47–48.

23. Constant, *Journaux intimes*, December 7, 1804, p. 422.

24. Ibid., May 3 and March 6, 1804, pp. 275, 302.

25. Ibid., March 17, 1804, p. 280.

26. Constant, *Cécile*, p. 189.

27. Mme de Staël to Jacques Necker, March 23 and 27, 1804, *Correspondance générale*, vol. 5, part 1, pp. 284, 293.

28. Mme de Staël to Jacques Necker, March 1 and 5, 1804, ibid., pp. 257–258.

29. Benjamin Constant, *Journaux intimes*, April 7, 1804, p. 288.

30. Ibid., April 9, 1804, p. 289.

31. Mme de Staël to Duke of Saxe-Gotha, April 28, 1804, *Correspondance générale*, vol. 5, part 1, p. 337.

32. Benjamin Constant, *Journaux intimes*, April 13, 1804, p. 292.

33. Constant, *Journaux intimes*, April 14, 1804, pp. 292–293.

7. Corinne and Adolphe

1. Benjamin Constant, *Journaux intimes*, January 26, 1803, p. 233.

2. Ibid., June 18, 1804, pp. 321–322.

3. Catherine Huber to her parents, December 4, 1789, in Kohler, *Madame de Staël et la Suisse*, p. 91.

4. Staël, *Corinne*, ed. Balayé, p. 521. See also Poulet, "Corinne et Adolphe."

5. Constant, *Journaux intimes*, August 24, 1804, p. 359.

6. Kohler, *Madame de Staël la Suisse*, p. 501.

7. Constant, *Journaux intimes*, January 23, 1805, p. 451.

8. Ibid., January 26, 1805, p. 453.

9. Ibid., December 9, 1804, p. 424.

10. Ibid., September 9 and December 28, 1804, and January 2, 1805, pp. 369, 434, 438.

11. Ibid., December 1 and 9, 1804, p. 424.

12. Mme de Staël to Benjamin Constant, November 1, 1804, *Correspondance générale*, vol. 5, part 2, pp. 446–447.

13. Ibid.

14. Constant, *Journaux intimes*, January 17, 1805, p. 448.

15. Ibid., September 7 and 8, 1804, p. 368.

16. Ibid., February 4 and 5, 1805, p. 459.

17. Benjamin Constant to Rosalie de Constant, June 24, 1807, in Constant and Constant, *Correspondance, 1786–1830*, p. 60.

18. Constant, *Journaux intimes*, May 8, 1805, p. 520.

19. Ibid., January 25 and 27, 1805, pp. 438–439, 453–454.

20. Mme de Staël to Vincenzo Monti, June 23, 1805, *Correspondance générale*, vol. 5, part 2, p. 605.

21. Constant, *Journaux intimes*, December 29, 1804, pp. 434–435.

22. Mme de Staël to Maurice O'Donnell, May 23, 1808, *Correspondance générale*, vol. 6, p. 431.

23. Mme de Staël to Benjamin Constant, May 15, 1808, ibid., pp. 420–421.

24. Necker de Saussure, *Notice*, p. cccxxvii; Constant, *Adolphe*, ed. Leuwers, p. 65.

25. Constant, *Journaux intimes*, October 20–25 and November 22, 1806, pp. 588–589, 597.

26. Staël, *Corinne*, ed. Balayé, p. 53.

27. Benjamin Constant to Claude Hochet, December 4, 1807, in Constant and Staël, *Lettres à un ami*, pp. 139–140.

28. Rosalie de Constant to Charles de Constant, August 18, 1807, in Kohler, *Madame de Staël et la Suisse*, p. 341.

29. Benjamin Constant to Claude Hochet, March 31, 1810, in Constant and Staël, *Lettres à un ami*, p. 170; Benjamin Constant to Rosalie de Constant, July 22, 1809, in Constant and Constant, *Correspondance, 1786–1830*, p. 94.

30. Rosalie de Constant to Charles de Constant, September 8 and October 14, 1807, Kohler, *Madame de Staël et la Suisse*, pp. 342–344.

31. Benjamin Constant and Rosalie de Constant, in Constant and Constant, *Correspondance, 1786–1830*, p. 104n.

32. Mme de Staël to Mme Récamier, April 20, 21, and 30 and December 16, 1808, *Correspondance générale*, vol. 6, pp. 349, 410–411.

33. Mme de Staël to Mme Récamier, c. March 1808, ibid., p. 388.

34. Charlotte Constant to Benjamin Constant, February 1810, ibid., p. 622n.

35. Benjamin Constant to Rosalie de Constant, November 14, 1809, in Constant and Constant, *Correspondance, 1786–1830*, pp. 109–110.

36. Benjamin Constant to Rosalie de Constant, December 9, 1809, ibid., p. 113.

37. Staël, *Corinne*, ed. Balayé, p. 57.

38. Ibid., p. 94.

39. Ibid., p. 431.

40. Ibid., p. 575.

41. Ibid., p. 578–579.

42. Ibid., p. 587.

43. Constant, *Recueil d'articles, 1795–1817*, pp. 85, 87.

44. Ibid., p. 86; Constant, *Mélanges*, p. 868.

45. Constant, *Recueil d'articles, 1795–1817*, p. 86.

46. Ibid., pp. 90–91; Simone Balayé, "Benjamin Constant lecteur de *Corinne*," in *Madame de Staël: Ecrire, lutter, vivre*, pp. 265–278.

47. Constant, *Adolphe*, ed. Leuwers, pp. 163–164.

8. The Flight to Freedom

1. Benjamin Constant to Claude Hochet, July 16, 1807, in Constant and Staël, *Lettres à un ami*, p. 128; Benjamin Constant to Charles de Villers, December 27, 1813, quoted by Harpaz in the Introduction to Constant, *De l'Esprit de conquête*, p. 23.

2. Mme de Staël to Mme Récamier, in Levaillant, *Une Amitié amoureuse*, p. 276.

3. Constant, *Cécile*, pp. 183–184.

4. Benjamin Constant to Claude Hochet, February 13, 1810, in Constant and Staël, *Lettres à un ami*, p. 119.

5. Benjamin Constant to Prosper de Barante, August 8, 1810, *Lettres à Prosper de Barante*, pp. 535, 538; Constant, *Recueil d'articles, 1795–1817*, p. 263.

6. Benjamin Constant to Mme de Staël, September 6, 1810, in Levaillant, *Une Amitié amoureuse*, pp. 241–242; Constant and Récamier, *Lettres, 1807–1830*, p. 41.

7. Mme de Staël to Mme Récamier, October 13, 1810, in Levaillant, *Une Amitié amoureuse*, p. 267.

8. Mme de Staël to Claude Hochet, July 19, 1811, in Constant and Staël, *Lettres à un ami*, p. 176.

9. Benjamin Constant, "Statement," April 19, 1811, in Staël, *Lettres à Benjamin Constant*, p. 147n.

10. Constant, *Journaux intimes*, May 8, 1813, p. 708.

11. Benjamin Constant to Rosalie de Constant, June 20, 1811, in Constant and Constant, *Correspondance, 1786–1830*, p. 146.

12. Benjamin Constant to Rosalie de Constant, July 2–6, 1811, ibid., p. 149.

13. Benjamin Constant to Claude Hochet, October 5, 1812, in Constant and Staël, *Lettres à un ami*, p. 225.

14. Constant, *Journaux intimes*, April 14, 1807, and February 15, April 8, June 27, September 27, October 19, and November 27, 1812, pp. 627, 687, 690, 693, 697, 698, 700.

15. Benjamin Constant to Claude Hochet, August 9, 1812, in Constant and Staël, *Lettres à un ami*, p. 221.

16. Ibid., p. 222.

17. Constant, *Journaux intimes*, June 18, August 6, November 2, and December 9, 17, and 24, 1812, and January 11, 1813, pp. 693, 695, 699, 701, 702, 703.

18. Ibid., June 28, 1813, p. 711.

19. Benjamin Constant to Prosper de Barante, April 7, 1813, *Lettres à Prosper de Barante*, p. 565.

20. Constant, *Journaux intimes*, September 6, 1813, p. 714.

21. Ibid., October 2 and 10, 1813, pp. 716–717.

22. Mme de Staël to Benjamin Constant, April 17, 1813, *Lettres à Benjamin Constant*, p. 38.

23. Ibid., May 20, 1813, p. 39.

24. Ibid., p. 41.

25. Lady Blessington, *Conversations of Lord Byron*, pp. 25–27.

26. Mme de Staël to Benjamin Constant, November 30, 1813, *Lettres à Benjamin Constant*, pp. 43–44.

27. Ibid., December 12, 1813, pp. 45–46.

28. Constant, *Journaux intimes*, October 25, 1813, p. 718.

29. Ibid., November 10, 1813, p. 719.

30. Ibid., November 30, 1813, p. 720; Mme de Staël to Benjamin Constant, January 8, 1814, *Lettres à Benjamin Constant*, p. 47.

31. Constant, *Journaux intimes*, February 7 and 8, 1814, p. 715.

32. Mme de Staël to Benjamin Constant, January 23, 1814, *Lettres à Benjamin Constant*, p. 58.

33. Ibid., p. 59.

34. Ibid., pp. 59–60.

35. Ibid., March 22, 1814, pp. 64–66.

36. Ibid., April 1, 1814, pp. 67–68.

37. Constant, *Journaux intimes*, April 4, 1814, p. 728.

38. Mme de Staël to Benjamin Constant, April 24, 1814, *Lettres à Benjamin Constant*, p. 69.

39. Constant, *Journaux intimes*, April 7, 1814, p. 729.

40. Ibid., April 8, 1814, p. 729.

41. Ibid., April 16, 1814, p. 729.

42. Mme de Staël to Claude Hochet, April 14, 1814, in Constant and Staël, *Lettres à un ami*, p. 244.

9. Reunion in Paris—and After

1. Mme de Staël to Benjamin Constant, April 24, 1814, *Lettres à Benjamin Constant*, pp. 63, 69–70.

2. Mme de Staël to Mme Récamier, August 18, 1814, *Lettres à Madame Récamier,* p. 254.

3. Mme de Staël to Benjamin Constant, August 18, 1814, *Lettres à Benjamin Constant,* p. 74.

4. Villemain, *Souvenirs,* vol. 2, pp. 26–27.

5. Constant, *Journaux intimes,* May 13, 1814, p. 732.

6. Ibid., May 18, 1814, p. 732.

7. Ibid., May 19, 1814, p. 732.

8. Ibid., May 24, 1814, p. 732.

9. Ibid., August 31, 1814, p. 739; October 13, 1814, p. 751; January 26, 1803, p. 233.

10. Mme de Staël to Benjamin Constant, April 17, 1815, *Lettres à Benjamin Constant,* p. 85.

11. Constant, *Journaux intimes,* September 6, 1815, p. 793.

12. Ibid., February 26, 1815, p. 774.

13. Ibid., November 29, 1815, p. 803.

14. Benjamin Constant to Rosalie de Constant, November 7, 1814, in Constant and Constant, *Correspondance, 1786–1830,* p. 203.

15. Constant, *Portraits, mémoires, souvenirs,* p. 280; Necker de Saussure, *Notice,* p. ccxci.

16. Constant, *Portraits, mémoires, souvenirs,* p. 283.

17. Constant, *Journaux intimes,* March 8, 1815, p. 776.

18. Constant, *Recueil d'articles, 1795–1817,* pp. 150–151.

19. Constant, *Journaux intimes,* March 6, 1815, p. 775.

20. Mme de Staël to Benjamin Constant, March 12, 1815, *Lettres à Benjamin Constant,* p. 79.

21. Mme de Staël to Mme Récamier, March 12, 1815, *Lettres à Benjamin Constant,* p. 152n.

22. Necker de Saussure, *Notice,* p. cccx.

23. Constant, *Journaux intimes,* April 1, 1815, p. 778.

24. Mme de Staël to Benjamin Constant, April 17, 1815, *Lettres à Benjamin Constant,* p. 88.

25. Auguste de Staël to Mme de Staël, May 11, 1815, in Jasinski, "En marge de deux lettres inédites," pp. 84–85.

26. Constant, *Journaux intimes*, March 30 and 31, 1815, p. 778.

27. Mme de Staël to Benjamin Constant, April 10, 1815, *Lettres à Benjamin Constant*, p. 83.

28. Constant, *Journaux intimes*, April 14, 15, and 18, 1815, pp. 779–780.

29. Mme Antoinette de Gerando to Camille Jordan, May 9, 1815, in Constant and Récamier, *Lettres, 1807–1830*, p. 198.

30. Constant, *Journaux intimes*, April 19, 1815, p. 780.

31. Ibid., April 23, 1815, p. 781.

32. Mme de Staël to Benjamin Constant, April 30, 1815, *Lettres à Benjamin Constant*, pp. 89–90.

33. Constant, *Journaux intimes*, May 20, 1815, p. 783.

34. Ibid., April 20, 1815, and November 14, 1814, pp. 780, 759.

35. Mme de Staël to Benjamin Constant, April 30, 1815, *Lettres à Benjamin Constant*, pp. 90–91; Constant, *Journaux intimes*, May 6, 1815, p. 782.

36. Mme de Staël to Benjamin Constant, May 15, 1815, *Lettres à Benjamin Constant*, pp. 93–94.

37. Constant, *Journaux intimes*, May 19, 1815, p. 783.

38. Mme de Staël to Benjamin Constant, May 23, 1815, *Lettres à Benjamin Constant*, pp. 95–96.

39. Ibid., May 28, 1815, pp. 97–99.

40. Constant, *Journaux intimes*, May 31 and June 2, 1815, p. 784.

41. Mme de Staël to Benjamin Constant, June 12, 1815, *Lettres à Benjamin Constant*, pp. 100–103.

42. Benjamin Constant to Rosalie de Constant, August 1815, in Constant and Constant, *Correspondance, 1786–1830*, p. 209.

43. Mme de Staël to Benjamin Constant, July 21, 1815, *Lettres à Benjamin Constant*, p. 105.

44. Ibid., August 11, 1815, p. 107.

45. Ibid., August 11 and September 1, 1815, pp. 106, 108–109.

46. Constant, *Journal intime et lettres à sa famille*, p. lvi.

47. Constant, *Journaux intimes*, January 16, 1816, p. 807.

48. Haussonville, *Femmes d'autrefois*, p. 211.

49. Constant, *Journaux intimes*, July 17, 1816, p. 818; Benjamin Constant to Mme

Récamier, June 5 and August 17, 1816, in Constant and Récamier, *Lettres, 1807–1830*, pp. 323, 326.

50. Mme de Staël and Albertine de Broglie to Benjamin Constant, February 23, 1816, in Staël, *Lettres à Benjamin Constant*, pp. 118–120.

51. Mme de Staël to Mme Récamier, February 17, 1816, *Lettres à Mme Récamier*, p. 263.

52. Balayé, *Madame de Staël: Lumières et liberté*, p. 226.

53. Constant, *Journaux intimes*, September 19, 1816, p. 822.

10. The Death of Corinne

1. Mme de Staël to Mary Berry, in Balayé, *Madame de Staël: Lumières et liberté*, p. 227.

2. Benjamin Constant to August Wilhelm Schlegel, in Balayé, "Benjamin Constant et la mort de Mme de Staël," p. 17.

3. Constant, *Journaux intimes*, February 5, 1805, p. 459.

4. Staël, *Considérations sur la Révolution française*, ed. Godechot, p. 389.

5. Staël, *Corinne*, ed. Balayé, p. 572.

6. Ibid.

7. Duc de Broglie, *Souvenirs*, in Balayé, "Benjamin Constant et la mort de Mme de Staël," p. 18.

8. Benjamin Constant, "On Mme de Staël," *Journal général de France*, July 18, 1817, in Balayé, "Benjamin Constant et la mort de Madame de Staël," pp. 21–22.

9. Ibid., pp. 27–28.

10. Benjamin Constant, "Nécrologie," *Mercure de France*, July 26, 1817, in *Recueil d'articles: Le Mercure, la Minerve et la Renommée*, vol. 1, p. 282.

11. Sismondi to Eulalie de Saint-Aulaire, December 13, 1830, *Espistolario*, vol. 3, p. 109.

12. Benjamin Constant to Mme Récamier, August 1817, in Constant and Récamier, *Lettres, 1807–1830*, p. 334.

13. Benjamin Constant to Rosalie de Constant, April 17, 1817, in Constant and Constant, *Correspondance, 1786–1830*, p. 226.

14. Rosalie de Constant to Benjamin Constant, May 11, 1817, ibid., p. 228.

Epilogue

1. Benjamin Constant to Prosper de Barante, August 1812, *Lettres à Prosper de Barante*, p. 561.

2. Staël, *Considérations sur la Révolution française*, ed. Godechot, p. 605.

3. Benjamin Constant, "Avant propos," in *Principes de politique*, p. 1100.

4. Benjamin Constant, Préface to *Mélanges*, in *Oeuvres*, p. 835.

5. Benjamin Constant on Staël, *Considérations sur la Révolution française* in *Recueil d'articles: Le Mercure, la Minerve et la Renommée*, vol. 1, p. 451; Staël, *Considérations sur la Révolution française*, p. 68.

6. Constant on Staël, *Considérations sur la Révolution française*, p. 453.

7. Kloocke, *Benjamin Constant*, p. 286.

8. Benjamin Constant, "Encore un mot sur le procès de Wilfrid Regnault," in *Recueil d'articles: Le Mercure, la Minerve et la Renommée*, vol. 1, pp. 358–360.

9. Benjamin Constant, Préface to *Mélanges*, in Levaillant, *Les Amours de Benjamin Constant*, p. 243; Mme de Staël to Benjamin Constant, August 15, 1815, *Lettres à Benjamin Constant*, p. 109.

10. Benjamin Constant to Joseph de Villèle, October 5, 1822, in Guillemin, *Pas à pas*, p. 55.

11. Constant, *Portraits, mémoires, souvenirs*, p. 53; see also pp. 47–48, 102–103nn.

12. Benjamin Constant to Emilie de Constant Rebecque, March 24, 1830, in Levaillant, *Les Amours de Benjamin Constant*, p. 246.

13. Vigny, *Le Journal d'un poète*, in *Oeuvres Complètes*, vol. 2, pp. 925–926.

14. Sismondi to Eulalie de Saint-Aulaire, December 13, 1830, *Epistolario*, vol. 3, p. 109.

BIBLIOGRAPHY

Andlau, Béatrix d'. *La Jeunesse de Madame Staël de 1766 à 1786.* Droz, Geneva, 1970.

——. *Madame de Staël.* Droz, Geneva, 1960.

Balayé, Simone. "Benjamin Constant et la mort de Madame de Staël." *Cahiers staëliens,* no. 9, December 1969, pp. 17–38.

——. *Madame de Staël: Ecrire, lutter, vivre.* Droz, Geneva, 1994.

——. *Madame de Staël: Lumieres et liberté.* Klincksieck, Paris, 1979.

Bastid, Paul. *Benjamin Constant et sa doctrine.* 2 vols. Armand Colin, Paris, 1966.

Bénichou, Paul. *Le Sacre de l'écrivain, 1750–1830.* José Corti, Paris, 1973.

Berlin, Isaiah. *Four Essays on Liberty.* Oxford University Press, Oxford, 1969.

Berthoud, Dorette. *La Seconde Madame Constant.* Payot, Lausanne, 1943.

Bertier de Sauvigny, G de. *La Restauration.* Flammarion, Paris, 1974.

Blennerhassett, Lady. *Madame de Staël.* 3 vols. Chapman and Hall, London, 1889.

Blessington, Lady. *Conversations of Lord Byron.* Ed. Ernest J. Lovell, Jr. Princeton University Press, Princeton, N.J., 1969.

Bluche, François. *La Vie quotidienne au temps de Louis XVI.* Hachette, Paris, 1989.

Boigne, Mme de. *Mémoires.* Ed. Jean-Claude Berchet. 2 vols. Mercure de France, Paris, 1999.

Bredin, Jean-Denis. *Sieyès, la clé de la Révolution française.* Editions du Fallois, Paris, 1988.

——. *Une Singulière famille: Jacques Necker, Suzanne Necker et Madame de Staël.* Fayard, Paris, 1999.

Burke, Edmund. *Reflections on the French Revolution.* Methuen, London, [1790] 1923.

Burney, Fanny. *The Journals and Letters of Fanny Burney.* Ed. Joyce Hemlow and Anthea Douglas. 12 vols. Clarendon Press, Oxford, 1972–1984.

Chateaubriand, François-René de. *Mémoires d'outre-tombe.* Ed. Maurice Levaillant and Georges Moulinier. 2 vols. Bibliothèque de la Pléiade, Gallimard, Paris, 1951.

Constant, Benjamin. *Adolphe.* In *Oeuvres.*

———. *Adolphe.* Ed. Daniel Leuwers. Flammarion, Paris, 1989.

———. *Adolphe.* Ed. Gustave Rudler. Manchester University Press, Manchester, [1919] 1971.

———. *Amélie et Germaine.* In *Oeuvres.*

———. *Le Cahier rouge: Ma vie (1767–1787).* In *Oeuvres.*

———. *Cécile.* In *Oeuvres.*

———. *Correspondance générale.* Ed. C. P. Courtney and Dennis Wood. 3 vols. Oeuvres complètes. Niemayer, Tübingen, 1993–2003.

———. *De l'esprit de conquête et de l'usurpation dans leurs rapports avec la civilisation européenne.* Ed. Ephraim Harpaz. Flammarion, Paris, 1986.

———. *Ecrits de jeunesse, 1774–1799.* Ed. Lucia Omacini, Jean-Daniel Candaux, and Mauro Barberis. Oeuvres complètes. Niemayer, Tübingen, 1998.

———. *Ecrits et discours politiques.* Ed. O. Pozzo di Borgo. Pauvert, Paris, 1964.

———. *Fragments d'un ouvrage abandonné sur la possibilité d'une constitution républicaine dans un grand pays.* Ed. Henri Grange. Aubier, Paris, 1991.

———. *Lettres à Prosper de Barante.* Ed. baron de Barante. *Revue des Deux Mondes,* vol. 34, 1906, pp. 241–272, 528–567.

———. *Lettres à sa famille.* Ed. Jean H. Menos. Savine, Paris, 1888.

———. *Journal intime et lettres à sa famille et à ses amis.* Ed. D. Melegari. Ollendorf, Paris, 1895.

———. *Journaux intimes.* In *Oeuvres.*

———. *Mélanges de littérature et de politique.* In *Oeuvres.*

———. *Mémoires sur les cent jours.* Ed. Kurt Kloocke and André Cabanis. Oeuvres complètes. Niemayer, Tubingen, 1993.

———. *Oeuvres.* Ed. Alfred Roulin. Bibliothèque de la Pléiade, Gallimard, Paris, 1957.

———. *Portraits, mémoires, souvenirs.* Ed. Ephraim Harpaz. Champion, Paris, 1992.

———. *Principes de politique.* In *Oeuvres.*

———. *Recueil d'articles: Le Mercure, la Minerve et la Renommée.* Ed. Ephraim Harpaz. 2 vols. Droz, Geneva, 1972.

———. *Recueil d'articles, 1795–1817.* Ed. Ephraim Harpaz. Droz, Geneva, 1978.

Constant, Benjamin, and Isabelle de Charrière. *Correspondance, 1787–1805.* Ed. Jean-Daniel Candaux. Desjonquères, Paris, 1996.

Constant, Benjamin, and Rosalie de Constant. *Correspondance, 1786–1830.* Ed. Alfred Roulin and Suzanne Roulin. Gallimard, Paris, 1955.

Constant, Benjamin, and Mme Récamier. *Lettres, 1807–1830.* Ed. Ephraim Harpaz. Champion, Paris / Slatkine, Geneva, 1992.

Constant, Benjamin, and Mme de Staël. *Lettres à un ami* [letters to Claude Hochet]. Ed. Jean Mistler. La Baconnière, Neuchâtel, 1949.

Constant de Rebecque, baronne. *L'Inconnue d'Adolphe, correspondance de Benjamin Constant et d'Anna Lindsay.* Plon, Paris, 1933.

Cordey, Pierre. *Madame de Staël et Benjamin Constant sur les bords du Léman.* Payot, Lausanne, 1966.

Courtney, C. P. *Isabelle de Charrière.* Voltaire Foundation, Oxford, 1993.

Deguise, Pierre. *Benjamin Constant méconnu.* Droz, Geneva, 1966.

Delbouille, Paul. *Genèse, structure et destin d'Adolphe.* Les Belles Lettres, Paris, 1971.

Diesbach, Ghislain de. *Madame de Staël.* Perrin, Paris, 1983.

Du Bos, Charles. *Grandeur et misère de Benjamin Constant.* Corrêa, Paris, 1946.

Fabre-Luce, Alfred. *Benjamin Constant.* Fayard, Paris, 1939.

Fairweather, Maria. *Madame de Staël.* Constable, London, 2005.

Fontana, Biancamaria. *Benjamin Constant and the Post-Revolutionary Mind.* Yale University Press, New Haven, 1991.

Furet, François. *La Révolution française.* 2 vols. Pluriel, Hachette, Paris, 1988.

Gautier, Paul. *Madame de Staël et Napoléon.* Plon, Paris, 1903.

Gibbon, Edward. *Memoirs of My Life.* Ed. Betty Radice. The Folio Society, London, 1991.

Glachant, Victor. *Benjamin Constant sous l'oeil du guet* [letters to Claude Fauriel]. Plon, Paris, 1906.

Godechot, Jacques. *La Vie quotidienne en France sous le Directoire.* Hachette, Paris, 1977.

Grange, Henri. *Benjamin Constant: Amoureux et Républicain, 1795–1799*. Les Belles Lettres, Paris, 2004.

Guillemin, Henri. *Benjamin Constant, muscadin, 1795–1799*. Gallimard, Paris, 1958.

——. *Madame de Staël, Benjamin Constant et Napoléon*. Plon, Paris, 1959.

——. *Madame de Staël et Napoléon*. Seuil, Paris, 1987.

——. *Pas à pas*. Gallimard, Paris, 1969.

Gutwirth, Madelyn. *Madame de Staël, Novelist*. University of Illinois Press, Chicago, 1978.

Gwynne, G. E. *Madame de Staël et la Révolution française*. Nizet, Paris, 1969.

Hasselrot, Bengt. *Nouveaux documents inédits sur Benjamin Constant et Madame de Staël*. Munksgaard, Copenhagen, 1952.

Haussonville, comte d'. *Femmes d'autrefois, hommes d'aujourd'hui*. Perrin, Paris, 1912.

——. *Madame de Staël et M. Necker*. Calmann-Lévy, Paris, 1925.

——. *Le Salon de Madame Necker*. 2 vols. Calmann-Lévy, Paris, 1882.

Herold, J. Christopher. *Mistress to an Age: The Life of Madame de Staël*. Hamish Hamilton, London, 1959.

Holmes, Stephen. *Benjamin Constant and the Making of Modern Liberalism*. Yale University Press, New Haven, 1984.

Jardin, André. *Histoire du libéralisme politique*. Hachette, Paris, 1985.

Jasinski, Béatrice W. *L'Engagement de Benjamin Constant: Amour et Politique, 1794–1796*. Minard, Paris, 1971.

——. "En marge de deux lettres inédites d'Auguste de Staël: L'Attitude politique de sa mère en 1815." *Europe*, January–February 1987, pp. 81–87.

Kelly, Linda. *Juniper Hall: An English Refuge from the French Revolution*. Weidenfeld and Nicolson, London, 1991.

King, Norman. "Libéralisme et légitimité: Madame de Staël, Louis XVIII et le comte de Blacas." *Europe*, January–February 1987, pp. 64–80.

——. "Madame de Staël et la chute de Napoléon." In *Madame de Staël et l'Europe* (papers presented at the Colloque de Coppet, July 18–24, 1966), Klincksieck, Paris, 1970, pp. 63–75.

——. "Le séjour de Madame de Staël en Angleterre (1813–1814)." In *Les Carnets de voyage de Madame de Staël*, ed. Simone Balayé, pp. 354–406. Droz, Geneva, 1971.

Kloocke, Kurt. *Benjamin Constant: Une Biographie intellectuelle*. Droz, Geneva, 1984.

Kohler, Pierre. *Madame de Staël et la Suisse*. Payot, Lausanne, 1916.

Lang, André. *Une Vie d'orages: Germaine de Staël*. Calmann-Lévy, Paris, 1958.

Larg, David Glass. *Madame de Staël: La Vie dans l'oeuvre, 1766–1800*. Champion, Paris, 1924.

——. *Madame de Staël: La Seconde vie, 1800–1807*. Champion, Paris, 1928.

La Tour du Pin, Mme de. *Mémoires*. Ed. Christian de Liederkerke-Beaufort. Mercure de France, Paris, 1989.

Lenormant, Amélie. *Coppet et Weimar*. Michel Lévy, Paris, 1862.

Levaillant, Maurice. *Une Amitié amoureuse: Madame de Staël et Madame Récamier*. Hachette, Paris, 1956.

——. *Les Amours de Benjamin Constant*. Hachette, Paris, 1958.

Luppé, Robert de. *Les Idées littéraires de Madame de Staël et l'héritage des lumières*. Vrin, Paris, 1969.

Mansel, Philip. *Louis XVIII*. Sutton, Stroud, Gloucestershire, [1981] 1999.

Mistler, Jean. *Madame de Staël et Maurice O'Donnell*. Calmann-Lévy, Paris, 1926.

Murray, Venetia. *High Society in the Regency Period, 1788–1830*. Penguin, London, 1999.

Necker de Saussure, Albertine. *Notice sur le caractère et les oeuvres de Madame de Staël*. In Staël, *Oeuvres complètes*, vol. 1.

Norvins, Jacques de. *Mémorial*. 3 vols. Plon, Paris, 1896.

Pange, Victor de. *Madame de Staël et le duc de Wellington: Correspondance, 1815–1817*. Gallimard, Paris, 1962.

——. *Le plus beau de toutes les fêtes*. Klincksieck, Paris, 1980.

Poulet, Georges. *Benjamin Constant par lui-même*. Seuil, Paris, 1968.

——. "*Corinne* et *Adolphe*: Deux romans conjugués." *Revue d'Histoire Littéraire de la France*, July–August 1978, pp. 580–596.

Reichardt, Johann Friedrich. *Un Hiver à Paris sous le Consulat (1802–1803)*. Ed. Thierry Lentz. Tallandier, Paris, 2003.

Rudler, Gustave. *La Jeunesse de Benjamin Constant, 1767–1794.* Armand Colin, Paris, 1909.

Sainte-Beuve, Charles-Augustin. *Cahiers I: Le Cahier vert.* Ed. Raphaël Molho. Gallimard, Paris, 1973.

——. *Chateaubriand et son groupe littéraire sous l'Empire.* 2 vols. Ed. Maurice Allem. Garnier, Paris, 1948.

——. *Oeuvres.* Ed. Maxime Leroy. 2 vols. Bibliothèque de la Pléiade, Gallimard, Paris, 1956, 1960.

Sismondi, Jean-Charles-Léonard Simonde de. *Epistolario.* Ed. Carlo Pellegrini. 4 vols. La Nuova Italia, Florence, 1933–1954.

Staël, Germaine de. *De la littérature.* Ed. Gérard Gengembre and Jean Goldzink. Flammarion, Paris, 1991.

——. *De la littérature.* Ed. Paul Van Tieghem. 2 vols. Droz, Geneva, and Minard, Paris, 1959.

——. *De la littérature dans ses rapports avec les institutions sociales.* In *Oeuvres complètes,* vol. 4.

——. *De l'Allemagne.* Ed. Simone Balayé. 2 vols. Flammarion, Paris, 1968.

——. *De l'Allemagne.* Ed. comtesse Jean de Pange and Simone Balayé. 5 vols. Hachette, Paris, 1958–1960.

——. *De l'influence des passions sur le bonheur des individus et des nations.* In *Oeuvres complètes,* vol. 3.

——. *Des circonstances actuelles qui peuvent terminer la Révolution et des principes qui doivent fonder la République en France.* Ed. Lucia Omacini. Droz, Geneva, 1979.

——. *Du caractère de M. Necker et de sa vie privée.* In *Oeuvres complètes,* vol. 17.

——. *Les Carnets de voyage de Madame de Staël.* Ed. Simone Balayé. Droz, Geneva, 1971.

——. *Considérations sur la Révolution française.* Ed. Jacques Godechot. Tallandier, Paris, 1983.

——. *Considérations sur les principaux événements de la Révolution française.* In *Oeuvres complètes,* vols. 12–14.

——. *Corinne ou l'Italie.* In *Oeuvres complètes,* vols. 8–9.

——. *Corinne ou l'Italie.* Ed. Simone Balayé. Folio, Gallimard, Paris, 1985.

——. *Correspondance générale*. Ed. Béatrice W. Jasinski. 6 vols. Pauvert and Klincksieck, Paris, 1960–1993.

——. *Delphine*. In *Oeuvres complètes*, vols. 5–7.

——. *Delphine*. Ed. Béatrice Didier. 2 vols. Flammarion, Paris, 2000.

——. *Dix années d'exil*. Ed. Simone Balayé and Mariella Vianello Bonifacio. Fayard, Paris, 1996.

——. *Lettres à Benjamin Constant*. Ed. baronne de Nolde and Paul Léon. Kra, Paris, 1928.

——. *Lettres à Madame Récamier*. Ed. E. Beau de Loménie. Domat, Paris, 1952.

——. *Lettres à Narbonne*. Ed. Georges Solovieff. Gallimard, Paris, 1960.

——. *Lettres à Ribbing*. Ed. Simone Balayé. Gallimard, Paris, 1960.

——. *Lettres inédites à Louis de Narbonne*. In *Correspondance générale*, vol. 2, part 1, 1960.

——. *Lettres sur les écrits et le caractère de Jean-Jacques Rousseau*. In *Oeuvres complètes*, vol. 1.

——. *Oeuvres complètes*. 17 vols. Treuttel et Würtz, Paris, 1820–1821.

Staël, Germaine de, and Pedro de Souza. *Correspondance*. Ed. Béatrix d'Andlau. Gallimard, Paris, 1979.

Starobinski, Jean. "Suicide et mélancolie chez Madame de Staël." In *Madame de Staël et l'Europe* (papers presented at the Colloque de Coppet, July 18–24, 1966), Klincksieck, Paris, 1970, pp. 242–252.

Stendhal. *Correspondance*. Ed. Henri Martineau and V. Del Litto. 3 vols. Bibliothèque de la Pléiade, Gallimard, Paris, 1968.

——. *Oeuvres intimes*. Ed. Henri Martineau. Bibliothèque de la Pléiade, Gallimard, Paris, 1955.

Talma, Julie. *Lettres à Benjamin Constant*. Ed. baronne Constant de Rebecque. Plon, Paris, 1933.

Tulard, Jean. *Napoléon ou le mythe du sauveur*. Fayard, Paris, [1977] 1987.

——. *La Vie quotidienne des Français sous Napoléon*. Hachette, Paris, 1979.

Vigny, Alfred de. *Oeuvres complètes*. Ed. Frédéric Baldensperger. 2 vols. Bibliothèque de la Pléiade, Gallimard, Paris, 1948, 1950.

Villemain, Abel-François. *Souvenirs contemporains d'histoire et de littérature*. 3 vols. Didier, Paris, 1855.

Wagener, Françoise. *Madame Récamier*. Lattès, Paris, 1986.

Winegarten, Renee. "A Concept of Liberty: Benjamin Constant." *New Criterion,* February 1995, pp. 30–37.

——. "Germaine de Staël: Against the Wind." In *Accursed Politics: Some French Women Writers and Political Life*. Ivan R. Dee, Chicago, 2003.

——. *Madame de Staël*. Berg, Leamington Spa, Eng., 1985.

Wollstonecraft, Mary. *A Vindication of the Rights of Woman*. Ed. Miriam Kramnick. Penguin, London, [1792] 1975.

Wood, Dennis. *Benjamin Constant: A Biography*. Routledge, London, 1993.

INDEX

chrétienne, Du, 47; *Possibilité d'une
constitution républicaine dans und
grand pays, De la,* 134–135; *Principes
de politique,* 184, 269, 291; *Réactions
politiques, Des,* 103; *Souvenirs historiques,* 105; *Spirit of Religions, The,*
14; *Suites de la contre-révolution en
Angleterre en 1660, Des,* 118; *Wallstein,* 184, 203, 207
Constant, Charles de (cousin), 8, 52,
205, 206
Constant, Charlotte (second wife). *See*
Hardenberg, Charlotte von
Constant, Henriette de Chandieu, Mme
(mother), 33
Constant, Juste de (father), 28, 80, 81;
characterized, 41, 42; death of wife, 33,
42; education and upbringing of BC,
33, 42, 43, 44, 46, 47; financial problems of, 42; mistress of, 33, 41–42;
relationship with BC, 41, 51, 111, 264
Constant, Rosalie de (cousin): as confidante of BC, 205; correspondence
with BC, 75–76, 135, 140, 170, 185,
194, 209, 210, 227, 254, 264, 269, 279,
286, 293; and gambling of BC, 189;
and GS, 7, 87, 95, 144, 205; on Juste
de Constant, 42, 111; on relationship
of BC-GS, 93, 204, 206–207
Constant, Rose-Suzanne de (grandmother), 33, 44–45
Constant, Samuel de (uncle), 80, 105, 118
Constant, Victor de (cousin), 140
Constant, Wilhelmina "Minna" (first
wife), 23–24, 53, 92, 166

Constitution: of *1814* (*la Charte*), 249;
of *1815* (*la benjamine*), 262; English,
292; of Hundred Days, 261–262; of
Year III, 77–78, 195; of Year VIII,
121, 123; of Year X, 147
Constitutional monarchists, 71–72, 147
Consulate: Concordat with Papacy,
145–146; criticism by BC, 122–123;
criticism by Necker, 122; dictatorship
of Napoleon, 125–126, 146; establishment of, 120–121; Parisian society
under, 137–138, 138; persecution of
GS, 127–132; and Sieyès, 121, 122–
124; Tribunate, 124, 126, 127, 136–
137, 142
Convent education, 35
Coppet: assemblies of writers and
thinkers at, 198, 204, 275; BC's visits
to, 9, 16, 86–90, 118, 139, 143, 175–
176, 191–192, 204, 209, 221, 226,
275; death of Necker at, 175–176;
during French occupation of Switzerland, 108, 111; funeral of GS at, 285–
286; GS's banishment to, 156, 230;
GS's life at, 68, 86–90, 118, 137, 138,
178–179; theatrical performances at,
204, 251, 271
Corinne ou l'Italie (Staël), 2, 184, 206;
BC on, 213–215, 283; betrayal theme
of, 166, 210–213; Byron on, 238;
death scene in, 280–281; GS as
model for Corinne, 180–181, 186;
and ideal man, 62–63; Napoleon on,
203; portrait of GS as Corinne, 287;
setting of, 197